DRUCKER'S MANAGEMENT BY OBJECTIVES

His primary European sources and their contributions to the ideas presented in his book:

'The Practice of Management'

by
Dr Peter Starbuck

1

Key Research Material Collated

For The

Degree of Doctor of Philosophy

Conferred by

The Open University Business School.

On

Dr. Peter Starbuck

Supervisors

Emeritus Professor of International Management

Derek S. Pugh ACSS

Emeritus Professor

Andrew W J Thomson OBE

FOREWORD

This publication is a part of ongoing research into Drucker's work and that of his identified influences. It is the second of six volumes in a set of four research works by this author.

Since its preparation in January 2005 further information has emerged regarding Drucker together with extensive research. Consequently, further observations, revisions and additions need to be acknowledged.

When Drucker was interviewed as (Pekar Jnr December 1992:17) he is reported to have said that he attended "*the first Montessori school in Austria*". Subsequent evidence is that he attended a progressive school which was not Montessori. My thought is that Drucker was indicating that he attended a progressive school in a manner which would be meaningful to his American audiences.

Readers are reminded that this analysis of Drucker's relationship with his influences covers his ideas which are evident in his first five books. Other scholars will have different opinions; this is why this volume has been published – to extend the international debate on Drucker's work.

Also acknowledged, is that Drucker's initial opinions on these influences changed with time.

ABSTRACT

The object of this research is to establish what unique contribution Drucker has made to the theory and practice of management. It examines Drucker's environment and development from his birth in Vienna, in 1909, up to and including the publication of his seminal management book *The Practice of Management* in 1954. It shows how Drucker evolved his ideas for the new society that was essential to replace the European totalitarian model. It examines the influences that helped Drucker develop his management idea that was based on a Christian Protestant society, which would provide man with freedom, status and function. His experiences and development are tracked as he moved from Austria to work and also study at universities in Germany, before leaving for England after registering his opposition to Adolf Hitler and the Nazis in 1933. His stay in England until 1937 is recorded before his permanent migration to America, where his interest in management ideas were propagated and developed.

This work is part of a much larger research project, which has examined the backgrounds and ideas of his influences and the reaction of his biographers and reviewers of his work. The findings of this research have been summarised. This research also seeks to determine whether Drucker could meet his own claim in *The Practice of Management*, that by integrating the functions of management, a 'discipline could be made of it!

CONTENTS

Foreword   5

Abstract   7

Abbreviations Used   15

CHAPTER 1 – DRUCKER'S BIOGRAPHY   17

America 1937- Onwards – Developing and Contributing
Period   17

Reflecting on Management 1946-1950   24

Taking a Central Position 1950-1953   24

CHAPTER 2 – THE EVOLUTION OF DRUCKER'S
IDEAS IN HIS FIRST FOUR BOOKS   27

End of Economic Man - The World of Despair   27

The Future of Industrial Man - Management Ideas
Germinating 1943   33

Concept of the Corporation - Learning about
Management in Practice 1944 – 1946   44

The New Society - Reflecting on Management 1946 – 1950   57

   'Society' – Previous Ideas   58

   Refinements of Previous Ideas   58

'   The Industrial Enterprise' – Previous Ideas   62

   Refinements of Previous Ideas   62

New Ideas   70

CHAPTER 3 – *THE PRACTICE OF MANAGEMENT*   75

Introduction   75

Purpose   77

Method   79

Previous Influences and their ideas that are carried
forward   80
Friends in American Management (1954: Preface viii)   89
References within the text   90
Case Studies   91
Selected Bibliography for further reading   91
Post Practice influence   92

CHAPTER 4 – DRUCKER'S SEVEN KEY IDEAS   95
1.   Management Will Be - Management by Objectives
      and Self Control (MbO)   97
2.   Decentralisation as the Preferred Structure   105
3.   The Integration of Productivity by Automation and
      Profit   109
      (i)   Automation   111
      (ii)   Profit   114
4.   Managers Must Measure   118
5.   The Entrepreneurial Function is: The Purpose of
      a Business –is "*to create a customer*"   126
      (i)   Marketing   126
      (ii)   Innovation   129
6.   People are Central to the Organisation   131
      (i)   Introduction   131
      (ii)   What does the Enterprise require?   132
      (iii) The Worker's Attitude   134
      (iv)   The Status Quo   135
      (v)   The Way Ahead – Supported by Case Studies   139
7.   The Manager's Job is Total Integration   145
      (i)   The Manager's Tasks   147
      (ii)   Managing a Business – Supported by Case
              Studies   148

(a)	The Need for Teamwork	149
(b)	What Business Are We In?	150
(c)	Delegation of Span of Control and Span of Managerial Responsibility	153
(iii)	Managing Managers	157
(iv)	Managing the Worker and Work	168
(v)	Time	172

The Impact of what was the Contribution of Drucker's Seven Key Ideas 172
1. MbO 172
2. Decentralisation 173
3. Integration by Productivity, Automation and Profit 173
4. Managers Must Measure 174
5. Entrepreneurial Function 174
6. People are Central to the Organisation 175
7. The Manager's Job is Total Integration 175
The Conclusion of *Practice* 176

CHAPTER 5 – REACTIONS TO DRUCKR'S WORK 179
Introduction 179
1. Book Reviews of *Practice* 180
2. The Work of his Biographers 180
   (i) Biographies about Peter F Drucker 180
   (ii) Chapters or Significant Entries on Peter F Drucker 181
3. Treatment of Drucker by Academics 182
   Introduction 182
   (i) Non-contentious theses on Drucker's Work 182
   (ii) Academic Reviews 183
   Economic Man 183

11

Future		184
Concept		185
Society		187
Practice		190
Summary		192
4.	Reference to Drucker in other writings	193
5.	Conclusion drawn from the Reactions to Drucker's Work	195

CHAPTER 6 – DRUCKER'S CONTRIBUTION TO MANAGEMENT AS A PRACTICE — 197

1.	As a Synthesiser?	197
2.	As an Originator?	200
3.	Did he "*make a Discipline of Management?*"	205
Conclusion		213

CHAPTER 7 – EVALUATION OF THIS RESEARCH — 217

1.	Personal Reflections on Drucker's Work	217
2.	What is My Contribution?	225
3.	What is My Research?	227
4.	The Arguments and Evidence that Support this Research	229

APPENDIX 1 – PETER FERDINAND DRUCKER TIMELINE FOR THE PERIOD 1909-1954 — 233

'Practice' Identifies Seven Major Integrated Ideas for Managers	248
Other Ideas That Have Emerged	249
Bibliography	253

Index   263
Endorsements of Peter Starbuck's Work on
Peter F. Drucker   271
Also By Dr Peter Starbuck   275
Profile – Dr Peter Starbuck   277

ABBREVIATIONS USED

American Telephone and Telegraph Company	AT&T
Chief Executive Officer	CEO
Chrysler Motors Corporation	Chrysler
Crown Zellerbach Corporation	Crown-Zellerbach
Federal Decentralisation	Decentralisation
General Electrical Company (of America)	GE
General Motors Corporation	GM
International Business Machines Corporation	IBM
Labour Unions	Unions
Management by Objectives and Self-Control	MbO
Montgomery Ward (& Company)	Wards
Return on Investment	ROI
Sears Roebuck & Company	Sears
Tennessee Valley Authority	TVA
The Ford Motor Company (of America)	Ford(s)
The United States of America	America

CHAPTER ONE

DRUCKER'S BIOGRAPHY

Drucker's life is now being divided into three periods: his formative years in Austria and Germany, an interim period in England, and his developing and contributing period in the United States of America.

America 1937 – Onwards - Developing and Contributing Period

In January 1937 Drucker left England for America. At twenty-seven years of age, he kept the promise he made to himself at the age of fourteen at the time of the youth rally. He had escaped *"pre-war"* by leaving Europe for America. In the four years in England, Drucker's career as a lecturer was placed on hold. His journalism and writing had further developed while his business career had developed from a nominal start in Hamburg as an export clerk, to an investment banker in London, one of the world's major capital centres. His exposure to further commercial situations and analytical training as a banker had added essentially to his skills.

Drucker's assurance of a part-income was an improvement on his initial arrival in England in 1933, as he quickly set up home in New York. He had an engagement to write for newspapers in London, Glasgow and Sheffield. He was also commencing work as a financial advisor and economist to a group of British investors and his previous employer Freedberg & Co. During the first few months of his arrival in America he began adding to his journalism by writing for the *Virginia Quarterly Review*, *The Washington Post Philadelphia's Saturday Evening Post*, *Harper's Magazine*, and *Asia*. This was Drucker's career development before his first book in English was published, *The End of Economic Man* (May 1939). *Economic Man* gave Drucker a wider intellectual recognition with important reviews by Sir Winston Churchill (1874-1965), detailed later. Jonathan Priestly (1894-1984) who wrote as J B Priestley (John Boynton Priestly), the distinguished writer on social affairs, wrote:

*"At once the most penetrating and most stimulating book I have read
on the world crisis. At last there is a ray of light in the dark chaos".*
(1939: Dust Cover).

That *Economic Man* established Drucker as an English language
intellectual is attested by many who quote him including Karl Polanyi, on
the *"English Evangelicals"* (1939:93) (Polanyi 1944:171). His fellow
countryman, Nobel Laureate Friedrich August Hayek (1899-1992),
complimented Drucker's analysis on Marxism and Russia, and his correct
observation:

> *"…that the less freedom there is the more there is talk of the 'new
> freedom'. Yet this new freedom is a mere word which covers the exact
> contradiction of all that Europe ever understood by freedom… The new
> freedom which is preached in Europe is, however, the right of the
> majority against the individual"*

(Hayek 1944: 21 & 118)

Because of Drucker's phenomenal output, his researchers have been
grateful for any guidance to help to categorise it, including Drucker's
own. It is my contention that when Drucker divides his books into two
main groups of Management, or Economics, Politics, Society, he
inadvertently misguides his readers because his management ideas are
developing continually in all of his writings. Because his holistic view of
management is based upon the Gestalt philosophy of reasoning that
accepts no total isolation of different disciplines from each other, the
result is that for Drucker management embraces the social, economic
and political elements of life. It is for this reason that his books cannot
be selected randomly when considering his management ideas. There is
evidence that he was already considering management issues as World
War II broke out, see *The Industrial Revolution Hits the Farmers* (*Harper's
Magazine* November 1939), which is referenced in Wayne Albert Risser
Leys' (1905-1973) 1941 book *Ethics and Social Policy* page 83. This article
was published after Drucker published *Economic Man* and before he
wrote *Future* both of which he classifies as Politics and Society.

18

In the months before World War II and after its outbreak Drucker's journalism continued with his analysis of Nazi Germany's economy and external policies. The *New Republic* a close following of government employees, the American intelligence services, and business policy makers. In 1940 he set up an independent consultancy to satisfy these demands which continued throughout the war.

Drucker was aware, as the war progressed, that the demand for his writing about Germany and Europe would diminish. He widened his range of topics from European history, economics, political affairs, and foreign affairs and began to write about philosophy, education, religion, economics and the arts, extending his readership to include "*Reader's Digest*" and "*The Review of Politics.*" As a leading magazine journalist he was writing much of his time. This was helping him to build a network of contacts, which would be one of his expanding strengths. Drucker later wrote that he didn't know what he wanted to do with his life, and this situation drifted until he was about thirty. The drifting had stopped when he identified his main life's work as the discipline of management. Much later at sixty he wrote that he still did not know what he wanted to do with the rest of his life as he always searched for new challenges within, and without management.

Drucker's return to teaching was at Sarah Lawrence College in Bronxville New York in the spring of 1941, the subjects being economics and statistics. He was engaged for one day a week until he was dismissed for failing to support a Senator Joseph McCarthy (1908-1957) anti-Communist Manifesto type witch-hunt of a colleague, having witnessed enough intolerance in Frankfurt. Despite being subjected to an FBI enquiry, Drucker's job was quickly replaced and by late 1941 he moved to Bennington College Vermont on a weekly basis, while also lecturing to small colleges throughout America, having visited over fifty by the time America entered World War II. By the summer of 1942 Drucker had moved his family and taken up a full-time appointment at Bennington, which was described as a highly visible woman's college.

He renewed his acquaintance with Karl Polanyi who joined the teaching staff at Bennington. He and Drucker continued a close friendship, although ideologically they were at odds. This was a pattern

19

in Drucker's life of respecting people for their intellectual capabilities while being at odds with their ideas. Another example is recorded in *Economic Man* where the *Introduction* (1939:vii-xiii) is by Henry Noel Brailsford (1873-1958), a supporter of Russian Communism and one of the most prolific writers on left-wing issues in the first half of the twentieth century; Drucker profiles Brailsford (1979:170-186).

Polanyi and Drucker were in accord that the evolution of society had not kept pace with economic changes and that it was imperative that this was brought about. Both started from the position that 17^{th}c England was the most developed country both politically and economically. {Polanyi's contention is that it is the tranches of The Enclosure Acts, between 1777 & 1795, which started with Statute of Artificers (1563) that began the social imbalance. This was followed by the action of magistrates at Speedhamland, Berkshire of 1795, which granted allowances to workers by making subsidised payments in relationship to the basic price of wheat calibrated to the size of the family, which was endorsed the following year 1796 by Parliament. For Polanyi this was the start of social disruption in England. The Industrial Revolution for Polanyi was a continuation of this sequence.} Drucker concluded that The Industrial Revolution was a separate pivotal event while recognising that other events affected its formation. It was at this point that their respective views further diverge. Drucker's society was based upon Christian individuality, status and freedom in a market economy. Polanyi argued that a market economy has never worked since The Industrial Revolution because labour, land and money were treated as commodities. The solution for Polanyi was a planned economy with man surrendering most of his status and freedom. Polanyi supported his argument by crediting Robert Owen (1771-1858), as the first to accept that industrial society had become too complex to accept that man could be a unique individual in a Christian sense. He must be considered as a part of a whole whose mutual interest would be protected by Owen's enlightened encouragement of Labour Unions (Polanyi 1944:85). Drucker while rejecting Polanyi's concept of society, still paid his respects by profiling Polanyi (1979:123- 140).

In the autumn of 1942 Drucker's second book *The Future of Industrial Man* was published. The reception of *Future* produced a range of reviews of which thirteen have been identified. The increase in the number from those on *Economic Man* confirmed that Drucker's impact was increasing. Henry Hazlitt in the *Yale Review* described the style as "*a combination of a German mysticism and a popular magazine looseness — but it is merely a brilliant blur.*" More representative of the reaction was Jacques Barzun (1907-2012) of The *New Republic*, (26 October 1942). Barzun deemed the book worthy of careful study "*that our scholars reserve for authors who have been dead a thousand years*". Quincy Howe, found in the author "*a tolerant inquiring spirit ... that our liberals and radicals can well afford to acquire*" (*Saturday Review of Literature*, 26 September 1942). These reviews and the others are detailed later. As a result of Drucker's growing recognition he was invited to join the "*American Political Science Association*" committee on "*Political Theory Research*". He felt his academic career had been launched. Drucker said that he knew that he wanted to keep on teaching at Bennington and was given the freedom to teach whatever subject needed teaching (1979:256). He taught philosophy, political theory, economic history, American government, American history, literature and religion. Drucker recorded that he had been involved in a dialogue regarding teaching at Harvard and Princeton, but remained at Bennington as Professor of Politics and Philosophy until 1949. One of the main reasons for the Harvard proposal not materialising was that the Dean restricted consulting to one day a week. Drucker's view was that management was a practice and needed to be practiced. His laboratories were his clients and their businesses, which could not be brought to the theatre, as with medical students; they had to be visited. The isolation of management students from practice has in Drucker's opinion producing an ongoing "*fault line*". In 1943 Drucker became an American Citizen (*Who's Who in America*: 2000).

Having settled into his teaching post in Vermont, his general consultancy work continued on political, social and economic affairs together with his writing. He also continued research "*on the political and social structure of industrial society, and on the 'anatomy of industrial order*'" (1979:258). Attempts at the end of 1942 to persuade business executives

21

to allow him access in their organisations resulted in rejection. *"Most of them like the chairman of Westinghouse Electric thought me a dangerous and "subversive" radical, if they understood at all what I was after"* (1979:258). Research in the Columbia University library was equally unproductive: *"the pitifully few books and articles that then existed in what we now call "management" – the very term was quite uncommon – dealt either with the rank-and-file worker at the machine or with such topics as finance or salesmanship."* Drucker felt so frustrated at his failure to commence his research that he described his efforts in New York as *"his one last effort."* (1979:258).

A few weeks into his *"last effort"* just before Christmas 1943, Drucker received a call to meet Frank Donaldson Brown (1885-1965). *"I've read your book, The Future of Industrial Man,"* said Brown:

> *"We in GM have been working on the things you're talking about – on the governance of the big organisation, its structure and constitution, on the place of big business in society, and on principles of industrial order. We don't use such terms, of course; we aren't political scientists, but mostly engineers or financial men. …Pierre Du Pont, who first delineated our structure when he took over a near-bankrupt GM in 1920, is long gone; Alfred Sloan, whom Mr Du Pont put in as president of GM… has been the architect of the Corporation and its chief executive officer for twenty years,… Our policies and structure are now almost a quarter century old; there's need for a fresh look. … you might be willing to look at GM as a political and social scientist, at our structure, our policies, our relationships inside and outside the company,… When you have a program worked out, I'll introduce you to Alfred Sloan. He is the most important man for the project. He is 'Mr GM'; the rest of us are supporting cast."* (1979:258-259).

Drucker accepted GM's commission to study their business. The result was the publication of his first book on management - *Concept of the Corporation* in autumn 1946.

The book did not go down well with GM's top management but was popular outside GM. On Drucker's academic career it had an adverse effect. Lewis Jones, president of Bennington College, told him:

22

"You're launched, on a highly promising academic career, either as an economist or as a political scientist. A book on a Business Corporation that treats it as a political and social institution will harm you in both fields" (1979:262).

Drucker said that Jones was right in this too. *"When the book came out, neither economist nor political scientist knew what to make of it and both have ever since viewed me with dark suspicion."* Drucker records that *"The reviewer in the American Economic Review was baffled by a book on business that was not "micro-economics" and complained that it offered no insights into pricing theory or the allocation of scarce resources."* Drucker also records that a *"highly sympathetic reviewer in The American Political Science Review ended by saying:*

> *"It is to be hoped that this promising young scholar will soon devote his considerable talents to a more serious subject"; and when the American Political Science Association next met, I was not reelected to the Committee on Political-Theory Research. ... thirty years later, economists as a rule were not willing to look upon the business enterprise except in economic terms, and political scientists, by and large, confine themselves to dealing with overtly "governmental" institutions and the "political process" in government."*

(1979:262-3).

Of the reviews a further six are considered later.

The positive effect of *Concept* on Drucker was to launch his management career and to convert his consultancy work into management consultancy. His claim that *Concept* started the management boom is one of the issues being examined in this research. *Concept* is still regularly quoted but for Drucker it was a stepping stone to *The Practice of Management*. However before Drucker was ready to write *Practice* he needed further preparation and would write another book. This period from the publication of *Concept* and the next book in 1950 could be described as 'Reflecting on Management.'

Reflecting on Management – 1946 - 1950

Drucker continued with his freelance writing, which included major articles. Also he continued developing his management consulting and teaching at Bennington College, while working on his next book *The New Society – The Analysis of Industrial Society* of 1950. He groups the book under the heading of Economics, Politics and Society but it is also in my view a management book because Drucker's idea is that management is central in the new society. This is confirmed by Drucker's first contribution to the *HBR* March 1950 "*Management Must Manage*" which is, in effect, a preview of *Society*. The book's intended audiences were the members of the new society. It is not specifically directed at Managers who are only part of the audience. *Management Must Manage* was the start of a relationship with *HBR*, which would set two records. The first was that he produced more Reviews than any other external contributor, and the second was that he has contributed over the greatest time span of any regular contributor (Letter HBR / Starbuck 19 November 1999).

In *Society*, Drucker's refines his existing ideas, develops new ones and begins the exploration of further ideas.

Taking a Central Position 1950 – 1953

As *Society* neared publication Drucker and his family left Vermont and Bennington College and moved back to New York for Drucker to become Professor of Management at the Graduate Business School of New York University. The engagement at New York lasted from 1950 to 1971. Drucker claims it was the first appointment ever as 'a professor of management' although Lillian Gilbreth achieved this in 1935 at Purdue University (Yost: 1949:337).

The New Society was, as the title suggests, about Drucker's vision of a new society. Rathenau had previously used the title for his book *Der Neue Staat (The New Society* 1919). The aim of Rathenau's book was to project policies that would protect citizens from their mistakes. Inadvertently he was laying the foundations for Nazi totalitarianism. While Drucker accepted many of Rathenau's ideas, Drucker's view of the new society differed fundamentally. Drucker's society was based upon American Christian free enterprise which, in the view of the *New Yorker* [*The Book Review Digest* 1951:258], was positioned somewhere between Communism and Capitalism with management's role integrated within society. *Society* received other positive and complimentary reviews as follows. It was a *"stimulating volume that is sure to be the book of the year in socio-economics"* (G G Higgins *Commonweal* 1 September 1950:164 [*The Book Review Digest* 1951:258]). It deserved *"the widest possible audience"* (The New York Times 14 May 1950:6[*The Book Review Digest* 1951:258]). *"Mr Drucker is regarded as one of America's leading experts on economics, social and political problems, and has a wide experience as a foreign correspondent, college teacher, international banker, and consultant to large businesses"* (H H *Springfield Republican* 4 June 1950:12 [*The Book Review Digest* 1951:258]). While commenting negatively that *"There are some minor irritations in this book"* S E Harris concludes, *"it is a stimulating valuable and provocative book"* (*New York Herald Tribune* 21 May 1950:6[*The Book Review Digest* 1951:258])

With the publication of *Society* Drucker had a robust model for society and an acknowledged reputation as a social commentator. He was now also immersed in management rather than the tentative outsider, who had started his research with GM for *Concept*. The evidence in *Society* is that Drucker's references are much more management related, which is evidence of his growing knowledge of other thinkers and writers on the subject. In the following four year gap between publishing *Society* and *Practice* Drucker's reputation grew. He developed his management consulting practice; extended his range of writing to include management related subjects, while continuing with his lecturing.

Concept has been founded on a management consultancy commission but centered on social organisation with the major American Corporation GM. *Practice* was also founded on a management consultancy commission. This time the client was General Electric Company (of America) GE, who commissioned Drucker's contribution for his management knowledge as part of their management review team, rather than asking for a social study. This provided further evidence of Drucker's progress as a management consultant and his now established standing in this discipline.

25

This chapter has explained Drucker's background, diverse experiences and his general development. It has provided a setting for his work to be examined now in detail.

CHAPTER TWO

THE EVOLUTION OF DRUCKER'S IDEAS IN HIS FIRST FOUR BOOKS

This Chapter will examine the development of Drucker's ideas and his consequential influences in these first four books.

End of Economic Man - **The World of Despair**

The full title of his first book is *The End of Economic Man – A Study of the New Totalitarianism* (May 1939). The first sentence is *"This is a political book"* (1939: xv). Although Drucker wrote that he needed to escape *"pre-war"* the book confirmed his obsession with it. The book tracked the historical events that caused the breakdown of European society between World Wars I and II starting with the development of Fascism that materialised first in Italy, then in Germany and spread into Austria. Reasons are given why the Fascists gained power, and also the Communists in Russia. The reasons are that the political and social structure had collapsed, leaving a vacuum and despair. People's lives had not only collapsed economically but also spiritually, as the Church had been powerless to fill the vacuum. The economic, political and spiritual world was bankrupt; people had lost the will for freedom, and had capitulated. Totalitarianism had filled the vacuum; it made decisions for the masses and gave economic hope. In Germany this had been achieved by building an economy that was based upon preparation for war.

A statistical analysis of the references in *Economic Man* confirms that Adolf Hitler (1889-1945) is the most frequently referred to with forty-one mentions followed by Karl Heinrich Marx (1818-1883) with thirty-eight. Although Hitler was a negative influence on Drucker's ideas he received even handed treatment from Drucker.

A management idea that Drucker did inherit from Hitler, albeit inadvertently, is privatisation, originally named re-privatisation. Drucker described that Hitler only wanted power and not to be involved in the day-to-day management of organisations except for control purposes.

27

Because the German banks were failing he reluctantly had to nationalise them for their survival. Once this had been achieved he returned them to private ownership by *"reprivatisation"* (*ibid*:118). This idea would re-emerge in Drucker's later writings and became acknowledged and adopted by the Thatcher Government as their *"privatisation"* policy. [Idea: Privatisation]

Marx, a recurring figure in Drucker's early writings, received rational intellectual analysis in *Economic Man* with credit being given by Drucker to certain of Marx's ideas on the labour market. However Drucker was totally opposed to Marx's political ideas. Of Marx as an economist he has Drucker's admiration but not his support. Drucker follows Schumpeter's line on Marx as an economist — that Marx asked the right question, which is the most important thing intellectually. What Drucker recognises is that Marx's socialist dogma was dependent on a proletariat, which only has their labour to sell.

Even a casual examination of the one hundred and thirty-three individual references in *Economic Man* demonstrated how extensive Drucker's preparation for his ideas were; he draws on history, philosophy, politics and economics, which links back to his time in Hamburg, where "(he) *read and read and read*" as he tried objectively to replace a world that had gone mad and attempted to discover a new purpose. A major part of that purpose later emerged as management. That he was prepared to examine the totalitarian philosophy and consider many alternatives before reaching his final conclusions is conspicuous in his work. An illustration is the work of Friedrich Nietzsche (1844-1900), whose *"God is dead"* was an anathema to Drucker, to the positive Christianity of Gilbert Keith Chesterton (1874-1936) and others to validate Søren Aabye Kierkegaard's (1813- 1859) ideas. He sets out on what later can be recognised as a journey of discovery – the discovery of management. It will take a different route from any taken before or since.

In *Economic Man* Drucker identifies several accepted or permanent influences. The first was Kierkegaard, who was described as an extreme Protestant whose relationship with God is purely personal. But even from this position society for Kierkegaard was utterly irrational (1939:

28

97). To endorse the need for an ecumenical dimension to one's personal life and to support Kierkegaard's position, Drucker includes Fyodor Mikhailovich Dostoevsky (1821-1881), describing his conversion from a French Revolutionist to what he perceived as the only solution: that of a Christian based society (*ibid*: 91).

Walther Rathenau (1867-1922), who is another permanent influence on Drucker's ideas (but with whom Drucker will not always agree), receives four mentions as a serious liberal political thinker – who as an opponent of Versailles from the beginning predicted it would lead to a military reaction from Germany (*ibid*: 60 & 110). Later connecting Rathenau to Hitler, Drucker wrote:

> "*I myself have heard him (Hitler) attack Walther Rathenau and his pupils for having advanced a totalitarian economy which - according to the Hitler of 1931 – would make the state the servant of its social structure*"
>
> (*ibid*: 118).

Rathenau the left-wing democrat "*was the first to preach totalitarian economics*" (*ibid*: 246). He did not see it would lead to fascism. In fact almost without exception these "*confirmed totalitarians*", the Nazis, came from his school. Contrary to what transpired, Rathenau the extreme nationalist saw totalitarian economics as:

> "*...the final step towards freedom and equality*"
>
> (*ibid*: 246).

Drucker's conclusion was that all forms of totalitarianism were unconstitutional and therefore illegitimate, but that the legitimate alternatives of socialism and capitalism in Europe had lost their appeal. Although *Economic Man* had a high theoretical content, as befits a constitutional lawyer, Drucker's management ideas could be seen to be emerging by sifting the ideas of his influences. Drucker was more prepared than any management writer before him to search widely for the solution to his problems in what could be described as a boundary-less search. The start was the ecumenical content of life such as

29

Kierkegaard's brand of Christianity, which should give man freedom, status, function and morality or integrity. Next was Rathenau's social plan to reorganise and have an integrated industrial order, as an alternative to totalitarianism. Kierkegaard and Rathenau provided the seeds of Drucker's management ideas, which were based on integrating major industry with a society that was fair to everyone. Drucker's perspective, as Rathenau's, was outward-looking towards society. This outlook contrasted with Frederick Winslow Taylor (1856-1915) and Jules Henri Fayol (1841-1925), whose focus was on self- contained businesses that were inward-looking. Drucker would later identify Taylor, Fayol and Rathenau as the three founding fathers of management. For Taylor the industrial plant was complete as a mechanical unit. For Fayol it was also a social organisation that spread into the households of the workers, but did not travel beyond into society in general. Drucker also drew attention to Robert Owen (1771-1858) for his concept of "*individual democracy*", "*the father of consumer's co-operation*" and for being "*that almost saintly figure of early capitalism*" (*ibid*:87). What was being established was that Drucker at this early stage of his work was identifying some of the major influences of 20[th]c management.

For Drucker the constitutional alternative to totalitarianism was American free-market capitalism. Drucker, like so many of this time, was uncertain about the future and could only offer America as an important 'safety valve' to Europe and a living example. His qualified hope (*ibid*: 41-42), was that it could lead:

> "...*toward the freedom and equality of the individual in the free and equal society.*"

> (*ibid*: 35)

Although Alexis De Tocqueville (1805-1859) is referenced for his religious view (*ibid*:85), Tocqueville held similar views to Drucker about the role of America in the early 19[th]c. The difference was that Tocqueville was more confident of the American ideal working, drawing his conclusions from being resident there, whereas Drucker was drawing his conclusions from afar. However Tocqueville signalled for Drucker the escape from 'pre-war' (Tocqueville 1835). Karl Emil Maximilian 'Max' Weber (1864-1920) added to America's attraction with his views that America was shaped by the early Quaker colonies creating a non-conformist Protestant society (Weber 1927). Many, including Drucker, followed Weber's view of America being a Quaker- created society as conventional wisdom, when *Economic Man* was written. During the following decades this view changed to include other immigrant groups. Rathenau was also attracted to America for different reasons, as he perceived that if Germany adopted their high wage potential for the workers, it would be a contributor to improving and stabilising the German economy and society. As part of a high wage package Rathenau rejected Taylor's and Ford's production methods as destroyers of the essential satisfaction that workers could achieve only by craft trained labour.

The idea that management has a part to play in society was emerging but not through the professional economist who "*seem(s) to have the power* [yet the] *actual developments have been taking a course which all economists – however much they differ among themselves – had declared to be "impossible"*" (1939:45-46). What Drucker was concluding was that they had misled those responsible for social and political developments for the need for a comparable change to balance the economic change that has already taken place. That they failed in their discipline had contributed to the breakdown in society. That economists should hold no responsibility for the social consequences of their actions, Drucker rejects. Economists Marx, John Maynard Keynes (1883-1946) and Adam Smith (1723-1790) are mentioned in the text but not Schumpeter. Henry Ford (1863-1947), one of Drucker's early management influences, was described in the text as "*...that grand old man of modern capitalism*" who is right and wrong at the same time when he "*forgets that economic expansion and increases are not aims in themselves. They make sense only as means to a social end*" (*ibid*:35). Also that "*the whole scientific system of classical economics collapsed when Henry Ford started out to obtain a monopoly by cheaper prices and large production in blissful ignorance of the "economic law" according to which monopolies reduce production and raise prices*" (1939:45). The Ford Motor Company was Drucker's first recorded interest in corporate management in a free-market economy. The

31

references to Rathenau at this juncture are related to society not corporate management.

Economic Man was completed with the American market in mind. It had been conceived in Europe at about the time when Drucker wrote the Stahl monograph. Drucker's description of Stahl was as one of the German Christian Conservatives who foresaw the events of the 1930s in the 1830s (*ibid*:83). On publication, *Economic Man* had considerable impact both inside and outside America. Amongst its potent messages was the regressive treatment of the Jews by Hitler. In America it established Drucker as an expert on the European scene and introduced him as an intellectual. Although he believed "*capitalism is doomed*" as far as Europe was concerned he viewed the American model as robust because it was different, as Ford had proved. The impact of the book was recorded in *The Book Review Digest* 1939. Listed without comments are reviews in *The Booklist, Christian Science, Monitor, Foreign Affairs, Manchester Guardian, The Spectator* and *The Yale Review*. Detailed were selected reviews as Julian Back Jnr in *Books* who describes the work as "*Like a cool shower*" that explained Fascism where countless had failed. Eli Ginzberg in *The Saturday Review of Literature* rated it "*A brilliant book*". M T Florinsky in *The New York Times* described the book as brilliantly written. Churchill, who was mentioned favorably in Drucker's text, produced a challenging review in *The Times Literary Supplement*. Although Churchill believed that some of the pieces fitted together too neatly, Drucker records that Churchill instructed that it became essential reading for British military cadets. Of the previous reviews full texts of Florinsky (21 May 1939) and Churchill (27 May 1939) were available for examination.

A further review not recorded in *The Book Review Digest* was by E W F Tomlin in *Life and Letters Today*, who compared *Economic Man* favorably with the outstanding contemporary books on politics by Balfour, Wyndham Lewis & Madariga. This essential book was a "*brilliant affair*". Tomlin described his review as an inadequate summary of what was becoming rare "*a really mature book*". Readers were invited – "*indeed urged*" – to verify this for themselves. The only critical review recorded in *The Book Review Digest* was by C T Schmidt in *New Republic*. He found Drucker's theory in itself so abstract as to need explaining.

There was a more general reaction to Drucker's forecast that Hitler would attack Russia despite their mutual neutrality treaty with Germany. This provoked attacks from the Communists, some of who alleged that Drucker did not exist, but that his work was that of a group of anti-Communist conspirators. Interestingly Drucker didn't make this forecast. He wrote that only a war could prevent an alliance. "*Actually this expectation of a Russo-German war was never much more than wishful thinking. Unless an unforeseeable accident happens there will be no war between Germany and Russia*" (1939:231). Drucker did not write that Hitler would attack Russia; he "*hoped*" he might, but suspected that he could not be that unintelligent.

The Future of Industrial Man - Management Ideas Germinating 1943

That Drucker would give considerable thought as to what needed to happen to lead the world away from totalitarianism was recorded in *Economic Man*. That it had been taking place was confirmed in the publication of his next book with a full title of "*The Future of Industrial Man, A Conservative Approach*" which was finished in the summer of 1942 and published later in that year. Drucker, having planted the seeds of his management thought, now saw them start to germinate. The book had but one topic: "*How can an industrial society be built as a free society?*" (1942:7). In the book Drucker gave his own views or draws from contemporaries or earlier writers. He continued the idea from his previous book that the problem was that the collapse of the social and political foundations of the Western world had spawned totalitarianism. To define society, Drucker writes, "*is as difficult as defining life, but for it to function it is worth repeating that society must give its individual members status, and function*".

Future is produced, like *Economic Man*, without an index and only a small number of footnotes. The following writers are referenced: Jacques Barzun (1907 -2012) for his books *The French Race* and *Race* (1942:15) {These are *The French Race and Theories of the Origins of The Social and Political Implications Prior to the Revolution* (1932) and *Race – A Study in Modern Superstition* (1937)}. Adolf Augustus Berle Jnr (1895-1971) &

33

Gardiner Coit Means' (1896- 1988) 1933 book *The Modern Corporation and Private Property* (1942:84); Marshall Edward Dimock (1903-1991) *No 11 TNEC Monographs*; James Burnham's (1905-1987) 1941 book *The Managerial Revolution* (1942:126); and Drucker's own *Economic Man* (1942:141, 280). Where there are one hundred and forty-eight references to different individuals, in *The Future of Industrial Man*, of these new references only twenty-two are repeated from in *The End of Economic Man*. This gives a net total of two hundred and fifty-nine at this date.

The influences are more integrated into the text than in *Economic Man*. Hitler and Nazism are the most dominant references politically with Marx and Marxism remaining conspicuous. Drucker tracks how politics had developed in Europe from ancient Greece. His conclusions were that the French Revolution spawned Marxism, and in particular Jean-Jacques Rousseau (1712-1778) spawned Hitler. In Drucker's opinion Hitler had succeeded not because there was a German type but because conditions were right. Drucker did not accept that there was an 'ideal type' of German character and that Germans are specifically different from other races. Rathenau in contrast believed that a German recovery was dependent on the 'ideal type' and their differences.

Drucker continues that England's Industrial Revolution also produced a wide divergence of thinkers but unlike in France, the outcome was a different political system. It was developing in the reign of George III, and it spawned the American democracy of The Founding Fathers. Drucker's conclusion was that the American Constitution was "*the*" political system. However, to fully convert from a mercantile society, it needed to complete the metamorphosis into a complete new American capitalist system. The progress of the metamorphosis had begun with the creation of big business, as the new preferred economic unit.

Drucker's management ideas are becoming more developed since their initial nominal references in *Economic Man*. Ford was attributed with reducing the old mercantile theory of monopoly by restricting supply to an absurdity. Ford increased production, reduced prices and made more profit than all of the old school monopolies put together (1942: 72-73). Ford also first used the assembly line as a radically new system of

34

production (*ibid*: 102). This assertion Drucker would later correct. Ford was attributed as being at the inception of the great innovation "*...of the worker as an efficient automatic standardized machine*" (*ibid*: 102). Ford was also mentioned for the popular support he received for both his opposition to the Unions and to the New Deal (*ibid*: 128). Taylor was mentioned in Drucker's writing for the first time in conjunction with Ford for his independent work, on "*...the worker as an efficient automatic standardized machine*" (*ibid*:102). Business giants were mentioned such as John Pierpont Morgan (1837-1913) (*ibid*:76, 254); John Davison Rockefeller (1839-1937) (*ibid*:254); and Andrew Carnegie (1835-1919) (*ibid*:254) to support Drucker's ideas of American economic success.

Three major economists appear in the text. Firstly Adam Smith (1723-1790), with regards to property, is described as "*a good deal more Marxist than Marx*" (*ibid*:93). But Smith, as a dazzling light of the English political scene of 1776, was eclipsed by the "*most dangerous of all liberal totalitarians, Jeremy Bentham (1748-1842)*" (*ibid*:230). Smith would later receive occasional general reference. Second, Marx received most attention for his political philosophy, but as an economist was described as pre-industrial (*ibid*:69) while Drucker noted that he agreed like the orthodox capitalist economist "*with the axiom that property is socially constitutive. They differ only on who should own*" (*ibid*:93). The third economist received very positive treatment:

> "*The only consistent and effective contemporary theory of capitalism – that of Professor Joseph Schumpeter – neither attempts to justify property nor tries to see property as constitutive in the social structure or as the motive power of economic development. Schumpeter centers on private initiative; the enterprising manager is both the justification and the motive power of this capitalist system. Capital plays a most subordinate part. Without the enterprising manager, Schumpeter regards it as wholly unproductive; it is nothing but an auxiliary to management. Professor Schumpeter is hard pressed to find a convincing justification for capital's claim to a share in the profits. One gathers that he would consider compensation beyond a service fee as an*

unjustified increment, and as a "surplus value" which properly should have gone to management"   (*ibid*:95)

For Drucker, in the period *"since James Watt invented the steam engine"* (*ibid*:3) society had moved from the mercantile economy, through the industrialization of the proprietorial owned enterprises of the Industrial Revolution. The change had had many consequences that Drucker identifies. The two which are the major concern of the book are that big business was not constitutionally legal, and that the disturbance of society brought about by industrial change had left an unacceptable and dangerous vacuum that will have to be filled.

With regard to the legitimacy of big business Drucker examines three sets of ideas. Firstly, that of Owen D Young (1874-1962) (described as *"perhaps the best representative of modern* (American) *corporate management"* (1942:89-90)) that the shareholders had lost authority to the directors as managers of the enterprise. For Young this situation should be formalised by removing the ownership rights that existed from the shareholders and transferring the legal title of the shares to the management. To compensate the shareholders, for what was a loss of property rights the shareholders would receive a *"wage"* for the use of their money. Drucker agreed with Young and concludes that his ideas align with the reality of the situation, whereas the legal situation did not.

The second set of ideas are those of Adolf Augustus Berle jnr (1895-1971) and Gardiner Coit Means (1896-1988). Drucker concluded that management power was legitimate as long as it was *"derived from individual property rights"* (*ibid*:79). But in conflict with contract theory *"in the modern Corporation the decisive power, that of the managers, is derived from no one but from the managers themselves"* (1942:80) therefore it was not legitimate. This divorce of management and control had been publicised by Berle & Means in their 1933 book *The Modern Corporation and Private Property* (1932:84). For Drucker, Dimock in his *No 11 TNEC monograph* and others had shown the trend as gathering momentum. In Drucker's later work he showed that Rathenau had preceded Berle & Means in identifying the transfer of power from the shareholders to the management (Rathenau *Von Kommenden Dingen* 1917- *In Days to Come* translation 1919:121). So had Young a few years later, but before Berle & Means see *Owen D Young A New Type of Industrial Leader* (Tarbell 1932).

The third set of ideas that Drucker considers are those of Burnham, {the American born academic Trotskyite who later became a supporter of American democratic ideals and worked for the Reagan Administration}. Burnham's ideas were set out in his 1941 book *The Managerial Revolution*. Burnham's hypothesis was that a management revolution was taking place regardless of the political system, whether totalitarianism or American democracy. In Burnham's management society, managerial power was legitimate and would inevitably lead to managerial rule. Drucker rejected Burnham's ideas like those of all Marxists or Trotskyist as flawed, stating that the *"managerial Society"* that Burnham predicts;

> *"...has been our society in the first third of the present century. And it belongs already to the past"*

(1942:127).

The support that Burnham's ideas received from managers was not endorsed by popular support for *"...mere managerial power; General Motors, though on the basis of their record probably more deserving of support, obtained none"* (*ibid*:128). (Drucker's compliment to GM was interesting, as his next book *Concept* was the result of a commission from them). Drucker's position on the legitimacy of the Corporation was that a way would have to be found to create this based upon individual property rights (*ibid*:128). The concept of Unions as alternative leaders was rejected. Union leadership and modern corporate management was simply a counter-balance. It was the negative to the Corporation's positive position. If the Unions took over management's power it would increase the danger of non-legitimate power (*ibid*:122-123).

Future contains several important ideas but the most consequential was Drucker's social idea. *"Economic Man... has also failed politically, socially and metaphysically. (As completely proven — see The End of Economic Man)"* (*ibid*:280). A plan was needed, but *"Planning as a philosophy thus rests upon a denial of freedom and upon the demand of the absolute rule of a perfect élite. As a political program it rests upon a probably false assertion*" (*ibid*:286). What was needed was a new form of planning; one that was flexible based upon unpreparedness such as that confronting the general staff of a future war and not the absolutist of preparedness (*ibid*:288-289). It was necessary to build on the social success learned from the war.

> "*The central fact in the social crisis of our time is that the industrial plant has become the basic social unit, but that it is not yet a social institution*"
>
> (*ibid*:297).

The answer was not total planning or a return to 19thc *laissez-faire* but the organisation of industry on the basis of local and decentralised self-government. Only a self-governing plant community would make possible both a free and functioning society giving status, and function, to its members and removing the greatest fear in a democratic society - that of unemployment and Depression effect (*ibid*:298). The "*self-governing plant community*" would later be named the "*autonomous self-governing plant community*." Man cannot always invent what he would like to have but has a duty to use the present institutions as much as possible. He will have to be radical in analysis, dogmatic in principles, conservative in methods, and pragmatic in politics. Centralised bureaucratic despotism must be prevented "*by building a genuine local self-government in the industrial sphere*" (*ibid*:291). Economic security would be imperative after the Western democracies have won the war (*ibid*:112). Centralised bureaucratic government must be replaced by Decentralisation (*ibid*:297-298) "*Freedom, as we understand it, is inconceivable outside and before the Christian era*" (*ibid*:154). Its only basis is man's imperfection (*ibid*:150). "*It is a faith – a faith in man's being at the same time as "proud and yet a wretched thing"*" (*ibid*:169). As the most advanced developed country, America had the responsibility to find the answer. Other countries would then have to follow her model.

Drucker maintains continuity from *Economic Man*. Of the four major influences the primacy of Hitler and Marx as the major evil forces in the world is maintained. However, by the conclusion of *Economic Man* Hitler has been exorcised as prominent in Drucker's mind. While Kierkegaard was not specifically referred to in the text, his influence was apparent, with the overt references to Christianity being central to Drucker's ideas. Also Tocqueville's name was absent, although his ideas were upheld in the text. Dostoevsky was carried forward, receiving a further mention in an idea of Drucker's in exploring happy slavery or responsible freedom (*ibid*:150-152). Referenced is Dostoevsky's 1880 book *The Grand Inquisitor* (*ibid*:150) and his proposition that man would rather be a happy slave than have the responsibility of freedom. Drucker agreed with Dostoevsky that freedom was a burden and also believed that it was an inevitable burden for a functioning society. This conclusion joins Kierkegaard and Dostoevsky's Christianity. Drucker supports Kierkegaard's view of Christianity and recognised that Dostoevsky was warning against a state that eventually led directly to Hitler. Ford was also carried forward with his influence on Drucker as the epitome of the American industrial capitalist. His innovative vision of modern industry has changed the way we work within the plant. Drucker recognises that what was needed now was a complementary change in society. Rathenau does not make the text but is the inspiration of Drucker's big idea 'the autonomous self- governing plant community' as evidenced in Rathenau's writing. See Lyndall Fownes Urwick (1891-1983) Chapter 6 Urwick 1956:122. [Idea: Autonomous self-governing plant community]. Others mentioned for their contribution to management ideas included Berle & Means, who would remain a constant influence on Drucker, Smith who was regarded as a foundation of the past; and Taylor, who after a low-key introduction would remain a major influence on Drucker's ideas. Schumpeter received his first mention. He would develop into the primary secular influence upon Drucker's management ideas. Young and Dimock had received their only mention.

Drucker confirmed in *Future* that his views on management would be wide ranging and based upon integrating each and any discipline that could make a worthwhile contribution, but only after passing the test of his close scrutiny. His view was also being established that management was a living discipline and must adapt to change in its environment because we were in an economy of "*free enterprise*" and "*private initiative*"

(1942:95) where management power has become a new and original power in society (1942:87).

Drucker's Stahl monograph had established him as a crusader against wrong. *Economic Man* reinforced the same position, being an attack on ideas that needed to be consigned to the past. In *Future* Drucker advanced his crusade as he was now examining the future. For Drucker the power of totalitarianism with a driving military purpose was being defeated. What was needed now was a legitimate constitutional organisation that must take its place. Drucker perceived that the new organ of society was already the mass production plant – the Corporation. Drucker wanted to make the management of the Corporation a legitimate government but had to accept Berle & Means' analysis that management was divorced from property rights meant it was not legitimate. Drucker would spend decades trying to evolve a format to make corporate management constitutionally legitimate – but fail. Of his idea, the autonomous self- governing plant community, which Drucker later described as probably his best idea, would only become workable in a few cooperatives, which Drucker never regarded as the corporate answer. What remained for Drucker 'in capitalism' was what would be the equivalent of the totalitarian 'military drive' – 'management'. It would be Drucker's "*life giving element*" or James David Mooney (1884-1957) & Alan Campbell Reiley's (1869-1947) "*vital spark*" *(Onward Industry!)* (1931, Page: 13). [Idea: Management as a 'life giving element'. It has become an original power].

In *Economic Man* Drucker examined man's political and society's problems of economic man. In *Future* he examined industrial man's social needs and the prospect of them being achieved by a humanised free market American capitalism, driven by the mass production plant. Industrial man's social needs would be met through the autonomous self-governing plant community. Progress in these two areas would provide for the increased economic necessities of man and his family, and also reinstate the social status that had been lost by the de-agrarianisation in the developing industrial societies; by the creation of the semi-skilled masses; and through deskilling by Taylor's Scientific Management.

40

Future received a range of reviews; some of these were listed in *The Book Review Digest* 1943 are *Bookmark, Political Science Quarterly, Pratt,* without being detailed while information is provided of reviews by D W Brogan in *The Manchester Guardian,* which was the most critical. He regarded the book as a lost opportunity to review the world order from an American perspective. He was suspicious that weakness of argument has been covered up by rhetoric. An anonymous review in *The Times Literary Review* agreed with Drucker that the existing institutions could not be converted, acknowledging that although it was a stimulating and provocative book, it was not always convincing. H J Laski in *The New Statesman & Nation* review was more neutral. He believed that the book *"fails to set the nature"* of the problem of *"massive complexity"* while acknowledging that Drucker was obviously, able and well read. Other reviews were supportive in principle. J H Landman in *American Academy* recorded the books as *"stimulating"*. Ernest Baker in *The Spectator* thought that there was much good and stimulating in an able book but found some of the detail distracting. Ordway Tead (1891-1973), one of Drucker's management influences, wrote in *Survey Gazette* that he considered the book was likely to arouse strong reader reaction although Drucker was too modest regarding his convictions. It was less important to agree with the writer than accept that the book was thought-provoking and should be read for this reason. Reviewed by Henry Hazlitt, who added *"let us admit it: Mr Drucker is 'brilliant'"* and further by Jacques Barzun, who found the book perfectly planned and *"each page is the fruit of much learning and long reflection"*. Barzun considered to whose work Drucker's relate. Barzun's conclusion was that Drucker was a new Walter Bagehot (1826-1877), close to Shaw but not close enough to Freud who belonged elsewhere. Revered Quincy Howe found only praise. For him Drucker stood out by understanding more fully than nearly all of the American intellectuals what Marx and Hitler really represented and for determining the point of departure for his own ideas. Liberals and radicals might spurn Drucker's book *"but what better have they to show over the years"*. Although not recorded in *The Book Review Digest* two further references were found. Freda Utley in *Common Sense* was amongst Drucker's supporters who believed that he had made an

41

original and important contribution. Amongst many other things Drucker had done was to try and bring "*ethics and politics back into politics and economy*" for both Europe and America. "(Not) *the least of the merits of the book lies in the author's complete freedom from racial or national prejudices – even if one does not accept his essential Christian philosophy*". An unidentified review in *Time* it is described as an essay that could not be disregarded.

The range and number of the reviews confirm that Drucker's reputation and recognition was increasing. Admittedly some of the reviews are critical but these may be engendered by the reviewer's political differences. A conclusion could be that the reviews are about equal in support or rejection. However I believe this is not the correct conclusion. Drucker appears to score better with the reviewers who display a comprehensive knowledge of the topics of Drucker's book. A considered conclusion is that Drucker's arguments work best when examined holistically and not just when viewed in a political or economic content. Whereas *Economic Man* had been pessimistic *Future* was optimistic, an attitude not prevalent in Britain in 1942 which was at the centre of World War II, which probably influenced the British reviewers who are in the main, critical of Drucker. What was conclusive was that GM reacted positively by commissioning Drucker to examine them within the context set by *Future*.

Drucker said that *Future* laid the foundation for his interest in the management of institutions. "*Out of this in turn came my first "management" book, Concept of the Corporation*" (1979:135). For him deskilling had removed the 'old' sense of workers' achievement. Drucker describes his plan to research management, through the political and social structure of industrial society, and on "*the 'anatomy of industrial order*" in his 1979 book *Adventures of a Bystander* (*ibid*:258).

Drucker had set out his theory to examine management from a different aspect than hitherto.

Concept of the Coporation - Learning about Management in Practice 1944 – 1946

Drucker related to John J Tarrant, one of his biographers, that *"When I got the assignment from GM I knew nothing about management. I gave myself a quickie course finding to my surprise that I could read all of the significant books about management in two days. There were just seven books on general management in all languages except Japanese and most of them repeated each other"* (Tarrant 1976:37). Drucker was advised to visit the American Library of the British born Harry Arthur Hopf (1882-1949), a management engineer as the Americans then termed management consultant, who was a management thinker, and writer. Hopf, who was a Drucker influence, was reputed to have the largest collection of management books in the world.

In an introduction by Drucker to Graham's 1995 book on Follett, *Mary Parker Follett Prophet of Management*, Drucker presented a different version:

> *"Most puzzling, perhaps, is her* [Follett's] *absence from the reading list Harry Hopf gave me. A successful consultant and authority on managing insurance companies, Hopf had built a magnificent business and management library numbering several thousand volumes at his farm in Crotonville* (also known as Ossining), *New York – which after his death in 1949 became the nucleus of GE's famed Advanced Management Institute. Hopf gave me a list of six or seven pages and assured me that it contained everything "of the slightest importance" on management. A most catholic list, it introduced me to Taylor, Gantt, and the two Gilbreths – husband and wife; to Ian Hamilton and Lyndall Urwick; to Robert Owen, Walther Rathenau, Henri Fayol, Cyril Burt and Hugo Münsterberg; to Elton Mayo, and Chester I Barnard. I owe to Hopf's list the realisation that there was a discipline of management waiting to be born. But Mary Parker Follett's name was not on the list. Her books, of course, were in Hopf's library; but evidently he did not consider them "of the slightest importance"* (Graham 1995:2). All of the aforementioned became

Drucker scholars. (Searches by this author could not establish the whereabouts of Hopf's library books).

Later Drucker told Jack Beatty that while researching *Concept*, he had asked GM executives if they could point him toward authorities on their obscure profession. "*I kept hearing about Harry Hopf*," Drucker told Warren Bennis.

> "*He was an insurance consultant and had built a library which became the nucleus of the General Electric Management Institute in Crotonville, New York. So I went out to visit Mr Hopf, who was an elderly gentleman and ailing. He had the biggest management library in the world. The only one. His library was an enormous room with thousands and thousands of volumes. My heart fell when I saw it. He said to me, "Young man, I understand that you are interested in management." And I said, "Yes sir." He said, "There are only six books here about management. The rest are all about insurance, selling, advertising and manufacturing." It turned out that three of them weren't quite management. So practically nothing existed.*"
>
> (Beatty 1998:101)

Drucker was contradicting what he previously wrote that there was "*more material than any man can read*" and that:

> "*...a large and steadily growing literature on business management which has been freely drawn upon in the study*". These included "*Chester I Barnard, James D Mooney and Ordway Tead, or the work done at the*
>> *Harvard Business School have contributed greatly to our knowledge of the Corporation as an organisation*" (1946:12).

Drucker's conclusion that, "*practically nothing existed*", was contradicted by Hopf in his 1945 paper *Soundings in the Literature of Management: Fifty Books the Educated Practitioner Should Know No 6*. Twelve books on Scientific Management start with Taylor's *Shop Management* from 1903 being the first date of publication, not as commonly recorded as 1911. Also included are Henry Laurence Gantt (1861-1919), the Gilbreths, and *The*

44

Gantt Chart (Clark 1923). Twelve indispensable works start with *The Philosophy of Management* (Oliver Sheldon 1923) followed by *Administration industrielle et générale* (*Industrial and General Administration*) (Fayol 1916), which Hopf notes was first presented as a paper in 1908, and continue with Paul Eugene Holden (1891-1983), Loundsbury Spaight Fish (.... - 1987) & Hubert L Smith, Mooney & Reiley, Walter Rautenstrauch (1880-1951), Chester Irving Barnard (1886-1961) and Ordway Tead (1891-1973). Twenty-four recommended works include Henry Clayton Metcalf (1885/1942) & Urwick, Tead & Metcalf, *Management and the Workers* re Western Electric (Roethlisberger & Dickson 1939). Drucker's conclusion is also contradicted by Urwick & Edward Francis Leopold Brech (1909-2006) in their 1945 book *The Making of Scientific Management Vol 1 Thirteen Pioneers*. And again by Hopf in his 1947 paper in response to Urwick & Brech's book entitled *Historical Perspectives in Management: A Critical Essay Embodying a Review of The Making of Scientific Management by L Urwick & E F L Brech*.

Later in 1956 Urwick edited another book *The Golden Book of Management*, which listed sixty- nine pioneers but did not include Barnard, Burt, Hamilton, Mooney and Tead on Drucker's lists (Urwick 1956). In 1984 a little known edition, in the UK, was published in America as *The Golden Book of Management New Expanded Edition*. William B Wolf had assembled the additional material. What Wolf made clear was that for inclusion in the 1956 edition as in the 1984 edition the pioneers had to be dead. Barnard, Mooney and Tead make this 1984 list with Drucker contributing to his identified influences of Brown, Harold Francis Smiddy (1900-1978) and Ralph Jerron Cordiner (1900-1973). Included in this list of new pioneers who are Drucker's influences are Nordling, McGregor, Sloan and Lillian Gilbreth.

Drucker's view that *"practically nothing existed"* he eventually contradicted. By 1974 of Hopf's library Drucker wrote;

> *"...there are no more than sixty or seventy volumes that properly could be called management. ..., the Hopf library contained everything written on management in any language (except Japanese) until the 1940s"*

(1974:12).

What has been confirmed by this examination of writers on general management is not that "*practically nothing existed*," before Drucker commenced writing *Concept* in 1943 but that Drucker was not aware of what existed.

After Drucker's first meeting with Brown's associates at GM, Drucker suggested that he change his report into a book. Brown agreed to the change. However Brown was skeptical whether a book on management was marketable, as were Drucker's publishers. Most managers did not realise they were practicing management. The general public had never heard of management although it was interested in how the rich made their money:

> "*A book on such esoteric subjects as organisation structure, the development of managers and the role of the foreman and middle management, was surely going to go unread.*"

(1979:262)

Drucker met Sloan, who was the chairman of the board of GM, and was told that Drucker's project was a decision of Sloan colleagues, which Sloan accepted. Sloan pledged access and co- operation for whatever Drucker needed. He told Drucker to act objectively and not be influenced by sensitivities, as the politics would start on the completion of the project. Drucker says that he did not completely heed this sound advice on what was his first assignment as a management consultant. Drucker learned from this experience and decided that to succeed; a management consultant must give his objective opinion and not patronize or flatter clients. After receiving the report the client was then free to act on the advice or otherwise, but it ought to be clear what the advice was. Drucker agreed with GM that he should be paid equivalent to his college salary while working for GM. Drucker spent the next eighteen months visiting plants across America, attending board meetings and examining GM's operations. By 1946 the product of his labour was the publication of *Concept*, which was published for the British market under the title *Big Business* because it was considered that the British wouldn't understand the American title. The book was an immediate success outside GM and has been regularly in print ever since. Drucker's career in management was established, which was not the declared intention. The intention was clearly stated:

> *"to research into the political and social structure of industrial society and the anatomy of industrial order"*
>
> (*ibid*:258).

The book was accepted as a management book. Drucker was continuing the transition from a constitutional lawyer to a management thinker and writer.

Concept was the first to describe the workings of a Corporation, not as an economic unit, *"but in the human relations both between the members of the Corporation, and between the Corporation and the citizens outside of it"* (1946:12-13). GM at the time was the largest corporation in the world with half a million employees. The book was also the first comprehensive study of Sloan's form of Federal Decentralisation or Decentralisation as it eventually became. To prevent confusion the term Decentralisation, which became generic circa 1960, will be used in this book. Sloan also used this term (Sloan 1964). The later description of 'M' form is also acknowledged. Drucker describes the components that make up Decentralisation and compares it with the main alternative Functional Decentralisation that he had identified as Centralisation (1946:127).

As part of Decentralisation, Drucker describes GM's Service Staff (*ibid*:54-55, 86-87, 226-227); these are head office services, where the divisional managers had discretion to use, or recruit their own. Drucker made clear *"that they have no direct authority whatsoever over the divisional manager"*. Drucker recommended their service as good value for money (*ibid*:54-55). GM and Drucker were opposed to the traditional *"staff and line"* approach to functions for two reasons despite their many other supporters. The tendency for *"staff"* function to become dominant rather than subservient to the *"line"* function and an aversion to borrowing from the military a term which seemed to imply the parochialism of the

47

trainee military mind. Business management needed imagination and an understanding of the outside (*ibid*:90).

What Drucker had learned about management from his research did not at this stage add up to an integrated framework, in fact related items are not collected together but often dispersed throughout the book. Later, as Drucker became more experienced, his ideas would be better integrated. While many are looking to ape the military for management ideas Drucker was identifying flaws and limitations in that approach. That the book had an index, albeit incomplete, was an improvement on its two predecessors.

For Drucker top of his management concerns were people. This area, because of its importance, needed considerable time and patience. Workers needed to be able to derive status, and function in the new organisation of society, the industrial mass production plant. Drucker recorded the importance of training and the mixed approach within GM's divisions. Training ranged from shop floor to graduate level. Its objectives were to supply the imperative need for "*life giving*" management for the organisation while enabling the individual to benefit from opportunities.

In Drucker's opinion business and management require order and patterns. Drucker concludes that although not perfect and still developing, Decentralisation was the most effective structure for a large multi-division business such as GM. The principle is that top management, whose job differs from that of operational managers, makes strategic policy decisions, which were then devolved to the divisions to perform the patiently agreed targets. Decisions needed careful consideration and examination. Quick agreements could be suspect and dissent should be encouraged to expose the alternatives. The decision-makers are the managers not the Unions, who have still to outline a positive role. Drucker views the role of John Llewellyn Lewis (1880-1969), the leader of the mineworker's union, as a negative one, of blackmailing society, denying equal opportunities, and penalizing efficiency and progress (*ibid*:161). Of business it was responsible for providing for its own survival and its own leaders. Foremen are an enigma being neither workers nor management. For Drucker this

48

anomaly would have to be resolved, as foremen represented untapped potential.

Another distinction about *Concept* was Drucker's challenge to the narrowness of the conventional view on profit. Drucker's starting point was the acceptance of the conventional view that the imperative of survival was that business needed to make a profit. Drucker's challenge was that profit was not the only measure for an organisation's success. Regard had to be given to the social requirement, both inside and outside the organisation. These are on-costs that have to be paid for, not as a surcharge that reduced profit, which would shrink the total national economy. The on- costs must be met by compensating performance from the processes of the organisation. However there can be no other yardstick for the success or failure of economic action but its profit (*ibid*:234). Although the business must make a profit in order to face yesterday's responsibilities, today's needs, and tomorrow's opportunities, the profit motive was not the sole rationale for business. Not only was profit an insurance premium against risk it was also the only source of capital for new equipment. Without profit, expansion was impossible. The higher the profit the faster the economy can advance, creating more opportunities (*ibid*:232). Drucker believed that profits in 1946 were too low to match the expansion that America expected (*ibid*:236). Expansion could only be funded by maximum production at the minimum of cost, which produces the maximum profit through mass-production. This was the original discovery of Ford, and was his greatest achievement and contribution (*ibid*:220). Having discarded the classical economists and Marx, Drucker footnotes three economists. (i) Keynes for his equilibrium economics, which Drucker believes, had been eclipsed by the dynamic theories of (ii) Schumpeter's *The Theory of Economic Developments* (1911) and (iii) Frank Hyneman Knight's (1885-1972) *Risk Uncertainty and Profit* (1921). Drucker concludes that Knight and Schumpeter were correct and that Keynes was wrong because equilibrium was not only unrealistic but was also undesirable (1946:235)

Drucker had now set himself a problem. Having accepted the fundamental importance of profit but rejected its accepted definition, he had to find a replacement. While the answer to this would emerge in his later works, the start of the solution is suggested in the advanced forms of measurement used by GM, which are also attributed elsewhere to Brown, as 'cost accounting and base pricing' and 'cost analysis' (*ibid*:123). These formed an essential part of GM's policy control and were components of what was regarded by many at the time including Drucker as the most advance cost accounting system. The foundations of this methodology were laid at du Pont (*ibid*:12). Later Drucker would develop on these ideas to help to define the measuring of profit. He has asked the question – what do we need to measure? The question he will add later was – how can we measure?

Accepting that taxes follow profit, Drucker's ideas are that they should be based upon a cyclical average rather than on annual profit. There should also be provision for business to build up an employment fund to spend on capital goods to create work during a Depression (*ibid*:276-277).

In Drucker's later work the contribution of Charles Erwin Wilson (1890-1961) the President of GM would be recognised for its practical application of management, organisational ability and progressive labour policies based upon respect for the individual (1979). GM's Wilson was known as "*Engine*" Charlie to differentiate him from the President of GE, also a Charles Wilson, who was known as "*Electric*" Charlie.

Many of the activities and ideas that Drucker refers to in *Concept* appeared, at first sight, to have no inter-relationship; they are as an agenda, setting out his programme for further holistic consideration that would result in more cohesive proposals through the integration of activities and ideas. He would establish that because they were interdependent they would have to be considered together and not as previously only in isolation.

Among Drucker's ideas that were emerging in *Concept* was the recognition of the needs and power of the market, which must have boundaries in the interests of social stability because society cannot allow labour, land or equipment or money to be treated as:

50

"commodities". "Labour is man. Land and capital equipment are his environment and his productive resources. Money and credit are the Social Organisation itself which brings together man and his resources"

(1946:256).

In the interests of society's stability the market could not be allowed to destroy them. Drucker observes that market limitations in society's interest had been the economic policy for a hundred years, citing Polanyi's 1944 book *The Great Transformation*. Drucker records that his only quarrel with Polanyi's profound book *"is that the author falls prey to the economic absolutism he so deplores in others"* (1946:256).

As with so much of Drucker's analysis, his focus was wide. He saw the market not just theoretically but also practically, as he concluded that, regardless of what managers would like to think, their customers were logical. [Idea: Game theory and risk assessment]. What the customers bought was what they perceived as value to them and in their own minds their decisions were logical. To satisfy the customer's needs the business needed to not only produce efficiently, although to managers they may appear illogical because they do not decide as they had forecast. It was also the managers' responsibility to create their own market opportunities by innovation. For the enterprise, market power by monopoly was not the answer to satisfying these requirements. The only answer was capitalism responsible to market forces. Ford was the first to see this with his mass production plant, the object of which was to produce more goods more efficiently. Although Drucker believed a better model was needed the object of the system was not to restrict supply (*ibid*:220). Drucker was now recognising fault lines in Ford's policies which eventually failed through his refusal to evolve management, or to accept that his market had evolved by maintaining that *"The customer can have any colour as long as its black"*. (*ibid*:90, 224, 239) GM recognised the function of the markets and evolved a policy of introducing annual models, which contrasted with Ford's retention of the *"Model T Ford"*, year after year. The effect was that GM overtook Fords as the world's largest automobile producer. But GM was not always infallible. Drucker examined GM's dealer business and concludes

51

that they had taken time to realise that they were in the second hand car market, as well as the new car market. GM's relationship with the dealers had become that of partner. Drucker comments briefly on the activities that would eventually become part of marketing - customer relations, advertising, and community relations.

Concept contained Drucker's first critical attack on Personnel Management when he described them as using 'gadgets' as psychological tests, which failed because they only established what people could not do, whereas Drucker's emphasis was on what people could do! Drucker questioned Personnel Management because it did not fulfill the promise of its title. It did not manage people (*ibid*:181 & 191).

Drucker continued that the whole industrial and management process was being handicapped because it was made up of separated sectors, which have too little understanding of or compatibility with their neighboring sector. This resulted in a problem of virtually no communications. [Idea: 'gadgets' ideas or practices that had a superficial appeal but failed to contribute what they promise. This identification would be continued throughout Drucker's work].

Drucker's belief at this stage of his career was that the Corporation or Big Business was the ideal model. He acknowledges that small businesses existed and had problems that needed resolving. He also believed that a combination of fiscal and banking policies prevent capital being made available for small businesses (*ibid*:111, 282 & 283). While attacking the American government's punitive taxation of small businesses he commended GM for their "*character bank*" which backs "*people potential*" rather than insisting on traditional asset collateral. [Idea: Character Banking equivalent of Venture Capital].

What was significant about the business activities recorded by Drucker was that they were all relevant, and represented much of the worthwhile management practice for the rest of the century. The activities that make up Decentralisation, which Drucker records, would be picked out by others to develop careers around the separate activities. All of the activities that Drucker recognises in *Concept* he would return to later to -develop and sometimes change. Drucker's description of the workings of GM was a stimulating commentary to which the additions of his own ideas gave his work its own character, distinctive style, uniqueness and its appeal to a wide audience.

What the book recorded was that Drucker was learning about management and his knowledge of other writers was increasing. On leadership Drucker refers to Chester Irving Barnard (1886-1961) and his practice of artificially testing managers in leadership situations (*ibid*:32). Drucker accepts that although no one knows if an untested manager will succeed, they must be tried out in practice, not artificially, because once an appointment has been made, removal gets more difficult the higher you go up the ladder. Drucker records his indebtedness to Mooney & Reiley (1931) for identifying with great force that modern industry, particularly mass production industry was a social organisation. Drucker later acknowledges that Rathenau identified this fact earlier (1989:77) (Rathenau 1917) and so did Weber (Weber 1922), but even Rathenau wasn't the first (1950:30). That the business organisation was a social organisation was germane to Drucker's ideas. Mooney & Reiley also provided the description of big business as the "*Corporation*", which Drucker used (1946:14). For Mooney & Reiley (although not specifically acknowledged in *Concept*) management was the "*vital spark*" – for Drucker it was the "*life provider.*" Drucker adapted Taylor's ideas, which focused on the manipulation of the individual. Drucker, while admitting that he knew nothing about production, he said that it needed to be implemented with a new theory of mass production technology that focused on the individual worker, and which tapped into people's imagination and initiative. However, listening to practitioners in the plant Drucker concluded that there was a need for - "*a new theory of mass production technology … (to) complement Frederick Taylor's famous studies*" where the focus is "*on the individual worker rather than on the individual manipulation*" (*Ibid*: 192). This was the start of a more critical analysis by Drucker compared to acceptance of Taylor's ideas in his later books. This continued beyond the late 1960s when Drucker began in effect to rediscover Taylor's contributions to knowledge, that it was "*Taylor's 'Scientific Management'* [that] *first applied knowledge to work…*" (1969:110-111)

The remaining two thirds of *Concept* was a variation or development of ideas from *Future* relating to the importance of the individual and the

53

need for income security against the 'demon' of Depression. For Drucker, man's place in the new world would be found in the autonomous self-governing plant community, where the worker would learn to develop managerial vision by managing social areas of the business as cafeterias, pensions schemes, health insurance, safety work schedules and general benefits. The development in these areas would create an understanding between workers and management as to what their respective jobs were and create inter-communication, which presently was non-existent. The workers involved would develop a sense of achievement and ownership that will motivate the worker, as shown in their co-operation on wartime projects. Drucker also drew upon the Hawthorne experiments, but did not credit Mayo. (1946:157)

Of the annual wage it was a bone of contention between management and workers. Management saw it as a cost, the worker as his and his family's economic essential. Drucker proposed that schemes should be set up whereby wage guarantees would be given to the neediest proportion of the workers, if economic recessions occurred. Unemployment was the curse of an industrial country. Also, business would be seen to fail if a Depression occurred again, if people were subjected to the same the consequential destruction caused by being unable to work, resulting in their exclusion from society.

Following on from *Future*, Drucker continued to support the American 'pluralist' society and introduced the David Eli Lilienthal (1899-1981) - managed TVA project, a mammoth environmental scheme to harness the power of the river, and stop the destruction of farmland by its regular flooding. The project was regarded as the largest state funded public participation scheme in the World, and was carried out during the New Deal Era. Drucker supported the idea that mammoth projects with a high social content needed state funding. It was part of a pluralist alliance but Drucker's advice is that politics should not interfere with management decisions. (*ibid*:3, 255, 272-3)

Based on his examination of GM and his own vision of society at large Drucker concludes that GM was one of the most advanced companies in the world and that it should proceed down the additional route that Drucker had identified, by leading America into the new social world order. Although free enterprise capitalism was working, it needed to work better. The danger was the return of Depression as people had demonstrated a need to work for status and function otherwise they would be socially destroyed. Again Drucker returned to unemployment, and proposed that an 'employment fund' was needed as a short-term bridge for their material requirements. He also struck a conservation note by stating that destruction of the world resources had to stop. America, the worst offenders had justified its actions by the need to survive the war. An omission in *Concept* is the recording of Sloan's obsession with any breaching of plant safety. For Sloan it was one of the few areas of error where there were no second chances for the perpetrator.

As the book was going to press in November 1945 a strike was called, which was to last one hundred and thirteen days. The Unions wanted to continue to have a big say in running GM and extend their progress from their pre-war position. The management wanted to return to the pre-war position of their control. *Concept* was considered by outsiders to be complimentary to GM.

Internally most of the top management believed it was a critical attack, the work of a Viennese Bolshevik despite Drucker restating his Christian beliefs (*ibid*: 136, 139-140, 142, 152-153, 242) and advocating the "*free market*". Sloan's view was that Drucker was wrong but entitled to his opinion. Wilson's attitude as President of GM towards *Concept* is not recorded.

It is appropriate to question what progress Drucker had made as a management writer from *Future* to *Concept*? The answer is considerable progress. His knowledge of what had been written about management was limited, but he displays an ability to build upon a portfolio of consequential writers. At large, *Concept* was a book about how "*Big Business*" worked, although the majority of its content was based upon Drucker's ideas and diverse influences – though direct references are not as extensive as in *Future*. Of the ongoing influences Christianity and Taylor were retained for the reasons previously stated. Ford was starting to be examined more critically. While maintaining that only the Corporation had the scale to train management, there was a point where "*bigness*" results in economic inefficiency. Drucker recorded that many observers believed that Fords' River Rouge Plant had reached this point and was now exceeding efficient size (*ibid*: 224). Schumpeter's short mention, coupled with Knight's similar ideas, elevates them and particularly Schumpeter above Keynes (*ibid*: 235). Burnham gets a single mention. Barnard is cited on leadership, while Mooney & Reiley are credited on social organisation and the term "*Corporations*". Hawthorne was highlighted for how people want to work. Barnard receives further mention with Mooney and Tead who are all recognised for their work on corporate organisations (*ibid*:12). The big addition from a personal influence is Sloan, and his team at GM. What should not be under-rated is the ongoing influence that Sloan and GM had on Drucker's ideas. Of these, the "*autonomous self-governing plant community*" had been further developed (*ibid*:182-191) and with it Rathenau's continuing influence by implication. Decentralisation had moved from a concept into a principle. The concept of profit, its definition and measure had started on what would be a long examination. Drucker's view that the purpose of a business was to innovate and satisfy the market to survive was now developing. Personnel Management and its related psychological tests had started to receive Drucker's critical attention.

The initial impact of *Concept* was recorded in six reviews in *The Book Review Digest* 1946. It listed without detail reviews by *Harvard Law Review* and E A Bedaar in *Canadian Forum*. The following reviewers were all anonymous. The *New Republic* regards it, as a "*valuable exposition but there is no marketing of facts and little keen analysis*". His thesis may "*be true but he had done little to prove it*". For the *Library Journal* it is in the form of a commentary, while the *US Quarterly* regarded *Concept* as "*meriting consideration as one of the first efforts of its kind*". And the *Weekly Book Review* comments are "*A thoughtful book – with many brilliant flashes of insight*". The reviews all recognised the importance of examining the Corporation as a social organisation and that Drucker is again looking at a topic of fundamental importance to society. A conclusion is that he was again displaying his ability to recognise and examine major issues.

What *Concept* recorded was that Drucker knew much more about management than when he embarked upon the project. It illustrated that

Drucker did not accept the identified boundaries of where the management discipline should stop but only where it should start. It also demonstrated his intention to write about his chosen new subject, as he believed it should be written about, regardless of controversy or consequences as had already been established, in his writing style in Germany. However, America was a place where he would not be exposing himself to personal danger. Hitler had been removed as a threat and was therefore relegated from prominence in Drucker's writing. Russia's Communism provided a replacement but was an unacceptable one, to capitalism. It was clear that Drucker wanted to span the whole management range, working from observation in a boundary-less environment. Drucker had convinced himself that management was the new social force.

The New Society - Reflecting on Management – 1946 - 1950

Society was a progression from Drucker's preceding books. *Economic Man* recorded the end of economic man and identified the need for a new society. *Future* explored what the new society had to satisfy an industrial production system that had moved forward into a new era carrying forward economic man as industrial man. The problem was that society and industry had got out of sync. The society of economic man was still trying to perform in the new economy of the mass production industrial era of industrial man that was creating terrific conflicts. Having confirmed that this was the position, Drucker identified a need to start to research the situation in practical terms, which had resulted in *Concept*.

Society records Drucker's positions at that date. His message is that this is an anti-utopian book; the aim is a *"livable society for our time."* (1950:333). His position was that management had mechanical functions as production, and measurement, but predominantly it is a set of social functions. Although to some extent the functions can be considered separately, they can only perform to their optimum if they are integrated. While Mooney, Follett and Barnard regard co- ordination as the cement of management functions, for Drucker co-ordination was a function, and

57

although it was essential it was not the cement. For Drucker the cementing agent of management was '*integration*'.

'*Society*' has two parts: -

1   Society
2.   The industrial enterprise.

These parts are compiled of what are basically repeats of previous ideas, refinements of them and new ideas.

'*Society*' – Previous Ideas

'*Society*' was based on Christian principles (*ibid*:333) and the belief that American free enterprise capitalism was preferable to the alternatives. However Drucker reiterates that it was dependent upon management to make it work. The call for status and function together with the right to expect opportunities for advancement in employment are all repeated (*ibid*:134-139). Burnham's ideas and Drucker's rejection of them are recorded (*ibid*:10, 45). That pluralism was working was confirmed with a reference to TVA (1950:9).

Refinements of Previous Ideas

> "*The true revolutionary principle is the idea of mass-production. Nothing ever before recorded in history of man equals, in speed, universality and impact, the transformation this principle has wrought in the foundations of society in the forty short years since Henry Ford turned out the first "Model T"*"

> (*ibid*:xi)

Mass production today was not confined to manufacturing "*but is a general principle for organising people to work together*" (*ibid*: xiii). It was being used widely as in medicine, journalism and the telephone industry (*ibid*: xiv). The consequence of this revolution, which was just as applicable in the Soviet Union as in the free world, is transferring the work of the masses from the farm to industrial employment (*ibid*:1). While the mass-

58

production plant was now accepted as a *social unit* it had not developed as *the new social unit*. The consequence of the transfer of work was that it had separated the worker from work (*ibid*: xviii). Responsibilities to the family were diminishing, and producing problems such as divorce and dependency on outside agencies to carry out what once were family responsibilities. While women had gained equality, the family had become a luxury and children have moved from being an economic asset to a liability (*ibid*: xxv). Before we had solved the imperative problem of a satisfactory social position for the industrial working class, they have numerically reached their peak in America, although they are still present in large numbers, and will be for the foreseeable future.

The Unions are still viewed as a negative non-constitutional force without a constructive role. Their restrictive practices are working against the interest of their members although they pretend to the contrary (*ibid*:106-107), while accepting that the Unions need the *"right to strike" to provide cohesion of its membership* (*ibid*:104). *"No government can allow a strike that endangers society"* (1950:314). Lewis is still viewed as a negative force. Amongst his demands were the rights of his members to a job even if one doesn't exist. (*ibid*: 88-90, 119-120, 122-123, 128, 212- 213).

Drucker asks the question *"Can unionism survive?"* The answer was not with Lewis's policies. The Rathenau inspired self-governing plant community had become the *"autonomous self- governing plant community"* (*ibid*:273). The workers' role had become clearer. They could organise social elements of management functions, as cafeterias, benefit schemes and shift schedules. Not only would the plant community give the worker a place and purpose in society that they presently lack, it would create a greater understanding by communication in both directions. The managers would understand the workers better, while the greatest contribution was that the workers would learn about the manager's task and develop *"managerial attitude"* (*ibid*:269). Drucker considered worker representation on Boards of Directors but rejects the idea as having been tried and failed in several Mainland European countries (*ibid*:271). Junior Boards of Directors have worked as with McCormick Spice Company in Baltimore. But they only work if the board members are in management positions.

59

But the importance of the plant community extended beyond the enterprise. It was central to a free industrial society. Although the modern state was expected to be and was a *"welfare state"* we were not talking about the *"hand-out state"*. The modern state's greatest threat was lack of responsible participation by its citizens. Although acceptable policies have to be determined by national government the modern welfare state would become both bankrupt unless local self- government was strong (*ibid*:317). Drucker asked how else would the members of society realise that payments were being made by the increased productivity of their *"efforts?"* His answer was that in an industrial society, the only meaningful units of local government are enterprise and plant community (*ibid*:318).

Drucker moved to a more constructive position on communication, which he had previously described as non-existent. He did this not by solving the problem, but by identifying some of the consequences. He set out his view that *"lack of communication"* was definitely not a technical but a social problem. Unless communications were established for the purpose of work industrial society would not be able to function or even survive (*ibid*:8). The solution was not more information from management, but the development of a listening culture enabling management to understand what was not being understood. Middle management and the worker would have to develop similar *"ears"*.

"Today industry hardly has the telephone: certainly there is no common language"
(*ibid*:178).

Drucker was in no doubt that the American workers wanted to work. But resistance to change was part of the complexity of the workers as a social animal (*ibid*:66). The workers' major concern was still the fear of unemployment, which was justified by the evidence of Edward Wight Bakke (1903-1971) (no reference given), who conducted studies into the disenfranchisement of the long- term unemployed in America and England during the Depression (*ibid*:27). The workers believed change always reduced the security of their wage. The consequence was that the fear of unemployment manifested itself into resistance to the essential changes that were needed for the enterprise's survival.

For Drucker, by careful planning to even-out fluctuations in the volume of demand, businesses could help themselves to reduce some of the extremes. Capital and maintenance expenditure, where possible, should be programmed for quieter times. Regrettably few businesses were using these practices. The Procter & Gamble Soap Company in Cincinnati had the most publicised employment guarantee scheme at the time. It originated from a plan to cut seasonal variations in demand. Although Procter's scheme worked it was not applicable to all industries. Drucker's conclusion was that the only solution was to tie-up income "*prediction*" with unemployment insurance (*ibid*:218-219). What had to be accepted was that some capital industries could not provide total guarantees as, for example in a Depression, their orders would dry-up (*ibid*:222). What was needed was a rational long-range wage policy related to an ability to pay, based upon "*changes in cost of living, productive efficiency or profitability*". The advantage was that it would remove the absurdity of the pressure of the emotional tension of a public debate and give what was badly needed for "*the enterprise a predictable wage burden*" and for the worker "*a predictable income*" (*ibid*:301).

For the unskilled manual workers, their opportunities were reducing. The trend of fifty years of need for unskilled labour had begun to reverse. The opportunities for the manual worker were being converted into the intellectual work of specialists (*ibid*:25). [Idea: The Knowledge Society]. The opportunities for workmen advancing to foremen were reduced as modern industries recruited college students (*ibid*:167-169). Drucker said that the "*crown prince by birth*" was more acceptable to the workforce than the "*crown prince by selection*" of the college-educated outsider (*ibid*:202). College students in overwhelming numbers had identified management as a career (*ibid*:24). For Drucker a college education should not be a passport to management, as by their nature, schoolteachers (*ibid*:173) would be unlikely to select "*the entrepreneurs, the innovators, the risk takers*".

61

'The Industrial Enterprise' – Previous Ideas

All of Drucker's previous ideas had been further developed and refined.

Refinement of Previous Ideas

For Drucker the preferred structure for the organisation was Decentralisation and not Functional Decentralisation (*ibid*:247-250), the reason being that Decentralisation was an integrated structure where the objectives of top management of the organisation were apparent to all the workers in the organisation. Functional Decentralisation was where the workers in the organisation only see the objectives of their own particular function, and operated in isolation from the overall aims as defined by top management. But for Decentralisation to work, each unit in the enterprise must have "*common citizenship*". If they were not related in their activities then each required separate top management and should be separate businesses. Decentralisation was not now universally applicable (*ibid*:255) as Functional Decentralisation was an alternative where there was no market test.

In Drucker's opinion management was spreading from the enterprise to other parts of society. In America there was growing concern with "*the organisation*". As managerial literature grew by leaps and bounds, the proposition seemed to be that "*the proper study of mankind is organisation*" (*ibid*:246), with organisations of the modern State, the Army and the Church all being subjected to management disciplines. "*Yet the sudden clamour for organisation bespeaks an acute disorganisation*" (*ibid*:246), which was the result of the use of 'gadgets' rather than principles.

Tensions in management groups resulted in attempts to create uniformity. Use of the army *staff and line* principle, which was focused on one future event, not only increased tension, but was ill adapted to the needs of the enterprise. Drucker was building a sounder argument for his previous rejection of "*line and staff*" (*ibid*:243-244) and distancing himself further from military ideas on management, as an inspiration for solving civilian problems.

Of influences on Drucker's management ideas, Sloan and the GM team were the basis for Decentralisation and the way forward for most enterprises. GM received praise for their 1947 *"contest"*, which yielded a record 175,000 replies from the employees on *"My Job and Why I like it"* (*ibid*:31, 141, 148, 151, 164-165, 179, 281). This was used as evidence that workers liked their work and wanted to work but they needed it to be meaningful. This was confirmed in the unpublished working paper *Profile of Charles Erwin Wilson* (1890-1961) December 2002.

Ford was still prominent, and was still credited with revolutionising how people work but Drucker noted that generally what was now termed as *"Fordism"* was being questioned by many as a method of work (*ibid*:xxviii). For Drucker, Ford's structure of business management by a First Minister was proved to have failed before his death in 1946. It was a method of *"management organisation - or disorganisation"*. *"To stay too long on the old basis is dangerous"* (*ibid*0:245). Drucker drew the analogy from history of France, which suffered by staying with Richelieu's success for too long (*ibid*:245). {For a fuller explanation see *Cardinal Richelieu and the Making of France* (Levi 2000)}. Ford got credit for providing the original example of what Drucker termed *"integration"*[1] or self-sufficiency, what would later be named *"vertical integration"*. Drucker returned to the divorce between ownership and control, repeating that this would have to be accepted (1950:15, 84) although he offered an alternative. Drucker saw Ford's transfer of shares into a trust, without voting rights, as a neat solution to the problem of management not being constitutionally legal. Shareholders would confirm by their action that they only wanted an economic investment. Alternatively if shares could be changed to 'bonds' it would be *"The best solution would simply to be to legalise the 'de facto' situation"*. Drucker's suggestion had already been identified as Young's ideas in *Future* (*ibid*:321). Drucker perceived an additional benefit in removing shareholder abuse by the minority, through aggressive and able shareholders (*ibid*:319, 323). As an alternative form of ownership, described as America's most successful co-operative, was The American

---

[1] Drucker changed his interpretation of 'integration' to mean the merging of all the functions of management. It is advisable to disregard this use of 'integration' and think in terms of 'vertical integration'.

Cast Iron Pipe Company which resulted from the owner on his death leaving the enterprise to the workers. Although there had been problems, it had developed the idea of the self-governing plant community and also a managerial vision with the workers. Drucker regarded it as a one-off rather than *the* national pattern (*ibid*:278-279) as had Weber (1922:45).

What the preceding paragraph has established is that Drucker had identified two separate but related issues. Both were concerns of society in relation to business ownership and management responsibility. What society no longer wanted was Old America of the all-powerful often megalomaniac owner {described as *"Caesars"* by other} as Ford. Transferring the power to the top management team solved this problem, because their power was acknowledged rather than covert. With the shareholding power transferred to the manager; society would have a recognisable and identifiable authority and be able to hold them responsible for their actions. Currently the managers could avoid taking this responsibility by sidestepping the issue by laying-off the problem to the shareholders. In essence Drucker was attempting to make power legitimate, which can only happen if it is linked to responsibility.

Further management writers were referred to in the text who would feature in Drucker's later writing. Taylor's influence was maintained but to a lesser effect. Although fifty years ago Taylor had split operations into their constituent parts they now needed to be rejoined together by co- ordination (1950:154-156). This fundamental problem would receive further attention by Drucker. Gantt was linked with Taylor in developing *"Scientific Management"*. Mayo and Fritz Jules Roethlisberger (1898-1974) were identified with the *"Hawthorne Study"*, which identified the enterprise is a social unit. This was something that Drucker regards as a *"rediscovery"* because for him it was first identified by François Fourier (1772-1837) and Comte de Saint-Simon (1760-1825) (1950:30). Drucker also credited Thomas North Whitehead (1891-1969) for his related independent contribution on Hawthorne with his 1938 book *"The Industrial Worker" – collected interviews of the Hawthorne Experiment*. Although Roethlisberger and Whitehead were recognised by Drucker, for their work regarding Hawthorne, it was Mayo, as the consequential influence on Drucker, who was considered in this research. Drucker referred to Mayo's 1933 book *The Human Problems of an Industrial Civilisation* and his 1949 book *The Social Problems of an Industrial Civilisation*, which are later examined in this text. Mayo and his associates were attributed with establishing that in addition to a formal organisation every industrial enterprise *"is an "informal" Social Organisation of the workers as well as of supervisory and managerial personnel"* (1950:157). Of the way that people work Drucker also examined a range of activities from featherbedding (1950:65) to Stakhanovite effort (*ibid*:66)

Of the economists Schumpeter and Knight's position as modern economists was maintained (*ibid*:36) while Schumpeter was attributed more clearly with the idea that the agent of expansion is the *"innovator"* not the *"capitalist"* (*ibid*:49). This will become a major plank of Drucker's ideas. Keynes received more attention, most of it adverse, for thinking in terms of the State as an economic institution *"rather than in terms of the 'isolated individual in the market"* (*ibid*:36), and for convincing business *"that all Depressions are, like that of the thirties in the United States"* (*ibid*:233-234). Drucker commented that Keynes' *"remedy of the 'reflation' of consumption is the very worst thing for it,"* (*ibid*:235) although his followers were by now prescribing massive purchases of capital goods (*ibid*:237). Drucker rejected Keynes' *"rhythm"* or *"business cycle"*, as being an inadequate substitute for *"a definite time span"* which Drucker believed was needed (*ibid*:52). Of other economists Smith and Marx each received further mention. David Ricardo (1772-1823), Cardinal Armand-Jean du Plesses de Richelieu (1585-1642) and John Stuart Mill (1806-1873) were considered but all were regarded as too old fashioned for modern society. Drucker had already disregarded old-fashioned economists as a solution to management problems in *Economic Man*.

Drucker's ideas on profit had developed considerably, although he continued to maintain that the *"profit motive"* was irrelevant. The problem was that without profit the enterprise would not survive. *Society* had recognised that the survival of the enterprise was in its own essential interest as evidenced by *"changes in the bankruptcy laws in every major industrial country in the last twenty years"* (*ibid*:22) which gave priority to the

65

going concern over all other groups. Drucker declared his first law of the enterprise to be *the law of loss avoidance* (*ibid*:44).

Obsession with profit was the wrong focus. Drucker listed what the enterprise must provide for to ensure its own survival before a profit could be declared:

- the current costs of doing business;
- the future costs of staying in business of replacement, obsolescence, risk proper, uncertainty;
- contribution to society for unsuccessful businesses;
- share of social non-economic services.

Having set down the parameters, Drucker reconfirmed two previously identified major problems. First, business does not know how to measure profit as its accounting was largely pre-industrial (*ibid*:51, 55). This was Drucker's continuation of his attack on the accountant's inadequate contribution, as he points out that managers have to play it by ear because they only have the most primitive measurement tools (*ibid*:189). Accountants fail on two counts because they neither reflect today nor chart the future. The second problem was that adequate profit was needed to protect the American way of life, yet there was hostility to profit within the plant and in society. There was a communication gap as no-one wanted to listen. When surveyed, the public replied that eight to ten percent was a "*fair return*" but when told this amount was $2 million it was regarded as excessive (*ibid*:71). The worker's hostility to profit was linked to the high levels of top salaries. Drucker defended the high levels on two counts. The net receipt after tax was not as high people believed from the gross declaration, and because salaries were hierarchical, as headroom was needed for those below to have space for their own differentials. Later Drucker would set ratios to prevent top salaries getting out of hand (1974:372). What Drucker did was to elevate the avoidance of loss and its bedfellow – profit – to a position of primacy in management priorities because pragmatically without survival the manager has nothing to manage. Drucker also further exposed how

66

incomplete were measurements of profit, which are continuations of his ideas from *Concept*.

For the enterprise to be maintained it had to become more productive to remain profitable and survive. Drucker declared his second law of the enterprise to be *the law of higher output* (1950:47). The problem was that society expected more and better-value goods from the enterprise, which was what management must deliver. The worker resisted by opposing reasonable levels of profit, which he saw as a charge against his wages. Workers also resisted increasing productivity as they saw higher output putting their jobs at risk. Drucker's argument was that workers were absolutely wrong, and were putting their jobs at risk by not contributing to the enterprise and maintaining its competitiveness (1950:49-50). This was the beginning of Drucker perceiving that profit and productivity were integrated.

For the worker within the enterprise, unemployment was still the major fear. Drucker suggested insurance, selected income platforms and progressive social benefits (*ibid*:274) and tax accumulation for capital works within the enterprise as in *Concept* (*ibid*:241). Drucker's own previous suggestion that major capital investment in the enterprise should be deferred in a Boom to create work in a Depression he now identified for himself was flawed for two reasons. Firstly; inabilities to identify in advance business cycles. Secondly the law of higher output demanded that capital expenditure was a priority to improve productivity in order to strengthen the business to withstand a Depression. Drucker argued that to improve security of employment, labour must be treated as a capital cost and rise and fall with the market. This would give a predictable employment plan and make guaranteed minimum wage possible. This was not a *"Guaranteed Annual Wage"*, which would only harm the worker if the economy could not live up to its promises (*ibid*:210-224).

Where the worker was displaced by technological progress Drucker examined a positive contribution from one of the national Union's President, Philip Murray (1886-1952). His idea was for a technological fund to compensate workers for changes within their industries during the changeover, with the obligation to give redundant workers six

67

months' notice. Drucker regarded the idea as impractical where whole industries were being restructured. Murray's plan had been made to work at (The Bell Telephone System) American Telephone and Telegraph Company but only because of a natural high turnover of telephone operatives (*ibid*:68-69). The problem remained of workers' resistance, with "*featherbedding*" and resistance to small changes "*sabotaged by the informal code of the plant*" (*ibid*:65 & 69).

Major changes were usually too specialised to be resisted except by wrecking machines. But the great majority of the workers did accept that technological progress was beneficial, a view that had fundamentally changed since the Luddites of a century ago (*ibid*:64 & 69). The root of the problem was the conflicting views "*between labour as a commodity and the worker as a capital resource*". The solution was to invest "*in the major productive resource of any enterprise, its labour force*" (*ibid*:69-70). [Idea: People are our greatest assets].

In *Concept* Drucker claimed to know nothing about production. In *Society* he was now examining productivity and was starting to make his contribution to the second stage of the work that Taylor and Gantt started – the concept of work and planning being integrated by the same person rather than by separate people. The starting point was the worker's relationship to the machine. The worker's unjustified long-term fear of increased productivity was coloured by the often-justified short-term loss of work. The problem was that the worker did not perceive, but should have, his increased productivity as an overall benefit. When Drucker identified how the workers and the Union resisted changes through featherbedding and informal plant structures and so on, he was demonstrating that he had moved considerably from a theoretician to a management specialist in a practical world.

Drucker's attack on Human Resources had temporarily abated as he now viewed their efforts as positive, in at least trying to identify the causes of the problem when seeking a solution. He concluded that responsibility for Human Resources should be spread across departments and embrace the whole enterprise and consequently they must be developed by the "*same organ that decides what the company's business is*" (*ibid*:191). It was a top management job. Psychological tests were again criticised as being a poor substitute for "*battle conditions*" (*ibid*:203) as Drucker conceded that there were maladjusted employees in any sample group. "*There is a legitimate place in the plant for the psychiatrist or clinical psychologist as there is for a plant doctor*" (*ibid*:285).

Drucker asked "*Is a Competitive Market Necessary?*" (*ibid*:257) by examining the Russian planned economy which was in a perpetual management crisis. Drucker concluded that the market was necessary as an impersonal outside check (*ibid*:260-261). Merely establishing that the Soviet system did not work was not a solution to the problem of free market capitalism. A balance had still to be found. Drucker agreed with Polanyi that there was no historical precedent for governmental and social institutions to be subordinated to economic performance (Polanyi *ibid*:33). Drucker maintained his previous position, that a combination of both status and function were essential for man in society. That this requirement was now being transferred into the market as again Drucker drew upon Polanyi's observation that:

> "*...the absence of 'function' in the market society is considered... to be one of the major reasons for its collapse*"
>
> (Polyani 1944)

For Drucker "*a society without status must become tyrannical*". Although status and function were different, they were so closely related they were inseparable, because they could only perform dysfunctionally if they were only present separately (*ibid*:136).

Drucker had arrived at the conclusion that there could be no such thing as a totally "*free market*". There must be some restraints by society. The first step, which he was consistent about, was that it was in the enterprise's long term self-interest to maintain its own self-regulation. If the enterprise did not recognise this, then eventually Government would be forced to intervene, which would always be more restrictive and often more arbitrary than if each enterprise had behaved within self-imposed restraints. For Drucker the shape and purpose of the competitive market was one of his core ideas.

Of the concept of managers and management there was a need to make further progress. The social and political tension within enterprises would not be resolved until management produced managers who genuinely put the interests of the enterprise above their own. Drucker recorded that at the date of writing only an identified few had succeeded (*ibid*:330-331). He defined the manager's job further as having three main parts - responsibility for survival, efficient use of its human resources, and planning for its own survival. It was necessary to develop managers as team players as part of succession planning because management by dictatorship was flawed because it prevented contribution by others (*ibid*:185 & 192). He again asserted that big business was the right model, because "*only if*" could produce and afford to develop managers together with all of the support departments for management to fully function. However, it was possible for business to be too big, which was when they had excessive layers of bureaucratic support. British Nationalised Industries were examples. In practice this arose when communications had broken down, which was a problem that small businesses could readily avoid (*ibid*:205). Ethically big businesses as a policy must treat small businesses, in particular its own partners, in a reasonable manner; otherwise the government (*ibid*:188) would introduce punitive measures. [Idea: This had a contemporary feel for three reasons: (i) the practice of big business to pay later; (ii) to use their excessive buying power to the detriment of their supplies; and (iii) partnering, which had become a fashionable management idea. Charles Handy pointed out correctly that it was an old idea and practice (Handy 2002:182)].

New Ideas

It was difficult to totally separate those ideas of Drucker's that were refinements of previous ideas from those that were completely new. An illustration was Knight and Schumpeter's contributions when Drucker wrote, "*by and large we have not yet developed an adequate theory of industrial economics.*" Even though the pioneer studies of Knight in his 1921 book *Risk Uncertainty and Profit* and of Schumpeter in his 1911 book *Theory of Economic Development* were both written more than thirty years ago

70

(1950:30). It could be argued that this was a new idea, or an extrapolation of the role of the innovator.

In *Economic Man* the one-'maybe hope' for Europe was a new society based upon American free market capitalism. Drucker now accepted that – "*One fact alone makes American reality totally untranslatable into European terms*" (1950:329-330), which was that one in eight American workers, excluding farm hands, were investors in industrial shares. Consequently Capitalism American-style did not have a translatable meaning in Europe (*ibid*:331). It remained unique, as it did in Tocqueville's day. Europe could not have capitalism on the American model. What was making the European conversion so difficult was that it had a proletariat that was difficult to convert. America never needed the conversion because it never had a proletariat. With Russia and the Eastern Bloc countries in mind Drucker concluded that for Marx's ideas to work, an agricultural proletariat was required (*ibid*:208-210). Although there were problems in American society, it was the Americans' responsibility to make it work by developing "*a functioning and free industrial society*" (*ibid*: xxvii). It would be the enterprise that would shape the system (*ibid*:10).

Drucker's idea of American capitalism was market-competitive free trade, not "*old capitalisation*", which still operated "*carriage trade*" capital markets that prevent the mass production and mass consumption system from operating (*ibid*:188). The tax system, which was in cahoots with the central banks resulting in young and growing enterprises being burdened by full taxes, was akin to expecting a boy to be as strong as a man. The actions of tax and the bank "*effectively disbars the new venture from access to risk capital*" (*ibid*:325) (see previous GM dealer "*character loans*" and Drucker's comment regarding small business taxation (1946: 111, 282 & 283).

Drucker saw his task for the future as developing a tradition and standard of "*management*", for which "*there is not even a word for it except in English*"[2] (*ibid*:194) despite the emergence of "*professional*" management (1950:22).

Drucker examined "*Why Managers Don't Do Their Jobs?*" (*ibid*:194) His answer was that there was a lack of ability to view the whole enterprise.

---

[2] This was later questioned but it illustrates that management has still to develop an accepted glossary.

71

Managers were still performing as specialists rather than as generalists (*ibid*:196), and were restricted by one-man rule and over-centralisation (*ibid*:200). A *"management attitude"* was required, with a need to spread it throughout the organisation by the new industrial middle class who were the middle management technicians and supervisors that were *"the nerve and circulatory systems of the enterprise"* (*ibid*:143). But always there must be clear boundaries between workers and management, because it was the role of management to manage (1950:269).

One of the many timeless ideas put forwarded by Drucker was his statement of management's first responsibility *"What is Our Business?"* *"It is management's responsibility to decide what business the enterprise is really in"* (*ibid*:185). Drucker was displaying his unique ability to give the manager a total focus. Later he would turn the question on its head;

> *"Peter Drucker – professor, management guru, and a formal consultant to GE – greatly influenced Welch by writing. If you weren't already in the business, would you enter it today? Welch pondered the or sell' any that did not meet this standard"* (Tichy & Sherman 1995 *question deeply, and acted on the answer. He insisted that every GE Business be No1 or No2 in the market vowing to 'fix, close*3:13 & 14).

It was in *Society* that Drucker's fundamental idea that the cement of all the activities of a manager was integration. As Drucker's ideas were formulating he began with his ideas being confined to the worker and his tasks (1950:2, 4-8 & 141-142).

What *Society* had done, was attempt to integrate the enterprise and its people into modern society within a free market democracy. Metcalf and his contributors had similar ideas in their 1926 book *Scientific Foundations of Business Administration*. They were not as developed as Drucker's ideas but they were just as contemporarily applicable in their time. Their aim was for a *"fair balanced society"* with an approach that included a philosophical, biological and psychological foundations incorporated into the basic principles of management all focusing on a practical approach. This new approach would replace the *"ugly"* society, which presently existed. Metcalf's contributors included *H A Overstreet, O W Caldwell, Thomas Nixon Carver, M P Follett, H S Pearson, Henry S Dennison.*

The initial impact of *Society* was recorded in nineteen reviews that were tabulated in *The Book Review Digest* 1951. Listed only are Robert Merrion in the *Chicago Sun;* Philip Dodd in the *Chicago Sunday Tribune;* John Maurice Clark (1884-1963), in *The Yale Review,* who was one of Drucker's influences. J E Cross in the *Library Journal;* R V Holt in the *Hibbert Journal;* David Fellman in the *New Republic, Cleveland Open Shelf, Current History,* and *US Quarterly.*

Of the following reviews that are quoted, all were complimentary and were generally anonymous, with the minority otherwise identified.

> *"A society for America that is neither capitalist nor communist"* New Yorker. *"Deserves wide reading"* Churchman. *"The book of the year in socio- economics - be sure to read"* Commonweal. *"A provocative, interesting book"* Kirkus. *"Substantial contribution more ambitious than Economic Man"* C E Noyes *Nation.* *"It is stimulating, valuable and provocative"* (as before) S E Harris *New York Herald Tribune.* *"What he has to say is so important that he is deserving of the widest possible audience".* *"He uses a natural commonsense"* L M Hacker *New York Times.* *"Penetrating social-economic analysis"* P F Brissendon *Political Science Quarterly* (see full review in Chapter 7). *"Well organised analysis of the most serious problems of our time"* J N Jackson *San Francisco Chronicle.* *"Mr Drucker is regarded as one of America's leading experts on economic, social and political problems and his wide experience as a foreign correspondent, college teacher, international banker and consultant to large business concerns. His scholarly book is a sound endorsement of the American way of life holds out"* and *"...hope for the future"* (as before) H H *Springfield Republic.*

Their compliments and their numbers confirm that he had achieved national recognition within his chosen field. The unanimity of the reviews confirmed that his message was being understood. The strength of Drucker's work was his willingness to tackle the most difficult aspects of management, which was the integration of people into the enterprise by rationally related principles, functions and policies. He accepted that he was only at the start of the journey and was not even approaching the destination. Much had still to be evolved but a 'gadget' would never resolve the problem. By identifying that people were the nucleus of all management, Drucker had a basis to *"discover(ed) management"*. His next task was to make people more productive or effective through management. When Alan Kantrow wrote - *Why Read Peter Drucker?* One of his answers was *"Integration of thought"* (Kantrow Jan/Feb 1980:77). It was an appropriate description for *Society*. By the publication of *Society* Drucker had recorded that he was immersed in management rather than being the tentative outsider when he first started his research with GM for *Concept*. The weakness of *Society*, if it was a weakness, was that Drucker asked many *"questions"*, which he left unanswered. However unanswerable questions of society about its own future were and were always likely to remain unanswered in a democracy, which was central to Drucker's vision of society. The precise future of a democratic society was always impossible to predict. The strength of the book was that it acknowledged that management was part of an unpredictable society, and therefore the manager's preparation should involve the widest self-development possible in readiness for his tasks. What my research established at this point was what Drucker knew about management and what his views were on society. It was from this foundation that he embarked on his further preparation before writing *Practice*.

CHAPTER THREE

THE PRACTICE OF MANAGEMENT

Drucker's previous management influences are examined and his new influences identified.

Introduction

The evidence was that Drucker knew much more about management at the time when he wrote *Practice*. This is confirmed by comparing the range of references in *Practice* with the 'quickie lists' of management writers that he had read in preparation for his work at GM and the resulting limited references in *Concept*. Retained from his earlier book in *Practice* were Mooney, Reiley, Urwick, Mayo, Taylor, Barnard, Gantt, and Schumpeter, who was highlighted as "*how much the author owes to this most fruitful modern economist.*" The influence of Sloan was acknowledged even though his seminal work "*My Years with General Motors*" would not be published until 1964. What was evident in *Practice* was that Drucker's working knowledge of business had widened beyond GM, and that he had developed into a management consultant of consequence, with heavyweight clients including GE, AT&T, Sears, and major railroad companies. Drucker was adding to and refining his knowledge of management through the extensive work he was doing for this impressive portfolio of clients. Harold Francis Smiddy (1900-1978) of GE was acknowledged as the Godfather of *Practice* although Drucker did not explain 'why' in his book. It was however known that Drucker and Smiddy had developed a good working relationship after the publication of *Concept* well before the GE proposal (Wren & Greenwood 1998:230).

Drucker was one of the consultant team at GE set up by Ralph Cordiner (1900-1973) (Tichy & Sherman 1993:271). Later Drucker would become the prime consultant (Wren & Greenwood 1998:231). The consequence of the work at GE was far reaching. "*The massive reorganisation of General Electric in the early 1950s* [was] *an action that perfected the model most big businesses around the world (including Japanese organisations) still follow."* (*The Coming of the New Organisation* Drucker *HBR* Jan/Feb1988:53)

> *"When Cordiner became president in 1950, he carried the reorganisation much further and by 1952 had created as intricate as sophisticated an organisational structure as had yet been devised for the large industrial enterprise."*

> (Chandler 1962:47)

Tichy & Sherman (1993:217) (source - Greenwood) emphasise Smiddy's contribution:

> *"The task force Ralph Cordiner put together was led by Harold Smiddy, VP of GE management consultation Services Division, a former consultant and partner at Booz, Allen and Hamilton, and president of the Academy of Management. Many of the ideas presented in the Blue Books by Cordiner bear Smiddy's trademark."*

Practice was about motivating individual human effort to achieve a common goal. Drucker's continuing emphasis was on people. His message was that all functions of management had to be considered simultaneously and they had to be integrated. Random selection and/or omission of functions would only lead to failure. *Concept* was, as its title suggests, about concepts. In *Practice* Drucker had moved forward to consider the practice of management as a discipline. His message for managers was that management has to be practiced even when managers know that some of the functions are only at an embryonic stage of development. Managers would have to use what they had, while identifying and accepting its limitations. They would also have to accept responsibility for helping further developments of management in general and the functions specifically. In *Practice* Drucker developed his ideas of the schedules of various functions of management that he began in *Society*. He also extended the use of case studies, which he began in *Concept* with its use confined to GM as the central case with ongoing references to Fords.

In *Society* GM, Fords and the Unions were again used as extensive sources while two new case studies were introduced. They were the previously referenced American Pipe Co (*ibid*:272-278) together with a passing reference to Procter and Gamble Soap Company as "*one of the more widely publicised employment guaranteed plan in existence*". Neither was further developed in *Practice* (1950:208). The extensive use of case studies in *Practice* would give Drucker's work one of its unique but overlooked characteristics that of practical messages fixed by "*memory hooks*". In *Practice* Drucker emphasised the essentiality of the development of principles of management and displayed a willingness to include and integrate where necessary other's sustainable ideas, which is Gestalt in practice as the "*foundation of learning*".

This Chapter identifies Drucker's Purpose and his Method. His influences are divided into six groups of which only the first is considered in detail in this Chapter.

The remaining five groups after being identified in this Chapter are mainly dealt with in later chapters.

- Friends in American Management (1954: Preface viii)
- References within the text
- Case Studies
- Selected Biography for further reading
- Post *Practice* influence

Chapter 5 examines Drucker's 'Seven Key Ideas' and concludes with the progressive messages that Drucker has culled from the most consequential of the case studies. The objective of Chapters 4 & 5 is to collect Drucker's eclectic presentation of ideas.

Purpose

The Preface (1954: vii & viii) sets out the purpose of the book, which was to help close the "*tremendous gap between knowledge and performance*" in management. It was not concerned with techniques; it was a practical book. The "*entire book is based upon the proposition that the days of the 'intuitive' managers are numbered*" (1954:9). It was written for the manager, the aspiring manager and the citizen, who needed to know about the functions of management. There was no reference to the needs of academics. The ignorance of the basics of management was 'almost universal' and was one of the most serious weaknesses of an industrial society. The book was not about manufacturing management or that "*of selling, finance, engineering or insurance- company investments*" (1954:92).

Practice was also intended to be a handbook for his consultancy clients:

> "*When I published Practice of Management…, that book made it possible for people to learn how to manage, something that up to then only a few geniuses seemed able to do, and nobody could replicate it. I sat down and made a discipline of it.*" (1986:9) "*European managers who have followed my books and my thinking right away saw my advocacy of management as a profession, as something that was a bit subversive, a bit revolutionary, and – in short – countercultural. In fact, in this light my book The Practice of Management was, and is, a sort of a manifesto in Europe*"

> (1995:302-3).

Practice was direct and authoritative and had a developed confidence compared with *Concept*, which was more investigative. The book was a guide rather than an orthodox textbook. Although containing some checklists, Drucker adopted a more flexible approach than most previous management writers and drew on a wider range of experiences. It was a new all- embracing type of management writing. Drucker, in *Practice*, had helped further to break the constraints of the textbook style, and written a book about a serious subject in a readable manner without trivialisation. It contained a mixture of concrete advice, and together with specific functions that required the managers to work through their own solutions, to fit specific situations and demands. Because so many elements were uncertain, objectives needed to be determined to create order out of chaos. But as with a captain sailing a ship, the course would

78

have to be checked, measured and adjusted throughout on what was, in effect, a voyage.

The concentration of the book was on business management, which was distinct from the management of other non-profit making organisations of society because it was:

> "...*the specific organ of the business enterprise, the vital principle that determines the nature of economic performance*"

(1954:7).

In *Practice* only two references were not drawn directly from management, although Drucker used them to reinforce his ideas. He related the Russian's discovery of "*management by the rouble*" to "*Our Lords Parable of the Talents*" (*ibid*:381) thus maintaining his Christian input. A story of Pitt the Younger was used to illustrate that management was about what was done, not about what was not done (*ibid*:148). A reference to Taylor grouping him with the philosophy of anti-democratic "*elitism*" that swept the Western World before World War I (*ibid* 4:278) did not appear to have any management relevance. That was until it was linked to the argument that work and its planning needed to be integrated into one person.

Method

Practice was written out of many years' experience in working with the management of companies, small, large and very large. The book owed much to the use of case studies. Wallace Brett Donham (1877-1954), the Dean of the Harvard Business School in 1919 introduced them as a teaching method (McNair 1954:vii) (Malcolm Perrine McNair 1894-1985). This was confirmed in *HBR* which included the first case study of "*The Star Copper Company*" (*HBR* No:1. Anon October 1922:425). Donham's decision to use case studies was prompted by Arch Wilkinson Shaw (1876-1962), a journalist and printer whose company worked for Harvard University in general and in particular printed the *HBR*. When he came to teach in 1911 at the then recently opened HBS, he complained that the students weren't learning anything practical. "*...they* *wouldn't recognise a problem if they saw one"* (*Lessons that simulated the real world* Skapinker *Financial Times* 12 November 2001).

Of Drucker's work researched together with a general examination of his subsequent books only Donham and Max Wertheimer (1880-1943) were not mentioned specifically, but their influences can be clearly identified.

Regarding footnotes, Drucker recorded that footnotes were not included except for direct quotations or where likely to be helpful in guiding readers to books that give full treatment to important subjects only touched upon in his text.

Previous Influences and their ideas that are carried forward

Christianity, where Kierkegaard's influence is implicit, together with the early Quaker influences as a bulwark of American Society as recorded by Weber and Tocqueville (see (i) Ethics and (ii) Political, Social and Managerial Society in Chapter 6). Drucker was now applying Christian principles more practically as the ethics of management and as forming part of a fundamental requirement of a manager, which was to have *"character"* which he brought to the job. It was something that could not be acquired. Although bad manners, incompetence and ignorance may be forgiven, a manager must never lack integrity. Drucker accepted that integrity was difficult to define, however; concentration on people's weaknesses was one of the actions that confirm that integrity was missing. While people's limitations had to be accepted, they should be seen as a challenge to the manager to make people perform better. The question should always be *"What is right?"* To put personality above the requirement of the work *"is corruption"*. Another danger was to ask; *"Who is Right?* (which) *encourages one's subordinates to play safe if not to play politics. Above all, it encourages them to 'cover up' rather than to take corrective action as soon as they find out that they have made a mistake"* (1954:155). Management should never appoint a manager who placed the importance of intelligence before integrity. Integrity of character must prevail, even over education and skill. A manager must put the interest

80

of the enterprise before his own self-interest, but in doing so he must not infringe upon the freedom of the individual (*ibid*:370-371, 376). The manager must lead by example and earn respect but he did not necessarily have to be liked (*ibid*:342). What managers must realise was that they were employing the whole man, which required that they demanded not merely a fair day's labour but also that all of the workers develop their potential. The aim was not acquiescence. The aim must be to build an aggressive *esprit de corps*. All of the foregoing was reflecting the influence of the Christian Protestant work ethic upon Drucker.

Marx's economics were described as "*the last important dupe*" for using muscle power as the measured unit of effort (*ibid*:39). Productivity was no longer based upon this tradition but on all factors of production (*ibid*:39). There had been inevitability in Drucker's writing that he would totally reject Marx, of interest is why it took so long? The reason for the inevitability was that Drucker's acclaim of Stahl was incompatible with tolerance of Marx. The evidence for my conclusion is that Marx was enrolled at Berlin University for his doctorate. Georg Wilhelm Friedrich Hegel (1770-1831) had headed the Philosophy Faculty from 1818 until 1831. Hegel believed in a Christianity of a form where the Universe was the power. Hegel's philosophical ideas left a choice of either left or right wing of politics, Marx chose the left, and also became an Atheist. The successor to Hegel's left-wing principles was Eduard Gans (1797-1839) who was the head of the Faculty of Law where Marx was enrolled. When Gans died unexpectedly in 1839 he was replaced by "*the severely reactionary Stahl*". Stahl and Marx were Jews by birth but were diametrically opposed philosophically, politically and religiously. For these reasons there could be no place in the University for Marx, who transferred to Berlin University. Marx's family was Christian converts and he was baptised only to reject Christianity whereas Stahl had converted and became a devout Christian (Wheen 1999:1-31).

Schumpeter's star continued to rise with Drucker and will be dealt with later in the text. Ford had undergone a metamorphosis and will also feature later in the text.

Rathenau's influence was implicit in the concept of the plant community; Drucker's development of the concept was to relieve managers of unrewarding jobs by giving them to the workers who would find them rewarding as arranging shift rosters, organising social functions to organise, and the management of benefit schemes that are essential to the organisation. Drucker's argument for these proposals was that workers would obtain satisfaction from these tasks while conversely, if they were arranged by management, they would only receive criticism from the workers for their performance. The experiences of 'organising' these functions would help to develop management vision in the workforce, (1954:301), an essential part of Drucker's philosophy, as was developing leadership skills (*ibid*:303). It would also develop motivation, self-control, and participation that would allow workers to become responsible citizens in the plant community (*ibid*:305). Drucker had tempered his idea that the "*autonomous self-governing plant community*" is central to the needs of society at large. In fact it can no longer be truly self-governing because, as part of a business, Drucker made clear that the worker could not participate in management decisions because it was only the manager who could manage (*ibid*:304). Even so Drucker included even this curtailed involvement as part of his manifesto of "*Motivating to Peak Performance*" (*ibid*:305). Owen was not mentioned in the text of *Practice* although Drucker aligned himself with Owen's general philosophy that making a profit was the essential to economic performance, as was the advisability of treating workers in a progressive manner.

Smith was given a by-line (*ibid*:385) but his relevance was discounted as being part of an economy where the businessman was a 'trader' (*ibid*:11). Keynes was not referred to in the text but was criticised by implication with those economists who saw the businessman as "*a concept of the 'investor' or the 'financier' rather than the manager*" (*ibid*:11). Drucker believed that the great store which economists placed upon primacy of the "*rate of capital formation*" was in fact a secondary factor as far as productivity was concerned. The fundamental factor in economic development had to be the rate of brain formation (*ibid* 4:40) [Idea: The Knowledge Society]. Drucker accepted that the standard advice of economists - to make capital investments in economic troughs and to invest in a boom - was common sense. But economists now doubted

82

whether there were real economic cycles. In any event the business cycles were too short in duration for heavy industry capital investments to be made only during the positive phase of the cycle because heavy industry had to work on fifteen to twenty-five-year programme. Even *"The greatest of modern economists, the late Joseph A Schumpeter, laboured mightily for twenty-five years…"* and could find cycles only in retrospect (*ibid*:86-87). {Schumpeter in his 1939 book, *Business Cycles: A Theoretical Historical and Statistical Analysis of the Capitalist Process* confirmed this conclusion. The reason that Schumpeter could not draw concrete conclusions was because for him it was impossible to predict major external factors or political decisions (*Ibid* 1939:1048)}. Drucker further criticised accountants. He cited accountants' inability to measure worker's attitude and failures by specific managers, or to acknowledge the intangibles of managers' performance and development of public responsibility. For Drucker it was the economist and accountants' bad luck that such items could not be quantified mathematically, but that this was no argument for them not being considered (1954:60-61). Drucker's criticism of *"old"* economists did not prevent him from recognising a new school of economists who were included in *Practice*. Their contribution will be considered later together with Schumpeter's main contributions of entrepreneurship and innovation.

Stahl's influence continued implicitly as Drucker contributed to enabling democratic and economic change to take place without causing a violent revolution. Berle & Means, Dimock and Young's, views on divorce of ownership and control were not repeated but accepted as a fact of life, as Drucker referred to management, and labour, rather than capital and labour (*ibid*:4).

Taylor was further examined and it was noted that few individuals had looked at work systematically until Taylor c1885. Scientific Management's contribution on how we viewed work and how it could be studied analysed and improved, was a lasting American contribution to Western society, as were the thoughts embodied in the *"Federalist Papers"* since which there have been few, if any, new insights. Since Taylor's testimony before the *"Special Committee of the House of Representatives"* there had been few, if any, insightful thinkers on the subject despite *"oceans of*

83

paper". *"There are of course exceptions - especially Mrs Lillian Gilbreth and the later Harry Hopf"*. Lillian Gilbreth's contribution was not identified but Hopf's was. Drucker wrote that Taylor's insight, *"as so often happens within the history of ideas is only half an insight"*. There were two faults. First, his insistence that work must be divided into a series of individual, mostly simple motions each carried out, if possible, by different workers. Possibly Taylor saw the need to integrate them, Hopf certainly did. As a case study Drucker used the analogy of the alphabet where words are the integration of letters. Drucker's contention was that where the analysis of work was concerned, man was an ineffectual machine and to use him as such was not utilising his specific qualities (*ibid*:274-276).

"The Second blind spot of Scientific Management is the 'divorce of planning from doing" (*ibid*:277) Taylor's discovery that planning was different from doing was one of his *"most valuable insights"*. On the principle that work would become more efficient the more we pre-plan rests the entire structure of modern management. From Taylor's idea flowed our ability *"to speak seriously and with meaning of management by objectives"*. But it did not follow that the planner and doer had to be different people. They were separate parts of the same job, not separate jobs. For Drucker, Taylor's divorce of planning from doing allied him to the philosophy of anti-democratic elitism that swept the world before World War I (*ibid*:278), as mentioned previously. Drucker concluded that the full benefit of Scientific Management was derived when doing and planning were integrated. He illustrated his argument with a comprehensive case study of International Business Machines Corporation, which was dispersed throughout *Practice* and considered later. Drucker re-identified Ford as one of the most thorough practitioners of Scientific Management, even though he had never heard of Taylor. Drucker reached the same conclusion on Ford's application of Scientific Management as on Ford's management ideas, which were, that from the time that Ford determined them, they remained static. Once an idea was engineered for work it remained unchanged (*ibid*:277-281).

Mooney & Reiley were not included in the text but were included in the Selected Bibliography. Their 'social organisation' and 'vital spark' were integrated into Drucker's ideas. Barnard also made it into the

Selected Bibliography but not in the text, while for Drucker, leadership was still a vital part of a manager's skills, as he concluded from his analysis of *Cyropaedia* by Xenophon (c 430-335BC) (*ibid*:156) that our knowledge of leadership has advanced little since c.360BC.

Gantt was identified as a prime example of one of the early pioneers of "*Scientific Management*" who demanded cartelisation in an attempt "*to make the world safe for professional management*". His ideas were part aligned with the German "*Rationalization*" movement of the 1920s, which were derived from Rathenau although Drucker did not mention him by name (*ibid*:10). Gantt was linked with Taylor, Fayol and the Gilbreths in a list of insightful thinkers on Scientific Management up to the 1920s. General Sir Ian Standish Monteith Hamilton (1853-1947) was not mentioned by name but his influence pervaded on the need for *esprit de corps*, which would later be subsumed into Drucker's definition of motivation. Also Hamilton and *Span of Control* was examined with Drucker giving some support to the conflicting idea of "*Span of Responsibility*", later to be known as *Span of Managerial Responsibility*. Urwick *et al* was included in Selected Bibliography for his writing on Follett. {Lyndall Fownes Urwick (1891- 1983) agreed generally with Hamilton on "*Span of Control*" but recognised the need for flexibility in application} (See Urwick in Chapter 5). Sir Cyril Ludowic Burt (1883-1971) received no further mention but he could now be regarded as having been rejected, as Drucker concluded that *IQ tests* were based upon a shaky theory. Hugo Münsterberg (1863-1916) after making a considerable contribution in the development of psychology also received no comment and could be regarded as being replaced by Mayo's and the other's later work. Tead's influence was referred to previously. Knight despite his extensive output and previous high rating, was not mentioned.

The Unions were still a negative but powerful outside force. Drucker devoted the minimum of references to them in the text and referred to *Society* where he carried out a full analysis. Management was criticised for not managing the Union element of the business and of leaving the initiative on labour relations to the Union (*ibid*:79). Drucker's conclusion was that management must learn how the Unions work and anticipate their demands to make them more beneficial to management. The focus

85

should be on returning the initiative to management (*ibid*:80). Presumably Drucker meant that management must not only anticipate the Unions' demand but present them to the workforce as a management initiative not wait until the Unions make their demands so that they can claim the credit.

Drucker's position on 'communication' had not moved as "*common understanding and common language … is usually lacking*" (*ibid*:123). But Drucker now accepted how difficult communication was; even with the best efforts management must continue to make in the interest of the enterprise. Management was reminded that conventional data presented in the conventional way meant nothing to workers. New techniques of communication were needed, as lack of information resulted in lack of incentive and performance (*ibid*:301). Drucker recommended through a case study the use of a management letter as follows [which is a Smiddy idea]: that subordinates write to their manager twice a year defining the subordinates' own job and that of the manager. The letter set out what a subordinate had to do to attain their own goals and what they expected from his manager to enable them to achieve their results. Once agreed it became the charter under which they operated (1954:126-128). This letter of mutual commitment between the supervisor and their manager was, in this writer's opinion, one of the cornerstones of making MbO work as intended by agreeing the individual's objectives in a manner that they are a personal commitment of performance.

The American worker's will to work and his willingness to make an unqualified commitment had been previously identified as being complex and was further examined in case studies. The enterprise had to "*employ the whole man*" and should be able to expect commitment, fairness, willing dedication and a willingness to accept change. Acquiescence was not what was required but a preparedness to help to build an *esprit de corps* and accept responsibility (1954:262-263). "*We know that regarding security of continuing employment it is the one really important security to most employees*" (1954:309). Since *Society* Drucker had discovered working examples to support these ideas and had resolved his outstanding issues regarding employment conditions with his major case study of IBM. Despite IBM's proven solution Drucker did not believe that it could be applied nationally. Drucker warned against doing nothing, because the *"guaranteed annual wage"* was only a few years' away, which would hurt both the worker and the enterprise (1954:309). He concluded that there could not be a national guaranteed wage, which was a change from his previous position. But what could be given and was needed was life insurance for workers. This idea was supported by a reference to the Resistoflex Corporation (1954:307) but the article in *Personnel* to which Drucker refers could not be traced. In comparison, Resistoflex insurance policies for personnel, as Drucker reported them, were nominal compared with IBM.

Drucker saw automation replacing the old mass production methods (1954:20, 280), as giving an opportunity to integrate work and its planning, which was something that IBM has achieved. See IBM case study (*ibid*:279). He rejected the speculation from *"the advocates of controlled economy and central planning - especially in Europe"* (1954:17) that workers and all but a few managers would be replaced by *"the push button factory of the future"* (1954:17).

Drucker believed the best preparation for management was a general education through formal schooling *"Or, as so many of the best have always done, he may educate himself"* (1954:368). [Idea: of responsibility for Continual Self-Development by Learning]. Drucker did not believe that young people could be taught how to manage. Management needed experience and maturity to assess and take risks (*ibid*:369). A case reference was made to the Jesuits' professional training, where it was found that it did *"not take"* until experience made advanced studies meaningful (*ibid*:37). As all managers needed further advanced education for tomorrow's tasks, they had to continue studying on the countless *"advanced management programmes"*. Drucker was identifying 'continual education' (*ibid*:370).

Drucker continued to reject the Army inspired *"line and staff"* function in business, which he linked to the warning of the danger of staff empires that confused workers and demonstrated authority without responsibility. The military system was designed for security first, with economic considerations secondary, and was not a starting point for management (*ibid*:7-8). Drucker admitted that specialists were needed

87

and so were specialist services, but he believed that central office staff should be as small as possible and staffed by people with operational experience, answerable to an executive or executives (*ibid*:237-238).

Drucker set the scene for the need for a practice of management. He believed that the Free World was effectively dependent on the skills of management for its survival, particularly those of the management of big organisations because of their capacity to produce for national defence at practically an instant's notice (*ibid*:4-5). On management's place in society, management was now a pivotal player in social history. It was a distinct leading institution since its emergence during the turn of the century. Seldom, if ever, in human history had a new institution proved so indispensable and been established with so little controversy (*ibid*:4).

Society made two types of basic demand on management, social and economic. It expected management to anticipate social demands and maintain employment as close to stability as possible (*ibid*:365). This included allowing for demographic changes by creating opportunities for workers and not excluding people unnecessarily on educational grounds. Old and disabled people should not be prevented from working as a policy (*ibid*:380) although it was necessary to ensure that they did not block progress and employment for younger workers (*ibid*:378). [Idea: It will have to be accepted that many people in the future will want to work beyond what was previously considered retirement age]. Management responsibility was not only for the enterprise itself and its own members (*ibid*:377), but must also act in the public interest (*ibid*:384). [Idea: Stakeholders]. While having the interest of society at large and of its own members, in particular, the enterprise should not take on the role of the state and should respect a pluralistic society (*ibid*:383). Nor should it assume paternal authority and demand the exclusive loyalty of its members (*ibid*:381). In Drucker's earlier works he had been moving towards advocating a mutual close alliance between employer and employed. Subsequently he recognised it as one of the potential dangers in *model* employment organisations that he identified in Rathenau's ideas.

Society also demanded that enterprises survived so that it could fulfil its obligations of tomorrow as well as today by planning for its own succession (*ibid*:376). Management was responsible for solving problems

88

as they arise. They should not be left for management's successors to solve. An example was a pension commitment that placed "*an all but unbearable burden on the production of the younger men*" (*ibid*:378). [Idea: Unsustainable pension burden has a resonance with today]. Drucker's overriding advice was for management to make sure that whatever is "*in the public good becomes the enterprise's own self-interest*" (1954:384). Society expected managers to act ethically and not abuse their power or betray the trust placed in them (1954:377).

The economic demand that society placed on the enterprise and its management to produce an economic performance that was wealth creating, by the generation of profit through productivity, placed in private hands what was an unprecedented permanent concentration of power (*ibid*:376). Profit as a responsibility of management was absolute and was only slightly ahead of growth as a priority, although Drucker's view of growth as a priority would change some decades later. Drucker acknowledged that not all organisations would be in sectors that are capable of growth even if they are efficient. Drucker noted that while paradoxically profit was recognised in the Soviet Union (*ibid*:380-381), yet in America there was a deep-seated hostility to profit in society in general. However, because a lack of profit threatened both societies' economic and social systems, American managers had a responsibility to overcome the national hostility.

For Drucker, management was the organ of society charged specifically with making resources productive reflected the spirit of the modern age (*ibid*:4). The American way of life depended upon growth from goods manufactured more productively, and upon making of profit to pay for the non-productive essentials of Government.

Friends in American Management (1954: Preface viii)

Among those named are James Carson Worthy (1910-1998), Brown, Sloan, and Schumpeter, all of whose influences could be identified. Cordiner, the president of GE was included in this section because he appeared several times in the text. Wilson of GM was also included because his contribution is integrated into *Practice* together with Smiddy, who was recorded as the "*Godfather*" of the book.

References within the text

Included in this list were those that contributed management ideas. It excluded casual references such as, Prince Bismarck (1954:335), or Ernest R Breech's appointment by Henry Ford II (1917- 1987), which although important to Fords only reinforced Drucker's established ideas. However, my criterion for inclusion was not dependent only on Drucker's specific attributions. Fayol was a "*name only*" inclusion in the text *(*1954:275), yet his functions of a manager's job are the basis for Drucker's MbO *(*1954:337-338). Drucker does explain why the others were included in his text. These include Carlson (1954:162); Joel Dean (1906-1991) (1954:25, 33, 72 &74); John Diebold (1926-2005); Otto Charles Doering (1872/3-1955) (1954:27, 31 &170); Ford (1954:18, 27, 96-98, 111-118, 164, 171, 224, 279, 284) Ford II (1917-1987) (1954: 114-115, 146, 244); Gantt (1954:10, 275); Frank Gilbreth (1954:275); Lillian Gilbreth (1954:275); William Barnes Given Jnr (1886-1968) (1954:139); Cameron Hawley (1905-1969) (1954:166); Alexander Richard Heron (1891-1965) (1954:310) Hopf (1954:175-176); Joseph Moses Juran (1904-2008) (1954:281); Oswald Whitman Knauth (1887-1962) (1954:25), Simon Smith Kuznets (1901-1985) (1954:40); Elton Mayo (1954:268);Cyrus Hall McCormick (1809-1884) (1954:36); Douglas McGregor (1954:270); Malcolm Perrin McNair (1894-1985) (1954:41); Rolf Nordling (1893-1974) (1954:163); Paul John William Pigors (1900-1994) and Charles Andrew Myers (1913-2000) (1954:271); Hubert H "*Speed*" Race (1899-1989) (1954:157); Rautenstrauch & Raymond Villers (1911-1985(not Villiers as in the text) (1954:75); Julius Rosenwald (1862-1937) (1954:27-28); Richard Warren Sears (1954:27, 33); Thomas Gardiner Spates (1890-1988) (1954:268); Taylor (1954:274-278); Theodore Newton Vail (1845-1920) (1954:40); Charles Rumford Walker (1893-1974) & Robert Henry Guest (1916 -) (1954:281,293); Frederick Leopold William Richardson Jnr (1909-1988) & Walker (1954:252);

90

Watson Snr (1954:253); General Robert Elkington Wood (1879-1969) (1954:28, 30, 32, 153, 170, 174) and Xenophon (1954:156).

Also referenced in the text were reports in: *Harper's Magazine - How to Place Bets In the Corporation Sweepstakes* of a Bank's Research into top managers' pay, relationships and performance of their enterprise (1954:171); *Business Week* of the Chesapeake & Ohio Railroad Employees' Participation (1954:301). Personnel Research Section, PR & P Branch, The Adjutants General's Office on the *Activities and Behaviours of Production Supervisors*" Report No. 946, Department of the Army, Washington DC 1953 (1954:316).

Also referenced are Drucker's own works: *American Journal of Sociology* (January 1953) *The Employee Society* (1954:264): (*HBR* May/June 1952) *Management and the Professional Employee* (1954:324); *Management Sciences* (Vol. 1 No. 1 – published January 1955) *Management Sciences and the Manager* (1954:389)* with a special thanks to Smiddy and also to Kendrick Porter (for their suggestions; *Concept* and *Society*,).

Case Studies

The wide-ranging minor and major case studies accumulate to circa one hundred and ten. A selection had been made of these for analysis of GM, Fords; GE; Sears; IBM and Crown-Zellerbach Corporation because they were influential on Drucker's basic ideas. Also included was the Chrysler Motor Company as it represented a different approach to automobile manufacture compared with GM and Fords. AT&T for its early unique contribution to management situations that differs from the others and TVA for being a public sector project, and American Pipe Co., uniquely it was an example of a 'Co-operative'. Also the Unions are included because they represent an ever-present power. Reference will be made to other case studies where applicable.

Selected Bibliography for further reading

The final list of influences is from Drucker's Selected Biography (1954:387-389), which was a reading list of management writers comprising thirty-six titles some with more than one author. Of this list, the work of eighteen has been excluded as they appear in the text of *Practice* and are included in three lists. The balance will be examined for their work on organisation including the previously mentioned Tead (1946:12 & 1954:388), together with Reginald Everett Gillmor (1887-1960) (1954:387), Urwick (1954:388), Holden, Fish, and Smith (1954:388), Bakke (1954:388) and Ernest Dale (1917-1996) (1954:388). For their work on ethics, social responsibility and society are John Maurice Clark (1884-1963), Boris Emmet (1885-1974) & John Edward Jeuck (1916-2009) (1954:387), Wayne Albert Risser Leys (1905-1973) (1954:389), Howard Rothmann Bowen (1908-1989) (1954:389), Clarence Belden Randall (1890-1963) (1954:389). Harwood Ferry Merrill (1904-1984) (1954:389) and his contributors: Harry Amos Bullis (1890-1963) , Donald Kirk David 1896-1979) , Richard Redwood Deupree (1885-1974), Allen Welsh Dulles (1893-1969), Ralph Edward Flanders (1880-1970), Clarence Francis (1888-1985) and Jack Isodor Straus (1900-1985) as was Follett, whose papers were collated by Metcalf and Urwick in their 1941 book *Dynamic Administration – The Collected Papers of Mary Parker Follett* (1954:389). For work on automation see Melvin Loescher Hurni (1911-1986), (1954:387 & 389) and John Diebold (1926-2005) (1954:387), and Diebold again for his contribution on computer potential and development. Porter and Edward Alexander Mahoney (1919-1994) for their work on extending the scope of automation by the use of cybernetics, which increases productivity and profit (1954:387) and George Katona's (1901-1981) contribution for his work on psychological influences on economics (1954:387).

Post '*Practice*' influence

TVA and Lilienthal as explained have been included because they represent Drucker's later, but predictable, extension of his ideas from business into the public sector. TVA and Lilienthal have been included in the general body of the text because TVA was referenced in *Society*.

Maslow for his 'hierarchy of needs' that related to incentives, work motivation and the limit on some workers not choosing to or wanting to take responsibility. Maslow's ideas are integrated in the text.

This chapter has identified how Drucker reconsidered some of his previously identified influences that had caused him to make adjustments to his ideas. Also it has identified who are the new influences and how they have been identified. This is in preparation for a later detailed examination of their ideas.

CHAPTER FOUR

DRUCKER'S SEVEN KEY IDEAS

MbO was the object of *Practice*. It was the essential integrator of the other six key integrated functions. The influences that Drucker considered in arriving at his conclusions are identified and considered.

Drucker's premise was that he was discussing a big Corporation that was capable of being managed, not one which was over-sized that could not communicate within itself, although management was as essential for them as for the Corporation. Small and medium sized businesses could not afford the cost of a top management team, but they had the advantage of being able to plan for shorter periods and are more adaptable. They had the disadvantage of not being big enough to plan for succession or to train and test managers. Also there was a tendency for one- man rule and the need to ensure that non-contributing family members such as *"Cousin Paul"* were paid to stay at home rather than de-motivating the workers by confirming their incompetence. Probably the greatest danger point was when an enterprise grew and had to change up into the next structure. What determined the size and complexity of the business was its management structures, not the number of employees. A water company with 7,500 employees serving thousands of consumers was a small company as far as its management structure is concerned. Whereas, a management consultancy business with 200 employees, where majority were consultants, was large by references to its management group — therefore under Drucker's definition it was a large company (1954:225-226).

Despite Drucker's eclectic methods the integration of his own and other's ideas had produced seven key ideas as a further development of his workable society.

Drucker's biggest idea in *Practice* was his brand of Management by Objectives and Self-Control. It was the integration of all the functions of management which must all be performed, but not necessarily, always in the same order, or with the same emphasis. It required all the functions to be capable of measurement, which gave the manager self-control as

95

opposed to being subjected to command and control. MbO was an exercise in integration. It was the implementer or dynamo to make Drucker's preceding most consequential idea *"the promotion of (Federal) Decentralisation"* in *Concept* productive. MbO and Decentralisation were part of Drucker's seven key ideas. The mechanics of MbO made the objectives productive.

Drucker's Seven Key Ideas:

1. Management will be - Management by Objectives and Self-Control (MbO).
2. Decentralisation as the Preferred Structure.
3. The Integration of Productivity by Automation and Profit: -
    (i) Automation
    (ii) Profit
4. Managers Must Measure.
5. The Entrepreneurial Function is; The Purpose of a Business is *"to create a customer"*
    (i)   Marketing
    (ii)   Innovation
6. People are Central to the Organisation
    (i)   Introduction
    (ii)   What does the Enterprise require?
    (iii)   The Workers Attitude
    (iv)   The Status Quo
    (v)   The Way Ahead – Supported by Case Studies
7. The Manager's Job is Total Integration
    (i)   The Manager's Tasks: -
    (ii)   Managing a Business – Supported by Case Studies
        (a)   The Need for Teamwork
        (b)   What Business Are We In?
        (c)   Delegation by *Span of Control* and *Span of Managerial Responsibility*
    (iii)   Managing Managers
    (iv)   Managing Workers and Work

(v)   Time

The Impact of what was the Contribution of Drucker's Seven Key Ideas:

1   MbO
2   Decentralisation
3   Integration by Productivity, Automation and Profit
4   Managers Must Measure
5   Entrepreneurial Function
6   People are Central to the Organisation
7   The Manager's Job is Total Integration

Conclusion of *Practice*

1   Management Will be - Management by Objectives and Self Control (MbO)

Drucker's MbO was not only Management by Objectives, where the manager would be controlled directly by others. For Drucker's MbO could be regarded as a "*philosophy*" of management (*ibid*:33-134). It rested as did the whole structure of modern management on Taylor's (see Profit 3(ii)) most valuable insight "*that planning is different from doing*" and Taylor's emphasis of the importance of planning (*ibid*:77).

The great advantage of MbO was that it made it possible for managers to control their own performance (*ibid*:28). To do so, the manager needed to know his goals and then have the information to measure them (*ibid*:29). MbO was dependent on the manager being able to measure all functions of the business including those that hitherto it had been considered impossible to measure. MbO was an aid to lift not lower performance.

MbO gave genuine freedom under the law. It commenced with top management, whose responsibility was to define the overarching policies (the objectives) of the business as identified in *Concept*. The starting point for the Chief Executive function was to ask the question "*What is our Business?*" (As posed in *Society*) to which in *Practice* has been added, "*What should it be?*" (*ibid*:46) Warnings were given that the question was regularly not asked and when it was asked it was more difficult to answer than

97

appeared at first sight. From this starting point the top management in the organisation could proceed to organise their work. In Drucker's view the job of the CEO was that of a team despite often being portrayed as a one-man job. It required a small team of two but preferably three people. Drucker wrote that there had probably never been a successful Corporation that had had a solitary head. Even Fords during its most successful period had Ford and James Couzens as a team (*ibid*:71).

The executive team was responsible for (i) those external relationships of the organisation, which were initially identified in *Concept*, and although some activities had more detail, their range had not changed; and (ii) internal spirit (*esprit de corps*), the creation of common citizenship, and the practical conversion of the Christian principles started at the top of a responsible organisation that gave the members freedom, purpose, status, opportunities for all, and promoted integrity as the overriding philosophy. The executive team was also responsible for providing as much security of employment as was possible.

The team had to set the objectives of the business while accepting the practical limit that these could never be a railroad timetable. They could only ever be as "*a compass by which a ship navigates*" (*ibid*:58). Regardless of the type of business, objectives remained the same although there might be a different emphasis. These objectives were "*market standing; innovation; productivity; physical and financial resources; profitability; manager performance and responsibility; worker performance and attitude and public responsibility*" (*ibid*:60).

Having established that the objectives were the same for every business, illustrations were given of the different emphases. One of these areas was 'time-span'. Production of a steam turbine will have a time-span of six years, {GE} whereas trees for wood pulp will take fifty years to mature {Crown-Zellerbach} (*ibid*:81). If a long term view did not prevail within the enterprise, then when "*the first cloud appears*" sudden cuts can destroy in one day what has taken years to build [Idea: warning against short-termism] (*ibid*:82). Although the emphasis of the objectives must be balanced against each other, the balance may change from time to time. Objectives also needed have to have regard for the future when obtaining results for today. It was not a mechanical job of staying within budget, but one requiring judgement, which could be achieved only if it was based upon a *"social analysis of the business"* (*ibid*:83-84).

In *The Evolution of Management Thought* (Wren 1994) referred to George Stanley Odiorne (1920-1992) (1965) and Ronald G. Greenwood (1981). Examination of their work provides the following interpretation of MbO by two close associates of Drucker's. Their ideas could be said to be the best informed.

Odiorne: Although Odiorne's *Management by Objectives – A System of Managerial Leadership* (1965) examined MbO in detail, Schumpeter's *Innovation and Entrepreneurship* {probably through Drucker's influence} was given more prominence than Drucker's work which only received two references. However Odiorne tracked Drucker's ideas and offered the following description of MbO:

> *"...management by objectives is essentially a system of incorporating into a more logical and effective pattern to the things many people are already doing, albeit in a somewhat chaotic fashion, or in a way that obscures personal risk and responsibility"* (Odiorne *ibid*: 56).
> *"MBO is a system of managing, not an additional managers job"*
>
> (*ibid*:77).

Odiorne, a student of Drucker's and the first person to write a full-scale book on MbO said, *"[Drucker] has been a voice of sanity in the graduate schools"* (Wren 1994:366) {Odiorne was one of Drucker's pupils}.

Odiorne followed his 1965 book with a paper *MBO: A Backward Glance* (*Business Horizons* October 1978). His research was wide ranging and recorded that a *"popular pastime amongst academics in uncovering the origins of MbO,"* which he cited as including Abraham & God, The Koran, and the philosophers ranging from Plato through to Marx. More objectively Arthur Moxham was recorded as the earliest tutor on MbO with Pierre du Pont as his student at the turn of the 20[th]c followed by Brown, Sloan, GM and later adherents.

Odiorne continued

"Drucker was undoubtedly forced into paying attention to MBO as a natural product of decentralization by the response of his audience in lectures and books. The fact that Drucker is a political scientist at heart, and a management scientist by request only, is often overlooked. For Drucker MBO was necessitated by the need for political changes in the Corporation. His belief was that structural changes were necessary from within the organisation to enable them and the capitalist system to survive... "[With] the observational skills of Tocqueville or a Darwin". He was probably closer to his fellow Austrians, Frederick Hayek and Ludwig Von Mises than he was to Douglas McGregor, Abraham Maslow or Rensis Likert."

Consequently Drucker was not motivated in his ideas by engineering efficiency

Odiorne recorded not only the impact of *Concept* and *Practice* but also work on MbO by a school of competent contributors. He also acknowledged that there were *"haters"* of the concept, who were vociferous rather than large in numbers. Some were employees of businesses where MbO was incorrectly used as a threat that *"employment will be terminated by cause"* unless performance targets are met. The malpracticers of MbO were *"the antiplanner* [who] *are a common type in both business and government"*.

Odiorne's considered conclusion was that: -

"MBO is a philosophy that reacts to the remoteness of bureaucracy and isolation from the leadership of the Corporation". It was a response to what top management demands and how people at work can meet the demands. *"It depends on human commitment self development and responsibility to produce results. It is based upon the creation of the future and forward planning rather than reacting to problems. It is about opportunities.*

MBO is based upon logic and is therefore easily proven to be job-related rather than related to caste, class, or personality". It helped resolve some chronic areas of management failure. It is a catalyst for correcting some of the long outstanding retarders to advancement by helping to determine performance, effectiveness, training, and rewards.

100

Greenwood: While Odiorne's references were wide ranging, Ronald Greenwood used Odiorne's two preceding works and also extensive alternative sources. Greenwood's work was *Management by Objectives: As Developed by Peter Drucker, Assisted by Harold Smiddy* (Ronald G Greenwood, Academy of Management Review 1981 Vol 6 No2 225 & 230). Greenwood, as the title would suggest, put Drucker much more in the centre of the MbO stage while Odiorne ranked him as the significant contemporary figure. Greenwood's conclusion was that:

> *"Drucker is often credited with "inventing" management by objectives. He himself has never claimed the distinction, but a perusal of the literature would lead one to a proper conclusion that Drucker was first to publish the concept and first to use the term."*

> *"MBO* (was) *conceptualized by Peter Drucker and first put into practice by Harold Smiddy, a long-time vice president of the General Electric Company and a close personal friend of Drucker."* [1954.p. ix]. *"Drucker was the first to identify that objectives have to be identified while earlier management theorists believed they were already known".*

> *"To Drucker, these activities "the work of managing as planning, organizing, integrating, and measuring the work of the organization" are the implementation of what he calls the real work of managing: of setting objectives based upon the question what the business is, what it should be? Although Drucker has made this point for the last thirty years it apparently has not yet been understood. For Sloan and Smiddy objectives were obvious; for Drucker they were anything but obvious. Drucker did coin the phrase MBO and made numerous contributions to its philosophy."*

> *"Drucker, on the other hand, found setting objectives to be the difficult, highly risk-taking aspect of the manager's job." "Drucker built management as a discipline and managing as a practice around the high risk taking decisions on objectives — something few others understood."*

The earlier systematic writers on management had focused on process, whereas for Drucker setting objectives was an intellectual exercise based upon conceptualism and analysis *"from which the process of management would flow"* [William J Greenwood/Ronald G Greenwood Personal Communication 22 November 1979]

> *"In answer to the question "Did you know anybody who practiced MBO before you wrote about it?" Drucker replied "A good many people in earlier times managed by objectives as Sloan." ... with probably Pierre Du Pont, before him"*

And, no doubt – *"Donaldson Brown"*.

For Greenwood:

> *"Peter Drucker put objectives into center stage and made them the core of the structure of a discipline of managing. Many other managers probably "invented" and used an MBO concept before 1954, but it took Drucker to put it all together, think through its underlying philosophy, and then explain and advocate it in a form others could use"*

(Greenwood 1981).

In a later reflection Greenwood was more definite of Drucker's contribution:

> *"Drucker did develop the concept there is no doubt about that".*
> *"MBO as it is understood today was conceptualized by Drucker and first put into practice by Harold Smiddy and his staff at GE"*

(Wren & Greenwood 1998:230-231).

Greenwood cleared up a misunderstanding that Sloan, was the first to use the term MbO. In his book on Drucker, Tarrant quoted Drucker as saying *"I didn't invent the term 'management by objectives' actually, Alfred Sloan used it in the 1950s"* (Tarrant 1976). *"Tarrant now says that he misconstrued what Drucker said about Sloan using objectives as a key to his management style to mean he used the term; in fact Sloan used neither the term nor the MBO philosophy*

(Greenwood 1981). Drucker reported that neither Sloan nor Brown at GM *"had [anything] to do with the term... [and] nothing to do with the concept as such" (Ibid* 1979b). But Drucker also claimed that Sloan *"practiced managing by objectives without considering it central to his management philosophy or to his style" (Ibid* 1981c)." Greenwood acknowledges that for Drucker MbO was central and the most difficult function for the manager, as confirmed in *Practice*.

For Drucker objectives had to be decided upon predictions which are always difficult. Predictions of between five to fifteen years in the future were always going to be 'guesses' - a 'gamble' or a 'hunch'. But what business needed was not a 'business forecast' in the usual sense but some better tools that would enable the business to continue without the fear of unpredictable business cycles neutralising their thinking. This was Sloan's philosophy. Drucker provided three useful tools (i) Test the assumptions against the sharpest set-back that our experience could lead us to expect; (ii) Use Bedrock Analysis, which was based upon events that have already happened and tries to find 'the why' of future events. {This is the start of Drucker's use of demographics, which should be included in this analysis}. But nothing was inevitable in the future, so Bedrock Analysis should not be used on its own (1954:89-91). It should always be used with (iii) Trend Analysis to limit risks. Trend Analysis attempted to analyse *"how likely"* or *"how fast"*. Drucker also referred to a new set of decision making tools 'Operations Research', which he identified as important but not new as most managers think as it was used by the *"medieval symbolical logicians such as St Bonaventure"*. However, the new tools had been brought into everybody's reach. Although mathematical information theory was in its infancy, potentially it would enable identification of deviations and action patterns (*ibid*:360-361). On the decision making process Drucker referred to his own wide-ranging advice on the difficulties of making decisions. He described the process of requiring an integrated approach that could never be achieved by a *single* objective. It was a rational activity based on *"definite assumptions"* and 'calculated assumptions' in his *"Management Science and the Manager* (January 1955), in which he acknowledged assistance for stimulation,

103

advice and criticism to Hurni, Smiddy and Porter. He also referenced *Practice* for a fuller description.

Drucker continued that once the executive team has been determined, the objectives of the business could be set in all of the key functions that are identified. What was important was how these decisions were made, in order to allow the business to obtain results for five to fifteen years hence. Drucker suggested three methods to be used to make the primary decisions, Activity Analysis, Decision Analysis and Relation Analysis. By using these methods the business could be analysed and the question of "*What is our business*" and "*What should it be*" can be answered in a practical manner. Only then could the structure of an organisation be determined. [Idea: The structure must follow the business not the business following the structure, which is flawed strategy] (1954:190-198). {This conclusion predates Alfred Chandler Jnr, who is generally acknowledged as the first to draw it (Chandler 1962)}.

That others had practised MbO before Drucker is not at issue. What Drucker did was synthesise the ideas and also identify the flaw in the previous methods of setting objectives. In doing so he created something new and made it possible for MbO to be applied as a discipline. In this respect Drucker had a substantial role in originating MbO not just in coining the name. Of Drucker's seven key ideas, MbO was the weld which brings together the other six. Its application increased the effectiveness of the others and gives them a consequence that they did not possess independently. What was apparent in this section was that the previously mentioned new influences were being worked into Drucker's ideas, including Smiddy's already highlighted letter between the manager and his subordinate. This was intended to enable the objectives of the business to be identified with the individual's contribution to which he had agreed.

Despite the large sample of Drucker's case studies none emphasise that management of a business was founded on it being the "*total integration*" of all the functions of an enterprise. That it was practised in successful enterprises was self-evident, otherwise they could not perform at the levels that they do. Although Drucker wrote that Hopf saw the need, it was Drucker that made it a central necessity followed closely by

Smiddy in his 1955 essay *Integration and Motivating for Effective Performance*. MbO was described as the integration of all the functions of management but not in a static pattern because the order and emphasis will change. That management was total integration of all the functions of an enterprise, may be the most important message in *Practice* because it is timeless and can be applied to all management philosophies not only MbO as he clearly sets down.

> "*At first sight it might seem that different businesses would have entirely different key areas — so different as to make impossible any general theory. It is indeed true that different key areas require different emphasis in different businesses — and differing emphasis at different stages of the development of each business. But the areas are the same, whatever the business, whatever the economic conditions, whatever the business's size or stage of growth*" (1954:60). "*When it comes to the job itself, however, the problem is not to dissect it into parts or motions but to 'put together an integrated whole'. This is the new task*"
>
> (*ibid*:289).

2   Decentralisation as the Preferred Structure

Looking back at the evolution of this concept in Drucker's thinking, it shows a tortuous journey. Drucker originally used the term Decentralisation in *Future* as an alternative to centralised despotism. He became aware of how it worked in an industrial setting during his studies of GM. There is however some confusion in the description, with Federalism and Decentralisation being used in an interchangeable way and also linked together. To remove the confusion Decentralisation is used throughout this book, as previously recorded. What is clear and what is important is that GM:

> "...*has become an essay in federalism - on the whole, an exceedingly successful one*" "*and further extension of Decentralisation are the answers to most of the problems of modern industrial society*"
>
> (1946:46).

Drucker listed eight advantages claimed for Decentralisation:

(i) Speed of decision based upon common knowledge.

(ii) Absence of divisional conflict.

(iii) A sense of fairness prevailing among executives due to the control of politics.

(iv) Democratic informal management which encouraged dissent during the formulation period. Once a decision was made it had to be accepted that the ultimate control was with the CEO's team.

(v) There was no elite privileged few.

(vi) That large management groups ensure a good supply of experienced leaders.

(vii) Objective measurement means that weak performance could be detected.

(viii) Patient agreement (as championed by Sloan) of policy evolution, which resulted in managers knowing the reasons for their objectives.

The outcome was the absence of edict management (*ibid*:47-48). Although there were service staff agencies at Central Office the:

> "*divisional manager is under no compulsion to consult or take their advice*"

> (*ibid*:54-56).

The service staff could only recommend, not 'lay down policies'.

Despite GM being a model for Decentralisation as identified in *Concept* its evolution into a fully decentralised corporation was not complete. Two of its very large divisions, Fisher Bodies and Chevrolet, had a Centralised structure and yet managed to be efficient. Drucker attributed their efficiency to the market check of the annual model change. But even Chevrolet had Decentralised its administration. The result had been a very successful 'speed-up' of production. While both Fisher and Chevrolet produced as effectively as the Decentralised divisions they failed at one of the imperatives of efficiency in that "*they do not discover and*

106

develop industrial leaders" (*ibid*:121 & 124-125). At this stage Decentralisation could be described as top management at Central Office agreeing with divisional managers their performance targets. These results were then measured based upon Brown's cost accounting systems. However, if there was no relationship between the activities in the divisions of the business then Functional Decentralisation had to be used with its own top management (*ibid*:247, 250 & 255). {What Drucker was also implying was that if, say, the process of the business in a simple sole unit as a quarry operation or a welding shop, then Functional Decentralisation's devolved authority within these types of units was the structure, because there were not any divisions to separate horizontally into Decentralisation}. By the time that Drucker wrote *Society* Decentralisation had become even more clearly the preferred structure of the two alternatives. In *Practice* it was still endorsed and *"is fast becoming the norm in the larger companies"* (1954:206). But divisions must have their own market, autonomous product and be answerable for performance by their own sets of accounts

For Drucker Decentralisation was endorsed by his case studies. However, there was some tempering of Drucker's views as Decentralisation and Functional Decentralisation were now complementary. Both had to be used in almost all businesses (corporations) (*ibid*:202-203). Drucker now accepted that his criticism of GM's structure in *Concept* cannot be upheld and that Functional Decentralisation was applicable in small businesses, and in growing businesses, up to the size at which Decentralisation becomes appropriate (*ibid*:202-203). Drucker described Functional Decentralisation as working better the more that it approached Decentralisation's delegation of authority in exchange for responsibility.

Drucker identified the criteria for determining the choice of structure. Once *"what the business is"* had been identified, the choice of structure could be determined by addressing three basic questions. (i) The enterprise must be organised for business performance; (ii) The structure must not direct efforts towards the wrong results; (iii) The structure must make possible the training and testing of tomorrow's top managers. The *"trying-out"* in actual management positions was imperative because

107

potential could not be the sole qualification for a management appointment. Experience confirms that once appointed removal of a president from an organisation *"is well nigh impossible"* (*ibid*:199-202).

Drucker demonstrated the benefits of Decentralisation through the use of case studies that will be examined later. These demonstrated that its application must be adapted to the business not the business to it. The following were the main reasons for Decentralisation becoming the dominant structure: (i) it focused the manager on results; (ii) it removed self-deception of unprofitable lines by removing the hiding place of costs in overheads; (iii) MbO became fully effective; (iv) it developed tomorrow's managers; (v) it tested manager's competence at a fairly low level.

The rules governing the applicability of Decentralisation were that there must be (i) strong divisions; (ii) businesses large enough to support management's needs; (iii) potential for growth in each division. It was a poor organisation that concentrated all mature lines into one division and all those with potential for growth in another; (iv) challenges for managers; (v) each federal unit (division) should work side by side with each other, with its own job, market and products, and be managed as independent businesses. Any joint ventures between divisions should be at the division's choice (*ibid*:206-215)

Drucker's conclusion was that Decentralisation had limitations if its rules were abused and also that the system should be as simple as possible, by having the fewest layers of management (*ibid*:218). One indication of maladministration was when layers are added. [Idea: Delayering or Re-engineering. For Drucker the ideal was to delegate authority so that responsibility for the decision was taken as low down in the organisation as possible]. In Drucker's view, Decentralisation was not the answer to every organisational structure but it was the best concept and could be applied a great deal more (*ibid*:15). Another structure that Drucker first introduced in *Practice* was the 'task force' team, which was the amalgamation of numerous specialists into a team that could be used within Decentralisation (*ibid*d:217). Later 'task force' teams would become a separate method of organisation, Drucker being amongst the first to recognise them. [Idea: Task force teams could and

108

should be set up within structures for special projects. This anticipates project management].

When the executive team had set the framework for its work and that of the other members of the organisation by delegation of responsibility, it must clearly reserve for itself *"a welfare clause"*. This was the right to act in the overall interest of the organisation for the good of all the members even though it might not be in the interest of a particular division (*ibid*:220). Although arguing for Decentralisation as the preferred structure, Drucker made the point that in the future, businesses may have to adopt different or hybrid structures. As the world changed so do all things, including management. In support of Drucker's contention Sloan (1964) later wrote that GM's Decentralised management model was not to be regarded as ever being a finished product. For Mooney & Reiley Decentralisation was being linked with co-ordination. Sloan was quoted by them to describe what a decentralised organisation is as *"a whole divided into a proper number of parts, each presided over by a chief executive who is held absolutely responsible for that particular part over which he presides"* *"...under no circumstances should instructions be given by any, regardless of that authority's status in the corporation, to that part, except through its duly appointed chief executive"* (Mooney & Reiley 1931:509). But for Drucker the cement of the organisation was integration not co-ordination.

3   The Integration of Productivity by Automation and Profit.

"The First Function of Management is Economic Performance". Management failed if it did not produce goods and services at a price that the customer was willing to pay. In doing so it must *"maintain the wealth producing capacity... entrusted to it"* (1954:7). Production at the right price satisfied the customer's wants, maintained profit, and replenished production capacity.

Drucker saw the American free market society as dependent on the above happening to ensure its survival (1954:6-7). He noted that in the last few years' productivity had become topical, but was little known and difficult to measure. It was the balance of *all* factors of production. It was different from the traditional standards of output per worker hour, because in a modern economy increase in productivity could never be achieved by muscle effort, only by substituting muscle with something else. One of the substitutes was capital equipment. The economist Kuznets established the benefit of equipment substitution through studies showing the direct relationship between increased productivity and investment in capital equipment in the United States. Kuznets' work relegated into a secondary position the traditional economist's view that productivity was related to increased capital formation (*ibid*:39-40). The publication that Drucker made reference to could not be found, but other works by the Russian-born American Nobel Laureate confirm his authority on the relationship between productivity and capital investment, such as his 1953 book *Economic Change – Selected Essays in Business Cycles, National Income and Economic Growth.*

Drucker defined productivity as the ability to produce more or better than all the inputs (*ibid*:12) or *"the greatest output for the smallest effort"* (*ibid*:39). It was results rather than effort (*ibid*:42). The principles of production were of serious concern not just to manufacturers, but to all businesses including distribution, and even advertising as identified by Harvard's McNair (*ibid*:41). See also his many publications including his book *Readings in Marketing* McNair & Hansen (1949). As with the other functions of the business, production was affected by the structure of the enterprise (*ibid*:43). But before objectives could be set for production the principles of production needed to be examined. Here Drucker's views had changed since he first wrote about the principles of production and praised Ford and Taylor as the great innovators *"of the worker as an automatic standardized machine"* (1950:102 & 286). Production management as practised fifty to sixty years ago was now hopelessly out of date as management had learned that the first principle of production is to bring the machines to the work, rather than the work to the machines.

Drucker's correction was that, the organisation of production had to move away from the two blind spots of Scientific Management. The first was that of breaking work down into the simplest operation to be carried out by separate workers. The second was derived from Taylor's most

110

valuable insight *"the divorce of planning from doing"*. But importantly, Drucker concluded that it did not follow that the planner and the doer had to be different people (1954:277-278).

For Drucker, since Taylor evolved the principles of Scientific Management, which was further developed by Fayol, Gantt, Frank, and Lillian Gilbreth, few new insights had emerged despite incredible efforts; the exception was Hopf and the further work of Lillian Gilbreth (*ibid*:275). It was the two blind spots that produced worker resistance to changes that prevent increased productivity (*ibid*:279). In relation to organising work Juran was credited with examining the assumption that man was a badly designed machine (*ibid*:281). (See *Quality Control Handbook* by Juran *et al* 1951, and the *Revised Editions* by Juran *et al* 1962)

(i) Automation

Drucker observed that the new mass production technology of twenty years previous was being replaced by a new principle of production, automation which he likened to a new Industrial Revolution (*ibid*:20). However like all revolutions he saw it as gradual, as people had yet to be trained in sufficient numbers. The old would continue as in the New York garment industry, which still operated in a similar fashion to the first Industrial Revolution of about 1750 (*ibid*:104). Automation was a technology. Like every other technology it was a system based on concepts where its technical elements are the results not the cause. Automation was based on three concepts. The first was Metaphysical, which is based upon the belief that behind the flux of phenomenon there are basic patterns of stability and predictability. The second was based upon the nature of work. It was not focused on skill as the integrating principles, as was the early individual production; nor upon Ford's mass production, which was focused for its organisation principles on the product. Its focus was on the process as an integrated and harmonious whole. The aim was for the best process that fulfils the criteria of producing goods in the greatest variety, at the lowest cost, with the least effort, all at the greatest stability. Possibly the more rigid the process, the greater may be the variety of goods produced. The third concept was that what was significant must be pre-established. This then was used to act "*as a pre-set and self-activating governor of the process*" it was setting up of the process that produces the planned result. The mechanics of control were secondary to the technology of automation (*ibid*:18-19). "*It is applying logic to work*" (*ibid*:93). It made Decentralisation more essential to give managers flexibility and autonomy (*ibid*:21).

Automation might be mass production with a conveyor belt, or the organisation of cheque clearing without the 'push button'. Drucker predicted that just as many of the pundits of the 1930s were wrong when they forecast that mass production would throw people out of work; automation (*ibid*:17) would have a similar effect of producing more job opportunities, not less. It would also accelerate the upgrading of workers skills with more managers and technicians needed. Drucker also questioned pundits' forecast that businesses would have to be bigger and concluded that in some instances smaller units may be pertinent. The production of raw steel was given as an example. The fashionable pundit prediction that Drucker challenged, was that the increase in capital would be tremendous. His view was that capital might increase but the force is 'brain power' (*ibid*:20-21). [Idea: Decades later, in the 1990s, Drucker identified brainpower as the new capital 'brain power' that replaces 'muscle' to increase productivity (*ibid*:40)]. But what was certain was that automation would change the nature of work (*ibid*:279). For Juran automation was also the integration of "*quality*" but although Juran was mentioned in the text, Drucker missed that essential linkage (1962: Chapter 22 Juran *et al*).

Drucker's position in *Concept* was that, while knowing little about production, he believed that a new theory of mass production technology was required, which focused on the individual worker and tapped into his imagination. From this position two things had changed. First Drucker had found the new technology which would produce continuous opportunities for decades to come. "*... in the consistent application of the new mass production principle and secondly in the application of the principles of Automation*" (*ibid*:105). The second change was that while Drucker still did not claim to have production expertise, he had now acquired the knowledge to define the principles. He could now tell the

112

managers that to adequately discharge their jobs they would have to understand the principles of production as being *"an understanding that efficient production is a matter of principles rather than of machines and gadgets"* (*ibid*:105).

Drucker set down what knowledge managers would need to acquire about the principles of productivity. To date there were three or maybe four basic systems of industrial production (i) unique production – e.g. as a battleship or skyscraper; (ii) mass production – old style, e.g. the production of uniform products; (iii) mass production – new style in which diverse production was assembled from uniform parts; (iv) process production – e.g. an oil refinery or chemical works. Each of the systems had their own basic principles that made specific demands on management. There were two rules of application: (i) the more vigorously and completely the set of particular principles were applied the more effective they were; (ii) each principle of productivity had its own requirements, application and limitations. These were least advanced in unique production and most advanced in process industries. Each had its applicability and progress from the least to the most advanced might not be possible. There were a further two general rules for managers: (i) when moving from one system to another, new things had to be learned rather than emphasis being placed on doing old things better; (ii) the better managers performed, the easier the demands of the principles were to meet (*ibid*:93-99). The manager had two basic productive sources, equipment and human resources. In fact only one was primary, the human resource, since it alone could make equipment productive. Therefore, a job must be engineered (*ibid*:284-90). Organising people for work, which is the manager's greatest productive resource, will be examined in a following section.

Drucker concluded that the manager needed to set objectives for productivity as in any other key function of the business. That equipment was required for manufacturing and almost all other activities of a business was a fact. Therefore the manager should see the limitation of the physical equipment as a trigger for the need for initiative to create new opportunities rather than accept the initial limitations as a constraint. But this demanded initiative, and was not supporting "*management by drives*", which Drucker identified as common in the manufacturing function. "*Management by drives*" was where resources were committed impulsively without any planning or forethought (*ibid*:92). This was not managing the situation. This was not an action of competence.

Of performance, productivity measurement was the only method of comparing the performance of managers in different units of the enterprise and outside [Idea: later became Benchmarking]. Production measurement measured the yield of the utilisation of the resources. The consistent improvement of productivity was management's most important job. [Idea: This is *Kaizen* see IBM] Productivity was also an area where a variety of factors make clear measurement difficult. Drucker used as a basic concept, Contributed Value [Idea: 'Added Value' or 'Value Added'], which for the first time provided a tool for setting goals for productivity improvements. The use of 'Contributed Value' should make possible the use of 'Operational Research' and 'Information Theory' as being able to identify alternative actions and predict their outcomes (*ibid*:69, 70 & 363). With these new principles of production, and the emergence of better techniques for setting objectives for productivity and progressive production alternatives were emerging for production.

Drucker noted that automation had been discussed almost exclusively as a production principle; however, in his view, it was a principle of work in general. The production manager would now have to be able to think across the other objectives of the business and integrate his speciality within the whole. This was a practical application of Wertheimer's Gestalt. Now the production manager's vision would not only have to be from management's view point but also from the customer's viewpoint, with regard for the external providers of distribution, materials, and customer services (*ibid*: 71 & 363-364). [Idea: Outsourcing].

(ii)   Profit

Profit received extensive examination in *Society*. Drucker started from his established position that "*the guiding principle of business economics … it is the*

114

avoidance of loss" the reason being that this enabled a business to fulfil its first duty, to survive (*ibid*:44). The 'profit motive' of the classical economists was rejected (*ibid*:34). What Drucker was not making clear was that no-one would enter into business merely to avoid loss. The presumption was that, once in business, avoiding loss when the 'business cycle' is in the downturn, is the guiding principle.

A decision about the nature of business started with profit and profitability but it was not the cause of the business but the result. The result was the consequence of the performance of the business of the marketing, innovation and productivity. Drucker's idea was that MbO was the integration of all functions of the business together with measurement, which was also a major function in itself. But profit was the only possible test, as Communist Russia discovered when they tried to abolish it in the 1920s (1954:44) only for it to be reinstated later as the first law of Russian management (1954:380-381)

But Drucker argued profit could not be a reason for the business because it would misdirect managers and endanger the long-term survival of the business. A management approach of 'short term' profit as being the single objective was flawed as it misdirected and harmed the business as the long-term essentials of research and replacement of obsolete equipment were neglected. It directed management towards the worst practice, that of short-term expediency (1954:59). [Idea: short-termism].

Despite the difficulty in defining profit, without it, the essential rationale for the survival of the business disappeared. Profit, according to Drucker, served three purposes: (i) it was the ultimate test of business performance; (ii) it was the "*risk premium*" for 'being in' and 'staying in' business. When profit was viewed as such there are no such things as profits, only costs; (iii) it supplied future capital for expansion and innovation through two sources: (a) retained profit and (b) through attracting external capital. This reference to external capital was a change in Drucker's previous position when capital could come only from the enterprise's self-generated funds of profit. However as before, the target was that the minimum profit level had to ensure the survival and the prosperity of the enterprise (1954:73-74).

Having argued the necessity of profit, Drucker was left with two dilemmas: the first was the need for higher profits for the survival of a progressive economic society, and second the resistance to adequate levels of profit from the public and the hostility of the workers to profit (1954:309-311). In Drucker's view the ownership of small shareholdings would not change the worker's resistance to profit (1954:310). This attitude stems from the enterprise having its origins in the economic sphere. Drucker referred to *Society* and his article *The Employee Society* (January 1953) in which he examined the consequences of American society becoming an employee society during the last fifty years. He noted that the majority of people expected to spend their working life employed, which had changed social values and demands. The age of the manager had caused the formation of another basic institution the Unions. The emergence of the employee society had created a tremendous challenge and opportunity.

Drucker believed that the current perception was that the enterprise existed in two economic systems, internal, and external. The worker believed that he operated in the internal system which converted in practice to his wages. The enterprise believed that it operated in an external system which was represented by what it received for its products, which were market determined. The manager's perception of the enterprise was that internally there were only costs, while externally were the results (1954:264-265), which created the profit or surplus essential for survival.

Drucker's conclusion was that the worker was opposed to the idea that profit was produced by the enterprise. The worker's belief was based upon the ancient superstition that as the producer '*he*' produces profit. The reality was that it was "*the purpose of the business to create a customer*" and that this market maintained employment. If this could be accepted then the outcome was harmony between employer and employee (1954:265, 310-311). Profit sharing might strengthen the message that performance created employment and income. But in Drucker's experience, income was what employees want most, rather than profit incentives.

116

The first responsibility of the enterprise to society was to operate at a profit because it was the *"wealth creating"* and *"wealth producing"* organ of society. Only slightly less important than profit is growth, by productivity. It was because of the importance of profit and its dependence upon productivity that Drucker saw them as integrated (1954:380). Drucker's conclusion was that the deep-seated hostility to profit was a threat to the social and economic systems of America and that management has the responsibility to overcome the problem (1954:382). What Drucker was arguing was that job insecurity was the worker's first fear. The workers believed that it was in their interest not to increase production because the maximum output equated to fewer workers to produce for a finite demand. Drucker's counter to this argument was that more productivity produced more goods, either resulting in lower prices or a better product. Both outcomes result in growth in the economy creating more demand and causing job security rather than reducing it. The next argument in the worker position was that if they did increase productivity then the profit from so doing was not theirs, nor did they have any interest in the profit. Drucker's counter argument was that without profit there was no job security for the worker; therefore their resistance to higher productivity and profit was exacerbating their greatest fear, that of unemployment.

When Drucker wrote that there were two basic productive sources, equipment and human resources, and concluded that only the human resource could make equipment productive, he was emphasizing the dependence of the enterprise on believing that the workers want to work. But the argument did not stop at this essential fact of life of the enterprise. By motivating the worker to achieve improved productivity only part of the complex equation was satisfied. Drucker continued that equipment, as a component of productivity, needed to be considered in a structured rather than an intuitive manner. New tools were available as exposed by Kuznets who had made the consideration of equipment as a replacement for labour a reality for measuring productivity. We were now moving to the next key idea of *"Managers must Measure"* and to answer the question of *"How Can We Measure?"* This is the topic of the next section, which will also consider with others the work of Dean in his 1951 book

117

Managerial Economics on the measurement of equipment and capital costs. Dean extended the traditional boundaries for what was measured. He considered that only running costs were being measure and not related capital costs. Additionally he extended the parameters that measured the declared profit. Also Juran's contribution on profit was through increased productivity, which was based upon reducing defective work by 'quality control'. Each gain he regarded as *"gold in the mine"*.

Drucker's linking of automation and profit had originality. His ideas on automation were an important record of the work of others. The importance was that it gave the general management reader accessibility to a new emerging principle of management. That Drucker missed the significance of Juran's work on quality control was not surprising as it followed Drucker's previous declaration in *Concept* that he was not an expert in production methods. But, because production was such a critical part of the management function, it could not be ignored. What Drucker was making was an important original contribution to his definition of *"what profit is"*. His earlier career as a banker and his grasp of economics were the foundation for his competence and expertise that aided this contribution. Profit or more precisely its close cousins, cash or credit were the essential imperative priority if an enterprise was to survive. In this section some of the influences that Drucker considered were showing in his ideas.

4.   Managers Must Measure

Drucker was first exposed to the importance of measuring the performance of business and the individual manager during his examination of GM's advanced costing systems as developed by Brown, which he praised as *"outstanding financial principles of control"* (1946:12). From this emerged Drucker's general criticism of the measuring professionals, the accountants, who were not providing or developing the wide-ranging measurements required by modern business. In fact such measurements as were undertaken were probably inappropriate as Drucker concluded that accountants, just like economists, measured only what could be quantified or receive mathematical treatment (1954:60-61).

118

He suggested a major overhaul of accounting methods might be required (*ibid*:69).

The basis for MbO was that the manager must be provided with the tools to measure his own performance, otherwise goals could not be set (*ibid*:128-129). Drucker believed policies must span all of the activities of management not just the small sample that had received attention to date. This was an ambitious aim, as some activities had no recognised form of measurement, while others were only at an inconclusive research stage. Later Kaplan & Norton extrapolated MbO into their book *Balanced Scorecard* (1996) a method of balanced objectives setting, which determined and measured the impacts the functions of organisations had upon each other (Kaplan & Norton 1996). [Idea: Balanced Scorecard]

The general criticism of accountants recorded in Drucker's early books was maintained in *Practice*. Drucker believed the time-honoured practice of accountants allocating overheads as a percentage across the board made realistic cost analysis impossible. It was necessary to focus on management's needs rather than those of the banker's, tax collector's and investor's folklore (1954:69). Also the allocation of parasitical overheads to "*productive*" costs was a cause of friction (*ibid*:42). He supported his view that accountants had failed to keep abreast of developments, citing a typical 1900 manufacturing business where managerial and technical overheads as a percentage of direct labour were 5% and 8% respectively whereas now in many industries the percentages were almost equal (*ibid*:40). Drucker quoted the view of an ex-accountant company president that business management could never be rational until it was freed from the unnecessary tyranny of the accounting year (*ibid*:75). That accounting departments were usually in conflict with the remainder of the organisation was not surprising. Accountancy departments had difficulty in setting objectives or measuring performance because they were responsible for five different functions: management reports, finance and tax, record keeping and custodial functions, and government requirements. Admittedly they all used the same data, but putting them together in the accounts department was not logical, as each had different priorities. The consequence was that this led to non-performance and confused objectives (*ibid*:204).

Moving on from his criticism of the contemporary accountants' lack of performance Drucker adopted a more positive approach, and effectively did a stock-take of ideas that would contribute to the accountant's role progressing since, there was no suggestion that the role could or should be disbanded. In Drucker's opinion the problem was that despite thousands of books on the functions of management, and on the management of a business, the requirements and the actions to progress ideas on accounting in management needed had been neglected, with two exceptions. There were two writers, both American, the first being Knauth the second Dean.

Like Drucker, Knauth in his 1948 book *Managerial Enterprise*, from a position of a basic belief in management and free enterprise, was critical of accountants while advocating the importance of profit and the measurement of capital. His views aligned with those of Berle & Means, and Schumpeter's while complementing Drucker's concepts (Knauth 1948). Drucker referred to Knauth's work as a short essay (1954:25). The work is a book of two hundred pages.

Dean, whose work was complementary to the work of Kuznets and Knauth, Drucker described as "*the most brilliant and fruitful of the economists analysing business today*" (*ibid*:33). Dean's views aligned with Drucker's in respect of economists and accountants whose measurement only works in a static economy (Dean 1951:14-15) while his "*Theory of Capital Rationing*" (*Ibid* 1951:586-610), described how to make capital investment by objective analysis rather than by intuition. Dean while questioning the validity of profit maximisation as an objective of business, also refined its meaning when applied to big businesses who were failing to measure effectively by emphasising marginal costs and revenues. Drucker concluded that Dean, in attempting to modernise maximisation of profit had qualified it out of existence (1954:33). Drucker made complimentary reference to other works by Dean including his 1951 book *Capital Budgeting* and his paper (*HBR* January 1954) *Measuring the Productivity of Capital* (1954:72-74). Dean identified that organisational facilities needed to be planned and their needs measured, because either under or over supply was extremely dangerous. Dean also emphasised the importance of measuring time with profit. For profit to be meaningful it must be set

120

within a time frame for what he termed *"consistent dollar profit"*. Dean in turn made complimentary reference to Drucker. Dean's contribution included his development of *"break even analysis"* and he was attributed with being an early practitioner of *Econometrics* the relationship between costs and volume. Drucker made no reference to these contributions. {The term *econometrics* was previously used in a different context to describe *"Pareto's Law"* in (1896). The 'Law' compared logarithmically the number of people receiving higher income than the average, in Schumpeter's (1952) book *Ten Great Economists from Marx to Keynes* (page 120)}.

Practice showed that Drucker had discovered new economists after rejecting the classical economists in *Economic Man* with only Schumpeter being retained, although Knight's alignment with Schumpeter had been previously recorded. The new economists referred to in *Practice* are Kuznets, Knauth, Dean, Rautenstrauch assisted by Villers, McNair and Katona. Knauth pertinently commented that *"Classical economists have lost touch with the colossal developments of the last fifty years"* But within the last twenty-five years economics had acquired a new virility (Knauth 1948:7).

What had emerged were some further profound questions regarding the forms of measurement used by Accountants. An example was the usefulness of the standard target for return on capital of 25%, because there was no standard answer to the question *"What is meant by capital?"* The following refinements were suggested by Drucker: that profit on equipment should be measured over the life of the equipment using discounted cash flow rather than an annual ROI (1954:74-75). Also the average for good and bad years should be considered together, using 'break-even point analyses'. But Drucker warned that there was still a problem because even with these refinements there were still unresolved issues, the major one being what to use as a yardstick to measure 'break-even point analyses' caused by the vulnerability to economic fluctuation of measurement. 'Return on Capital' made sense but it was as *"rubber elastic"* because original investment distorted the current results and avoided issues such as currency exchange rates. What the management profession needed to start with was a rational investment policy (*ibid*:76). Yet accountants and economists in general again had failed to provide an

121

answer. A working compromise that many managers and Accountants used was to calculate 'invested capital' at today's prices, but even this had limitations if the market prices of equipment as in Depressions produced lower base costs (*ibid*:77-78).

But it was necessary to have a method to make budgeting possible, as capital investment policy had to be set (*ibid*:76) before determining how to measure profit. Drucker's idea on measuring 'return on invested capital' (ROI) was taking the original investment adjusted for inflation or deflation as the base, then projecting the current net profit after depreciation against the original gross investment (*ibid*:78). [Idea: Return on Invested Capital. Drucker said that he has no theory to support his ideas, but the method as crude and simple and would not fool any manager into mistaking it for precision (*ibid*:78)]. The measure of profit was a problem, as 'profit' could be turned into a 'loss' merely by changing the rate of depreciation (*ibid*:81).

Drucker also examined other functions of management where progress had been or needed to be made. Taylor had established that work could be measured but Drucker's view was that this important start needed to be progressed into the psychology of work (*ibid*:274). Annual customer surveys to gauge customer satisfaction were being carried out by only a few identified progressive managements, and this needed to be extended (*ibid*:65).

Reports could be used to measure progress but should not be used as tools for control from above, but for the person who filled in the report (*ibid*:133). Reports and procedures were amongst the most misused of the necessary tools of management (*ibid*:131). Every five years they should all be put on trial 'for their lives' and killed off if they were no longer essential (*ibid*:133).

Some businesses were building an Employee Relations Index, of suggestion schemes, absenteeism, turnover of labour etc. While accepting that a start had been made Drucker regarded the practice as a stopgap until real objectives could be set, based on knowledge (*ibid*:80).
No effective means of measuring advertising had been discovered despite the work of experts as McNair (*ibid*:41). {However McNair's greatest contribution to management ideas is in marketing and controls in the

122

wholesale and retail trades. Even a random search reveals that his work spanned from 1920 to the mid-1960s. Most of his work had been as a Harvard academic}

Drucker referred for the first time to the Americans Rautenstrauch and the industrial engineer management writer Villers for their 1949 book *The Economics of Industrial Management* whose 'break-even point analysis' permitted fairly accurate prediction of returns under various business conditions (*ibid*:75). They differed from Drucker on accountants, and gave them credit for permitting a business to know 'where it is' without having to wait for a stock-take, (Rautenstrauch & Villers 1949:240). This conclusion, which Drucker did not mention, was only partly correct. Accountants were still dependent upon stock takers and technical information from others to complete their conclusions. However Rautenstrauch & Villers agreed with Drucker, that the 'Balance Sheet' and the 'Profit and Loss Statement' were not adequate tools by themselves for decision-making (*Ibid* 1949:35).

Although there remained enormous gaps in what needed to be measured and the techniques so far developed, it was still Drucker's objective to develop measurement. For him responsibility started with the CEO and the Board. The CEO must set the overall objectives of the business, carefully assessing all parts and must measure performance and results (1954:83 &159). By setting the objectives and monitoring where no measure currently existed, yardsticks could be developed by using the new analytical techniques. The CEO would have to become, in addition to his other activities, *"a first rate analyst and synthesizer"* (*ibid*:167). Survey and analysis would establish some of the rules.

As an illustration of the proper use of measurement, Drucker made reference to GE's travelling audit team, which visited every management unit at least once a year. A report was then sent to unit managers as an aid to assist self-control rather than being used as a form of control from above. In Drucker's opinion the system engendered trust, this was evident in GE managers. Drucker contrasted this with an unidentified business which operated an audit unit reporting to the president who used it as a tool of confrontation. The outcome of the work of the 'President's Gestapo' was that management objectives were directed at

123

"*passing*" the audit not at best performance. Drucker wrote that he was not opposing the view that managers should be held strictly accountable for the results of their performance, but that by using measurement to aid MbO and self-control then better results would be obtained (*ibid*:130). Results would be harmed rather than improved if an integrated approach was not taken. Isolating one objective has a danger of destroying other objectives if the overall effect of the actions was not taken into account.

Despite reference to Gantt, Drucker did not refer to Gantt's contribution of the Gantt Chart or the Bar Chart as a method of measurement as previously noted (Clark 1923). In his later work Drucker acknowledged that Gantt's work was the forerunner of Critical Path Planning, and PERT (Programme Evaluation Results Technique).

Juran was included in Drucker's text for his contribution to the Human Resource school in challenging the idea that man is a badly designed machine (1954:281). However, he omitted Juran's work on "*Quality Control*", which extended into measurement, by including measurement of waste, reliability of products, and the use of interchangeable parts, of which the advantages included reducing inventory costs. For Juran avoiding costs through quality control was a philosophy that pervaded all parts of the business and not just manufacturing. It is described as "*gold in the mine*", which is a theory of profit enhancement. For Juran all activities of the business were costs, and costs needed to be controlled by measurement (Juran 1951:318).

Drucker had accepted that some areas are more difficult to measure and set targets for than others; this was supported by Katona's unique contribution with illustrations in his 1951 book *Psychological Economics*. Katona criticised his fellow economists for failing to consider people's irrational actions when forecasting people's purchase decisions. Here Katona was confirming the point that Drucker made in *Concept* regarding the need for businessmen to accept that the customer was always "*right*" even when acting illogically. Katona, like Drucker was applying Gestalt (Wertheimer) by joining previous unrelated disciplines together. This time the disciplines were economics and psychology in a practical application of holisticism.

Drucker believed that rewards should be targeted on performance with the removal of non- performers, as the danger of a passive policy was safe mediocrity (1954:45). Jack Welch's translation of Drucker's policy on personnel performance was, to look after the top 20%, because they were driven by passion and they made things happen. The middle 70% did the job and kept the company running. The bottom 10% were the weakest and you should talk to them maybe once, maybe twice. If they did not improve you called them in and "*fire*" them (Skapinker: *Financial Times* 13 February 2002).

As an emphasis of the difficulties in the area of effective measurement Drucker used a brief 'case study' to endorse his practical advice by quoting the late Nicholas Dreystadt of Cadillac "*Any fool can learn to stay within his budget. But I have seen only a handful of managers… who can draw up a budget that is worth staying within*" (1954:84). This has a resonance with three British events that are still within recent memory. The Channel Tunnel suffered an enormous cost over- run, of five times, with no certainty that funding costs are included in this figure. When this error was coupled with unrealistic traffic predictions the result has been that the Tunnel has still to make a profit since opening in 1994. The new British Library, London, had a seventeen-year time overrun partly caused by the bookshelf design being incorrect originally, and also after the first re-design. No-one wanted to talk about costs. The Millennium Dome was just another project where the construction costs were out of control, with income failing to meet predictions because the attendance predictions were based upon fantasy attendance figures of 12 million visitors per annum. The result was that the Dome was still losing money after its initial closure.

Drucker's conclusion used a biological analogy that cash or credit was the life-blood of an enterprise to the extent that the body corporate was literally just that. The enterprise, like an animal's body, could not function and died without its essential blood. Flowing from this was an imperative to be able to measure accurately all activities that contribute to consuming the blood. This was why managers *must* measure not only the traditional areas of production, but also *all* activities of the business. This lack of breadth was why accountants were failing and why Drucker identified in *Economic Man* that economists would be unable to solve the problems of society; hence Drucker's identification of the 'new economists' who were extending the ranges of what could be measured beyond the old traditional limits. The business world, where every activity could be objectively measured, may appear Utopian, but it was a much fairer idea than a system where those who aren't measured, measure others. Drucker identified accountants as the most dominant in this measuring group. Impartial measurement for all was essential to Drucker in that it removed arbitrary control and enabled self-control. It also enabled *"freedom under the law"*. Again Drucker was drawing upon his new influences.

For Drucker measurement was a tool of management not a shackle to the manager's task. Although systems were needed for order, they should never be too rigid to prevent rewards for contribution (*ibid*:148). Entrepreneurial performance or motivation should be recognised and paid for, but it should also be realised that performance could not be bought (*ibid*:150-151). The problem of the conflict between short-term, and long-term objectives should always be considered because organisation's survival depended on it (*ibid*:65).

5. The Entrepreneurial Function:
The Purpose of a Business - is *"to create a customer"*

This epigram is probably Drucker's greatest monument (*ibid*:35) because it captured the primary purpose of a sustainable business (although later he added a coda *"and get paid"*). Of all of his major ideas the entrepreneurial role in business has had the greatest long-term acceptance. It follows from the purpose of the business being to create a customer that any business has only two basic functions. They are the entrepreneurial functions of, marketing, and innovation.

(i) Marketing

It is the imperative need for survival that makes marketing of either a product or service the first function of business. This is what sets a

126

business organisation apart from other social organisations such as the State, Church, Army or School. An organisation that fulfils itself through marketing is a business, whereas any organisation that did not or where marketing is incidental should never be managed as one. Drucker identified McCormick, who by 1850 was the man who *"invented the basic tools of modern marketing: market research and market analysis, the concept of market standing, modern pricing policies, the modern service—salesman, parts and service supply to the customer and instalment credit."* McCormick's contribution was so consequential that Drucker termed him as *"the father of business management"* whose ideas were not imitated even in America for a further fifty years (*ibid*:35-36).

The examination of the market of the enterprise started with two recurring questions. The first *"What is our business?"* In answering this question the business could establish where it was and then set marketing objectives. Drucker's position was that in most businesses there were seven marketing goals not one. (i) The standing by measurement of existing products in present markets; (ii) The standing by measurement of the desired position in new markets; (iii) Existing products that should be abandoned (later called Yesterday's Breadwinners) (1964:48); (iv) New products for existing markets; (v) New markets that should be developed by new products; (vi) Retail, distribution, and pricing policies, to achieve the objectives; (vii) Service objectives to give to the customer better service than competitors. Only the customer, through *"regular systematic unbiased questioning"* could decide this. GM customer surveys have already been mentioned. Additional emphasis was given by a short case study of a hospital supply company president and chairman, who visited two hundred of their six hundred customers each year (1954:64-65).

As a continuation of the answer to the question *"What is our business?"* Drucker stated that the following questions needed to be asked. *"Who is the Customer?"* actual and potential. *"Where the customer is?"* *"How does he buy?"* *"How can he be reached?"* Drucker illustrated the answers by several case studies including references to Sears, Montgomery Ward, an electrical manufacturer, Cadillac and Packard. Retailers such as Sears reached their customers through mail order and retail stores, while

Wards did so through retail stores. The electrical manufacturer obtained access to their customers through electrical contractors.

Drucker then asked the question *"What does the customer buy?"* which was a question that was aligned to his question *"What is our business?"* In answering the first question *"What does the customer buy?"* Drucker compared Cadillac, a division of GM, Packard, Chevrolet and Fords. When a customer bought an automobile he basically bought transport particularly with a mass- market product such as Chevrolet and Fords. However, when a customer bought a luxury product such as a Cadillac, Drucker questioned if the customer was purchasing transport or prestige and whether Cadillac was competing with other luxury purchases as diamonds or mink coats. Cadillac's continued success was because ownership symbolised that the owner had arrived. Packard had succeeded through the early Depression because they had a product, which portrayed *"conservative solvency and security in an insolvent and insecure world"*. By the mid-thirties the customer was more confident. Cadillac matched their changed perspectives. Packard no longer did. The result was that in a boom market Packard had to merge to avert disaster (*ibid*:50).

Once the current position of the enterprise had been identified the future could be considered by asking, *"What will our business be?"* Both questions were necessary because a manager had to work in two time zones, the present and the future. In considering the future, there were four questions: (i) Market potential and trend; (ii) Competition that is decided by where the customer buys; (iii) Innovation and knowledge that will change customer's wants; (iv) Customers' needs that are not being satisfied. The actions in response to these questions would separate the growth businesses, which anticipated where the market would go, from those that depended on the tide of their industry or the economy, since those that *"rise with the tide will also fall with it"* (*ibid*:53 & 54). The answers to the questions that Drucker had set were supported by short but pertinent case studies.

The Marketing Manager's role was central to a business as the designers needed information on new products and/or design and development modifications to existing ones. Juran insisted that quality and after-sales performance are part of the marketing and sales function (Juran *et al* 1962). For Drucker similarly, purchasing depended on marketing's unique information. But conversely marketing was dependent on all these functions to perform its two jobs of marketing and selling. For Drucker both marketing and selling carried equal weight but they were both the responsibility of the marketing function. This was another example of Drucker's integrated approach as he was in disagreement with ideas that marketing and selling were separate functions, or that the title was *"sales and marketing"*, which in Drucker's opinion was putting the chicken before the egg (*ibid*:197).

A case study supports Drucker's argument. GE during the previous ten years had placed customer needs and market appeal at the centre of its design. The authority of the marketing function had been elevated and confirmed in the 1952 annual reports (*ibid*:37). This was a change from the general attitude of American management of fifty years ago in which *"The sales department will sell whatever the plant produces"* (*ibid*:36). Today the emphasis was on production for market needs! Drucker had previously referred to Katona for his identification of the psychological influences that impact on people as customers and why it should be considered in sales forecasts. {McNair, who produced an extensive range of research papers on the retail trades, as previously noted, was the only specialist marketing writer referenced by Drucker, however, not for his marketing skills in general, but for those in advertising}.

The evidence of McNair's pioneering work was evidenced by his paper *"Significance of Stock- turn in Retail and Wholesale Merchandising"* in the first *HBR* (*HBR* October 1922 Vol 1. No: 1.) Noted is that another of Drucker's influences Donham was on the editorial board of the *HBR*.

(ii) Innovation

The second function of business was innovation. Marketing alone did not create a business enterprise. For Drucker there could be no long-term growth without innovation as a business could exist only in an expanding or changing economy. It is interesting to examine what Drucker had actually written here. *"A business enterprise can only exist in an expanding economy*". As a quote this is accurate but it is a perfect example of why Drucker can be misunderstood and selectively misquoted. If the quote is continued then the meaning changes to something quite different "*or in one that considers change both natural and desirable*" (*ibid*:37).

Innovation did not provide economic goods, but better goods more economically. For Drucker a business did not necessarily have to grow bigger, but it had to constantly grow better (*ibid*:37). Innovation takes many forms. Economists favoured lower prices because they could apply their quantitative tools, but alternatively it might be new or better products, or the application of existing products to new uses, such as refrigeration for Eskimos to keep food from getting too cold. This was a new product because it created "*new conveniences or the creation of new want*" (*ibid*:37-38). Innovation did not necessarily mean lower prices because what was important was the value perceived by the customer, which might even result in higher prices (*ibid*:51-53). Innovation should extend through all businesses. Every managerial unit of a business needed clear objectives for innovation (*ibid*:38-39).

For Drucker change was the nature of business, observing that changes arising out of innovation were so well known that they did not need much detailing. He supported his position with brief case studies on a range of businesses such as an insurance company, a Christmas toy wholesaler, a welding consultant, and a branded goods enterprise (*ibid*:55-57).

In every business there were two kinds of innovation, the product or service, and the skills and activities needed to implement them (*ibid*:65). For typical businesses five goals were listed for innovation. (i) New products or services required to reach market objectives; (ii) Replacement of the obsolete; (iii) Product improvements resulting from technological change and new market objectives; (iv) New processes in retaining market objectives; (v) Innovation in all major areas of activities such as accounting, administration, labour relations, or design, were needed to keep up with current knowledge and skill (*ibid*:66). Creating a culture of innovation was an objective but the difficulty of measuring the results had already been noted (*ibid*:65). Innovation was the driving and most powerful force in business. What Drucker was saying by

130

implication was that when the question was asked *"Are we in the right business?"* we might discover that innovation had anticipated the question and already changed the nature of the business (*ibid*:55).

Drucker's statement that the purpose of a business was *"to create a customer"* should have come as a *"wake-up"* call to the businessmen who received his message. A minority had anticipated his call. Some listened and changed while the majority continued comfortable in the old economy, which was still serving the needs of a society catching up from the shortages of World War II. Although Drucker's book was directed primarily at an American audience, if the foregoing conclusion of the *"customer"* message was relevant in the American market it was even more so for British businessmen, whose priority was Union appeasement or Union avoidance. Marketing for most was some irrelevant American new-fangled idea, while innovation, even if they had heard of Schumpeter, was regarded as some academic's irrelevance. For the majority only time would prove the relevance of Drucker's messages, which reflected old and new influences.

6.   People are Central to the Organisation

This section is divided by Drucker into five sections (i) Introduction; (ii) What is required by the Enterprise; (iii) The Worker's Attitude; (iv) The Status Quo. Section (ii) to (iv) Set down the problems. (v) The Way Ahead was a commentary on the solutions to problems that Drucker had found in his major case studies, references to books, published papers, and his own ideas.

(i)   Introduction

It is a current coinage of the last decade or so that *"people are our greatest asset"*; a term that emerged from (Drucker 1974). For Drucker people occupied the central position both within the enterprise through their direct membership, and on the outside as customers of the enterprise in particular and also as members of society in general. As in his previous books a substantial space was devoted to people matters.

131

The emphasis of the responsibility of the individual worker to perform was carried forward in *Practice* and further emphasised. Further developed was the concept of team effort as it was as a member of the team that the individual would make his contribution to the objectives of the business. But as a member of the team the members would bear self-responsibility. They would be expected to measure their own performance, which would vary because they were human beings. This was not implying a welfare organisation where the contributors carry the non- contributors, because The First Principle of an Organisation is that the individual's strength becomes part of the group's (1954:260). Although the technological changes that were ahead would increase the number of jobs carried out by individuals, Drucker believed that for the majority of work the team of two or more would be the prevailing rule (*ibid*:291). But the enterprise was more than teams and individuals; it was a community of human beings bound by common beliefs and principles. Without common beliefs and principles the organisation is dysfunctional (1954:61). Everyone in the enterprise was a worker. The business enterprise required at least three groups: managers; ordinary workers skilled or unskilled manual or clerical; and professionals (*ibid*:324-325).

One of the theses of *Practice* was that there were no such things as labour "*considered as an inanimate resource*". The goal of all groups of labour was the achievement of managerial vision (*ibid*:324-425). It was fortunate that people wanted to work otherwise the manager's job would be impossible (*ibid*:266).

Once Drucker's parameters were accepted the issues faced were four-fold: (i) What was required by the enterprise; (ii) The worker's attitudes; (iii) The status quo; (iv) The way ahead.

(ii)   What does the Enterprise require?

Drucker had identified the need for more productivity to remain competitive, and the creation of profits as a means to ensure the enterprise's survival. Because the enterprise was a social organisation the only way it could meet its performance objective was through its people. The key to this was another Drucker manifesto "*Social Organisation for*

132

peak performance" – the motivation of its members. He set out the ideas of his manifesto. It was performance, rather than happiness or satisfaction (*ibid*:283). That fear by the worker for his job was a thing of the past, was all to the good. Its removal did not signify the collapse of motivation because fear was never true motivation, although it could have been interpreted as such (*ibid*:259). There was a need for motivation to be developed. He did not regard this to be *"employee satisfaction,"* which was a meaningless palliative common in his contemporary America. He continued that satisfaction was passive acquiescence. The old external fear needed to be replaced, with internal self-motivation, which only responsibility would provide. But responsibility could not be bought for money nor was money on its own the answer. There were four necessary goals to create the responsible worker: (i) Careful placement; (ii) High performance standards; (iii) Information for the workers to control themselves; (iv) Participation to give managerial vision. Drucker reiterated his previous view that although the employees could not participate in managing the business strategically they could acquire managerial vision by running support services as part of the autonomous self- governing plant community (*ibid*:296-305).

Through acquisition of management vision, the deep-seated resistance of the worker to profit should be overcome. The false belief that workers were defending their security by resisting increased productivity and the related creation of profit Drucker saw as one of the key problems of the time. The reality was that no profit equalled no jobs, just as much as 'No sale' equalled 'No job' (*ibid*:309-312).

Drucker's reference was to Heron's 1954 book *No Sale No Job*. In his book Heron examined the management of the worker and work. His ideas spanned across several of Drucker's *"key ideas"*: productivity, profit, marketing and worker's attitudes. Heron made complimentary reference to Drucker on the need in the employee society to return work to the worker. To summarise Heron's message: the customer buys; therefore everybody needs sales, as they are the ultimate job creators (*ibid*:309-312).

Drucker did not believe that profit-sharing was a primary motivation of the worker. It might reinforce management commitment but the most important factor for the worker was job security, which could be achieved only by performance (*ibid*:311).

(iii)   The Worker's Attitude

Drucker's view of the manual worker had changed from that of the somewhat isolated individual controlled by Scientific Management and driven by several fears as depicted in Drucker's earlier books. The worker still had a fear, that of loss of income. The Union issue was prominent in *Society*, therefore Drucker only needed to summarise that Unions were part of the industrial society that could wreck the business through wage demands and their intentions to deprive management of control (*ibid*:79). The guaranteed wage sought by the Unions would be a burden that business could not carry. But because the nature of work was changing, Drucker noted the appearance of new groups of workers. The manual worker had become semi-skilled and was required to exercise his judgement. Some workers had advanced from being skilled workers to become supervisors or technicians. Also three new groups had emerged: clerical workers, professionals/specialists and managers. As a result the manual plant worker's attitudes had changed. The worker now saw himself as a member of his immediate group and related as an individual to that group. Drucker noted that this had been established by Mayo together with The Hawthorne team, and that it influenced the workers' attitudes to the task (*ibid*:259-260 & 78). The outcome was that the workers could choose if they wanted to work or not and control the speed at which they worked (*ibid*:251-256 & 289). Again we were reminded that the workers' choice was influenced by the deep-seated erroneous attitude of the manual worker that increased productivity and increased profit destroy security and incomes. Drucker suggested that new technology gave an opportunity to correct this long-term problem, which was as much in the manual workers interest as management's (*ibid*:306-309). But change would meet resistance unless it strengthened security (*ibid*:263).   The worker was demanding citizenship in the industrial society not the right to be a member of a welfare society. The enterprise was demanding change of the worker. This could be achieved only by positive action (*ibid*:262-263).

(iv)   Status Quo

While accepting that the workers' need for security was foremost, Drucker noted that security could not ever be without limits. It could never cover unprecedented catastrophes, since immortality could not be promised (*ibid*:306-307). While the Union's demand for the total "*guaranteed annual wage*" could not be acceded to, neither could it be ignored. The conflict between the enterprise's view of the wage as an inflexible cost, and the employee's demand for predictable income and employment, was a dispute that would have to be resolved as discussed fully in *Society* (*ibid*:306). Policies of work simplification related to old industry. The evolution of how work was carried out had changed the way people worked and the prospects for control. The machine was no longer pacing the worker, it was the worker who paced the machine (*ibid*:301 & 259): as work had become more complicated (integrated), the worker resented being left behind as a cog, as he perceived his opportunities diminish (*ibid*:258 & 264). Treating every worker the same, whether they were 'highly motivated' or near 'moron' was poor engineering as it lowered rather than lifted the whole performance (1954:261).

Drucker observed that the close supervision of "*Span of Control*" was not always applicable, as it was dependent upon how management had been developed in specific enterprises. While the evidence was that "*Span of Managerial Responsibility*" was applicable, the process needed to be further developed (*ibid*:136-137). See following case studies of GE, Sears and IBM.

Management needed to accept that it had abdicated responsibility for labour relations, which had been left by the enterprise to the Unions (1954:79). The function of management with this responsibility was Personnel Management. Drucker continued his previous critical examination of Personnel Management but now, as with his criticism of accountants, he made constructive suggestions to correct some of the

135

shortcomings. His technique displayed a common pattern in his work of identifying the problem, or asking the right question. He then examined practice in the selected area. If the practice was sound then he moved on to the next target. If practice was absent this was recorded. If it was deficient he recorded his criticism. Sometimes a solution was offered there and then, or the topic would be returned to in a later work as he constructed a partial or comprehensive answer.

An important illustration of this technique was his treatment of Personnel Management. The question was asked, "*Is Personnel Management Bankrupt?*" (*ibid*:267). Drucker's answer was that because its assets exceeded its liabilities, then it was not bankrupt but it was insolvent because it did not deliver what it promised, which was to manage the worker and work (*ibid*:281). [For this statement to be accurate in British terms insolvent would replace bankrupt.].

Personnel Management had now been divided into two parts: Personnel Administration and Human Relations. In both parts the sum total of people and their efforts exceeded that of any other field of management (*ibid*:267-268). Drucker's view was that both branches of Personnel Management grew out of World War I. Drucker credited Münsterberg's contribution in his other writing. Drucker's view was that apart from some additional work on the Unions, basic knowledge had not advanced since one of Personnel Administration's founding fathers, Thomas Gardiner Spates (1890-1988) wrote in the early twenties (*ibid*:368). The first work that has been discovered in this research was a book *Industrial Relation Trends* (1937) (source American Library of Congress, not available in the UK). However Spates wrote "*I decided to make a career of the personnel function*" (*Ibid* 1960:38). This is evidence that Spates was active in the early twenties (see *The Scope of Modern Personnel Administration* (Spates 1948) and *Human Values Where People Work* (Spates 1960). While agreeing with Drucker that Spates' work was very clear and complete, Spates himself credited Metcalf and Tead as the authors of the first textbook on Personnel Management in 1920 (*ibid*:7). Drucker continued to praise McGregor's work in identifying the sterility of Personnel Administration for being based upon three misconceptions that: (i) People don't want to work; (ii) The job of managing the worker

136

is a specialist job rather than part of the manager's job; (iii) The role is dominated by 'problems', 'headaches' and 'fire-fighting' (1954:27), see also McGregor's later book *The Human Side of Enterprise* (1960).

Drucker observed that even the best current text book on the subject, *Personnel Administration* (Pigors & Myers 1947 First Edition) spent 301 of its 321 pages *"on the programmes that the department itself organises and manages"* (1954:270-271). For Drucker, progress must be made to replace what has become a *"hodgepodge"* of unrelated functions including the *"unpleasant choices"* of placating the Unions, filing, housekeeping, social work, and the fire-fighting that grew out of World War I (*ibid*:268-269). Pigors & Myers' proposals were that Personnel Administration became a staff function along with buying, accounting, or research, and needed to be properly organised. Its role was to set policies and agree them with the CEO. Its role was not to take away the manager's role of supervising worker or fire fighter. Regarding Pigors & Myers, Drucker could have added that for the authors Personnel Administration grew out of a need to solve problems, which confirms McGregor's general criticism of writers on Personnel Administration. Also Pigors & Myers stated that Personnel Administration should be a separate function for the specialist not a sideline for the supervisor (Pigors & Myers 1947:12-25), again, one of McGregor's criticisms. Drucker's position was that the personnel function was not a separate but an integrated function, using Sears and IBM's case studies, where Drucker would agree with the authors' position that good management was people (*ibid*:5). By 1965 Pigors & Myers had tempered their position in the 5th Edition of their book, that the personnel expert was only an advisor to the line manager whose job was managing Human Resources. If the Personnel Administration had any authority it was the authority to establish policies and procedures as highlighted in *Review of Personnel Administration – Policies not Purpose* (Evans – Vaughan *The Manager* September 1965).

Drucker concluded that Human Relations was only in a little better shape, having made little progress since the work of Mayo and his Harvard colleagues around 1928. Novelty had been added but it was no substitute for sound principles. There was much talk but little sound development. It was like giving a fractious child soothing syrup; it was a

137

palliative not a cure of the problem. Drucker acknowledged that of the "Human Relations" pioneers *"indeed I owe myself their discipline"* *"though their achievement is great, it is not adequate"*. (*ibid*:267-273). In Drucker's opinion gimmicks such as believing that financial rewards were a substitute for poor organisation were part of the problem not the solution (*ibid*:306). Attempts to determine the *" 'average work load' for the 'average worker' are based (wholly) upon a disproven psychology which equated learning speed with learning ability"* (*ibid*:261). The use of Employee Relations Indices whatever they measure, was a stopgap (*ibid*:80). Personnel Administration scored no better in dealing with the demands of the professional employees as Drucker recorded that their problems could not be solved with traditional concepts (1954:327).

Drucker saw some progress being made by Walker & Guest in their 1952 book *The Man on the Assembly Line*, which analysed the role of the worker in a major car plant. This will be examined in the next section. Professor Juran was credited as a writer of standing on Scientific Management who was making a serious contribution along with Walker & Guest in organising work *"according to properties of the human resource"*. Drucker recommended various papers by Juran (1954:281). Juran's much later work *Made in America: Renaissance in Quality* (Juran *HBR* July/August 1993) confirmed his earlier concerns, while working at Western Electric in 1924, that departmental barriers prevented changes in working practices for improved quality being extended across the plant. The transfer would have increased job satisfaction. For Juran the quality of work was a key factor of motivation (Juran 1951:1-14).

Drucker referred to his own paper: *The Employee Society* (January 1953) in which he wrote *"American society had become an employee society in the last fifty years, where people expected to spend their lives as employees."* This had set the ethos of American society. It had caused management to emerge and as a consequence the Unions. These changes had produced a tremendous challenge and opportunity for the student of society. However, in order to make the necessary adjustments, better tools for analysis would have to be developed as the three contemporary methodologies of quantitative, psychological, and anthropological analysis, had proved inadequate (1954:264). Follett was not mentioned in the text, but

Drucker was aware of her ideas and contribution, which he would acknowledge in his later work. Her influence is noted later.

(iv)   The Way Ahead – Supported by Case Studies

Drucker had now identified the problems and moved to find a solution. He has identified that the new way of working would be automation which he used generically to separate old and new methods of organising work. The common denominators were that the two parts of Taylor's Scientific Management, the function of the work task itself and its planning, needed to be integrated and carried out to varying degrees by the workers carrying out the work task. As an example of how this would work, a case study of a telephone engineer was described. His job was integrated now, and depended on his judgement rather than his old manual skills alone. [Idea: New technology would need a technical worker who was not a manual worker in the old sense. The technical worker would require self-management skills and a need for continual learning to be able to perform the contemporary demands of his work (1954:281)]. For Drucker it was becoming clear that workers would have to plan better than many managers were currently capable of. But this was only the first step in essential change. The second step was that Personnel Management needed to become integrated in the work of the workers and their work and not treated as separate work of specialists.

On offer then were the two opposing theories of Personnel Management. The first was that people don't want to work, or the second, which Drucker expounded, was that Personnel Management was not a separate speciality but part of integrated management (1954:270-271). Drucker continued later that the worker wanted to work was confirmed by the response to GM's 1947 employee survey *"My Job and Why I Like It"*. Drucker, who was one of the judges, claimed that the results preceded and also proved the works of Rensis Likert's and Frederick Herzberg's *"hygiene factors on motivation and demotivation"* (1979:276). [Idea: Hygiene Factor]. That it was possible to provide the worker with function, opportunities and status, was supported by the research in Walker & Guest's in their book (1952:281 & 293). Drucker

139

took the automobile assembly line as the epitome of working control and recorded that Chrysler in the early 1940s found that the "*utility man who moved around the 'line' had greater job satisfaction than those controlling one operation.*" Walker & Guest's research was conducted in 1949 in one of the most modern, but unidentified, car plants in the world. The research showed that the workers wanted to obtain greater job satisfaction and in return were prepared to provide greater production. The workers employed on repetitive tasks felt isolated and lacked social contact because the noise made it impossible to talk. Workers and the Unions accepted that the assembly line was an integral part of industrial society. However the way it was being utilised was regressive. The average range of work was two operations in two minutes. There was no worker influence on the pace of work, tools used, or methods. Tasks took two hours to learn. Because of the low skill level on the "*line*" there was little progress from the bottom to the top through promotion. Although there was no general dissatisfaction with pay in the plant, lack of promotion in the "*line*" gave specific dissatisfaction because it denied the American ideal of the possibility of "*rising in the world*" (*Ibid*: 1952:160).

The positive conclusions of Walker & Guest were that the majority of workers were not critical of the foremen, whom they regarded as doing their job, and that they were satisfied with the Unions. They also believed their jobs should be expanded to include several skills, and workers rotated to different jobs as in another plant where ten tasks were learnt. Workers should also be able to build up "*time breaks*" and have breaks to interact with others. Workers saw the immediate solution to their present predicament was by obtaining promotion to foreman, or transferring into other departments such as the maintenance crew where the variety of work and its control made time for social contact were possible. Mayo was mentioned in the text. Walker & Guest recommended that the workers should have an opportunity to help predetermine tools and techniques and Drucker was used as complementary support for the idea. Drucker's:

> "*The Human Being in Industrial Production*" 1950 was referenced. Drucker's point was that, "*predetermination of tools*

and techniques has gone too far when it completely precludes any participation of the workers..."

(*Ibid* 1952:153).

Drucker concluded that Walker & Guest's survey confirmed that many workers were in the wrong job. He also criticised as too restrictive, a GM technique where they had concentrated on placement of workers but only for their first ninety days. Drucker stated that systematic and continual placement was *"one of the most important tasks in the management of worker and work"* (1954:294). On it rested the worker's continuing desire to work. It gave the worker function, opportunity and status. What Walker & Guest's 1952 book demonstrated was a part solution to the problems of providing function, opportunities, status, security, and freedom, in return for responsibility and managerial vision. To complete the equation Drucker turned to two of his major case studies, Sears and IBM, and reverted to the question of the role of Personnel Management.

In respect of Sears, Drucker turned to Emmet & Jeuck's 1950 book *Catalogues and Counters – A History of Sears Roebuck & Company.* Although Drucker did not quote them directly Emmet and Jeuck recorded that *"in top management there is no recognition of specialised personnel functions"* (*ibid*:547). Drucker wrote that it was no accident that personnel work at Sears started with managers, not with Personnel Administration. The individual store managers conducted their own Personnel Management as part of their integrated role as manager.

IBM in their personnel policy was the opposite of those where the rank and file workers do as they are directed (1954:254). Drucker regarded IBM as answering more of the questions of managing the enterprise than any other of his studies of successful enterprises. Of Drucker's criteria for 'the complete' Corporation only a Decentralised structure was missing at the time of Drucker's review. Subsequently, IBM would adopt Decentralisation within the following few years.

Drucker drew on the work of Walker again and a new partner Richardson for their 1948 book *Human Relations in an Expanding Company.* The book was a study of IBM and Drucker's interpretation of it provided a description of the new way of working - automation and the

141

integration of men and machinery. IBM had previously provided the answers to the problems that Walker & Guest identify in *The Man on the Assembly Line*. By moving the design of work to the workbench the workers could determine how the work could be done, set their outputs, and pace themselves to create *"time-banks"*. The *"foreman"*, whom Drucker defined as the *"first-line supervisor"* who might also be called *"chief clerk or section manager"* (1954:313), acted as an assistant to the workpeople, helping them to determine the best work practices. Preferably the name foreman, and especially supervisor, should be changed to manager as the terms foreman and supervisor had connotations of the old *"team boss"*. The danger was that the retention of the old names could aid a return to the past (*ibid*:318-322) which ensured by influence, the required output of the enterprise was achieved, which was subtle measurement. What Drucker described was an environment where workers were trained for as many opportunities as possible and where they could influence events (*ibid*:251-256). By widening the scope of the job IBM had increased productivity (*ibid*:286), and was able to create opportunities for semi-skilled workers and create a supply of home-grown foremen and managers. IBM succeeded in its promotion policies because only those respected by their colleagues were promoted. Because the supervisors were tested IBM was not plagued by the problems of other businesses, where there were fewer than half the successes in supervisor appointments. The foremen and 'job instructors', who were selected from the shop floor, were assistants to the work force (*ibid*:140). Because the two parts of work identified by Taylor were integrated through the production details being *"worked out on the production floor"*, production was enhanced. In 1936 IBM replaced traditional payment methods, paying incentives and making workers salaried with benefits including overtime payments. Each worker was evaluated based on their individual speed and aptitude to calculate their maximum production. In IBM there were no norms. The foremen assessed the workers' aptitudes, arranging, retraining and continually review placement. The workers' job was widened to combat assembly line monotony. Working as a team and improving products and value – see further explanation in Chapter 8. [Idea: This is *Kaizen*], IBM was also

142

able to maintain employment while competitors were not. The fear of the workers *"working themselves out of a job"* had been removed, solving the big problem identified by Drucker of the worker relating higher production and profit as being against their interest (*ibid* IBM Story: 251-256 & 310-311). Drucker referred to his own article; *Productivity is an Attitude* (*Nations Business* April 1952), which examined how workers' motivation controlled their output. Also connected was the idea that growth needed people to change (1954:259) as the IBM work force did by relating to their business and developing managerial vision.

Drucker used another example of the employees' co-operation in producing a plan for improving the organisation of their diesel engine shop at the Chesapeake & Ohio Railroad by reversing a work simplification programme. Drucker complimented the management who took out a two- page advert in *Business Week* (14 November 1954) to publicise the work of its employees. Drucker referred to the occurrence as a story reported (1954:301).

To summarise what Drucker had adopted from the IBM study was that the worker could be given function, status and security and from this he obtained freedom. In return the worker responded with responsibility and managerial vision. IBM was a reproduction of Drucker's definition of automation as a method of working, rather than being a particular specific process (*ibid*:28).

Following on from the example of Sears integrating Personnel Management, Drucker recorded that IBM did something similar but provided more detail. The foreman *"(supervisor) handles all the relations of his department... for instance with the personnel department"* (*ibid*:319). IBM had demonstrated another of Drucker's tenets - that Personnel Management must be an integrated function in the business.

The IBM study also resolved the problem that Drucker identified in *Concept* that the foreman's status was an enigma as he was neither worker nor management. Drucker concluded that this anomaly would have to be resolved as they represented untapped potential. However, as recognised at IBM the foreman was clearly management. In *Practice* as previously noted Drucker referred to *Activities and Behaviour of Production Supervisors* Report No 946 into the role of the foreman.

The report was a survey primarily for military use of large civilian organisations to identify what role the foreman carried out. The object was to enable a job specification to be established, in order to establish reasonable expectations and rewards for results rather than based on intuition. Military research could not be conducted because of the demands of the Korean War. Drucker reported that forty-one activities of a foreman's work were identified, which resulted in a job overload. Drucker concluded that the solution to the problem was not to make the foreman's job smaller but to arrange it properly. The foreman also needed proper promotion opportunities otherwise he represented "*a criminal waste of Human Resources*" (1954:316-317). My conclusion is that if the Army had read Richardson & Walker they need not have conducted their study. Also if they had examined Taylor's *Shop Management* (first published in 1903) where he concluded that the military type of organisation for the foreman would not work, they would have increased their knowledge before embarking on their survey (Taylor 1911:94). Taylor went further "*Throughout the whole field of management the military type of organisation should be abandoned*" (*ibid*:99). Drucker concurred with Taylor's view regarding the military. For Drucker the military's purpose as not primarily economic and never could be (1954:8).

Drucker noted that IBM organised the foreman's job properly, by not believing that he was a superman. They reversed the trend of narrowing the job and increased his authority (*ibid*4:318- 320). Support staff was provided to assist with routine activities and specialised work such as training, thus freeing the foreman's time for the people tasks, and other priorities. The foreman was paid commensurate with his responsibilities rather than being paid less than his workers were, for the privilege of being called "*foreman*". {What Drucker did not report was that in the production department the foreman to worker ratio in 1940 was 1:58. By 1947 it had reduced to 1:44 and similarly in other departments (Richardson & Walker 1948:20-21). This was unique in any event but even more so as it had occurred in a period of considerable growth and increased productivity}. Apart for this last omission, what Drucker had provided was as near a complete picture as identified by Richardson & Walker. {What Richardson & Walker also identified was that during the

144

time of their study that the founder of IBM Watson's personality was deeply stamped on the business particularly Human Relations and that he practised an "*open door policy*" to all employees (*Ibid* 1948: 7, 8 & 10)}. Drucker records that GE was considering adopting IBM policies.

The points that Drucker had been making sum up his position "*people are central to the organisation*". For many managers labour and the Unions were the worst problems they had to face. But dumping them into a separated Personnel Department would not solve the problems, as Drucker had proved by his case studies that this was bound to fail, because people are central to the organisation and need to be treated as such. *Practice* demonstrates that the work of the earlier modern pioneers of Personnel Management of Mayo, Spates and Tead & Metcalf had all been influences on Drucker's matrix of ideas. Amongst his identified contemporaries Drucker was acknowledged as being at the centre of, and contributing to the developing ideas in this area.

7.   The Manager's Job is Total Integration

Drucker sets the business manager's role within the context of society. The emergence of business management was a pivotal event in social history. It had grown so rapidly without opposition because it was indispensable (1954:3-4)

The First Function of business management was economic performance, which separated it from other organisations (*ibid*:7 & 11). It had changed America's economics by creating a marketing revolution in the fifty years since 1900. Europe however was different; it had no understanding of the function of marketing as a specific business function, which was the reason for its stagnation (*ibid*:36). The real danger for America was to follow Great Britain's lack of management vision and effort, that had caused its decline from 1880 (*ibid*:5). Although the free world was dependent on business management for its survival (*ibid*4:4-5), Drucker stated that management's pivotal role was only to be "*one*" of the leading groups of society (*ibid*:10). This is a more tempered view than Drucker's earlier position where management was the leading group.

In Drucker's view the manager was the product of the new economy of process. The manager had eclipsed and in effect replaced the old economy of the trader and financier (*ibid*:11). The enterprise relied on the manager for its performance. The manager made the enterprise and was "*the life giving element of any business*" (*ibid*:12-13). So much so that *Practice* could appropriately have been entitled "*The Practice of the Manager*". Managers were the enterprise's most costly resource, but paradoxically economies could not be made by reducing their number, as more, rather than less, would be required (*ibid*:13 & 21).

For Drucker, although the functions of management could be analysed separately all are important and no part could be neglected. All must be integrated as Hopf had recognised earlier, and Drucker had begun to recognise in *Society* when he began redeveloping his ideas and concluding that work had to be integrated, as a manager could not separate them in his work. From this analysis he concluded that management was a multi-purpose organ (*ibid*:15-16), which was very complex (*ibid*:13). A practice rather than a science (*ibid*:9). However, no description of management would be complete unless it took into account the new method of working – automation. Its adaptation would be gradual but whoever succeeded in it would achieve world leadership (*ibid*:21-22).

Drucker saw the manager as managing by MbO as previously described (*ibid*:8). The manager's performance would not be determined by knowledge, because the ultimate test was achievement (*ibid*:9). In a case study to support the need for performance Drucker quoted GE's Cordiner that "*there has been a growing realisation in American industry that...*" opportunities exist to develop human resources, particularly managers. In GE there was an opportunity "*to increase productivity 50 per cent in the next ten years through better management alone*" (*ibid*:181). The manager would be expected to provide leadership, which would achieve the purpose of an organisation in "*making common men do uncommon things*". Leadership, Drucker identified as being of the utmost importance. There was no substitute for leadership. Although it could not be created, promoted, taught, or learnt, management by using the right practices could bring out whatever leadership there was in the group. It "*is the lifting of a man's *vision to higher sights"* and raising performance beyond the individual's normal limits. Nothing develops the spirit of management better than operating polices of responsibility, high performance and the respect of the individuals and their work. *"It is not "making friends and influencing people'";* this was Drucker making a slight at Dale Carnegie, who wrote a book entitled *How to Win Friends and Influence People* (1926). In support of Drucker's argument that leadership could not be taught, despite thousands of years of trying, he wrote that man knew no more than when Xenophon in Ancient Greece (1954:156) wrote *Cyropaedia*. This was Xenophon's account of his role as a military commander when he fought for the Spartans against his native city Athens in BC 401. {The book covers all the aspects of visible leadership, such as shared values, training, spirit, communications, equality, free speech, resourcefulness, personal development, organisation, objectives and their implementation, behaviour in victory, treatment of prisoners, and finally payment by the fair division of spoils.

Xenophon's conclusion was that the activities of leadership had been completed when the spoils were divided because rewards only occurred when all activities were complete. Drucker concluded that a tutor could not teach leadership, although the mechanics of war just as the mechanics of management could be taught, and that teaching improved performance (*Cyropaedia* by Xenophon translated by Walter Mille 1914). Drucker's conclusion was that there had never been enough naturally occurring leaders yet, society was now demanding more, called managers. The way forward was to allow managers to learn how to perform their job, which was to manage. It was the practical substitute for leadership. But for this policy to succeed it would require placing the best manager in each management job.

(i)   The Manager's Tasks

According to Drucker the Manager had three tasks: (i) Managing a business (1954:8); (ii) Managing managers; and (iii) Managing workers and work (*ibid*:13). Although not strictly speaking a management function there was an ever-present additional dimension (iv) Time.

(ii) Managing a Business – Supported by Case Studies

Drucker asked the question *"What is managing a business?"* The answer was deciding what business it should be engaged in and then setting possible rather than desirable objectives (1954:45). It was not profit maximisation. After deciding on this definition Drucker drew heavily on his major case studies to illustrate what the definition means in *Practice*. This confirmed the fundamental influence of GM from the *Concept* period. The messages conveyed in the case studies were clearly visible if GM was used as a template to compare how the other case study businesses operate.

The case studies selected for examination in this research were because they were a representation of Drucker's ideas. They were Unions, American Pipe Company, GM, Fords, GE, Sears, IBM, Crown-Zellerbach, Chrysler and AT&T.

The Unions had been under examination by Drucker since Page 17 in *Economic Man* when he reported on:

> *"one of the most embittered labour conflicts in German History – when the Nazis together with the communists supported the strike against the official trade unions…"*

(1939:17).

Drucker's prolonged examination had produced a consistent conclusion that the Unions were not a positive contributing force, because they had failed to identify a constructive role for themselves.

American Pipe Company was considered and rejected as an industrial model because Drucker believed co-operatives would not provide the widespread dynamic enterprises that the free market economy requires. The lesson was that management still needed all the skills, authority and responsibility in a co-operative as in other profit-making organisations. Drucker alluded to some initial teething problems in the organisation after the original owner had 'gifted' the business to the workers. Eventually the workers resolved that their role was the traditional one of subordinates to the managers with management having and needing authority to manage.

148

Drucker noted that co-operatives had been made to work previously. He is probably alluding to the regularly quoted example of the German Zeiss Optical Factory.

(a)   The Need for Teamwork

Drucker used GM to illustrate how managers managed the business. The CEO's job was not the job of an individual, as previously identified in *Concept*. It was a team of preferably three rather than two, since evidence showed that two people were likely to retire together, breaking continuity. Sears, GE, and AT&T were identified as having teams. In the teams one man was likely to stand out as a "*strong team captain*", as the first among equals such as Sloan at GM and Wood at Sears. But they should strengthen their colleagues' position and never undermine them (1954:17& 174). Drucker wrote that no business was likely to be better than its top management (*ibid*:158). He mentioned Brown by name and Wilson by his title as President at GM (*ibid*:170); Ford II and Ernest R Breech at Fords who got but a brief mention (*ibid*:114); while at the GE, Cordiner, who was described as a notable example of top Management. Drucker drew attention to Cordiner's 1953 speech to the *HBS "Efficient Organisation Structure"* (1954:166-167). Cordiner's team was the most extensively described by Drucker with Cordiner as the President and his team of group executives who were effectively the Deputy President and Vice-presidents of major functions of the business such as Research, Marketing, or Management Organisation (1954:170). No personalities were identified other than Cordiner. Cordiner's speech could not be found; however his 1956 book *New Frontiers of Professional Management* set out his philosophy. The book aligned with what Drucker had been writing. The book also contained an early record of a 'mission statement' and although later than Given (1949), Cordiner's mission statement was more purposeful than Given's, which followed.

Drucker identified both the old team of Rosenwald, Mr Loeb (legal adviser), and Doering at Sears, as well as their successors, Wood and Mr Houser, but not the company's unnamed president (*ibid*:170). IBM's team was not referred to, probably because Watson Snr was so dominant. Of his information on IBM's working practices, Drucker attributed to Richardson & Walker (*ibid*:252). Drucker gave general advice on the composition of the Board of Directors and illustrated the advantages of competent non-executive directors by recording in a brief case study of Merck and Company who attributed their effective board as a major factor of its success (*ibid*:177)

(b)   What Business Are We In?

Having examined how the top team of the business should be arranged, Drucker moved to the next question: "*What business are we in or should be in?*" The purpose of the question was to determine where customers perceived value and were prepared to pay for efficiently produced products that generate a profit. [Idea: No business can do everything but every business has a strength that it should play to (*ibid*:43). Those ideas were later adopted by Peters & Waterman (1982) with their "*stick to your knitting*", and Hamel & Prahalad's (1990) "*core competencies*".

GM's assessment of what business it was in and how it could exploit its strengths through its own developed management was described in *Concept*. Although Drucker was an advocate of businesses developing their own managers, he accepted that sometimes it did not work and outsiders needed to be recruited. Case study references are made to Fords and Sears. Fords after the "*one-man rule*" of Ford (1954:109-118 & 164) had reorganised as an executive team bringing managers from GM to provide new ideas. Sears did similarly with Wood in 1924 when it wanted to develop retail stores from its base business of mail order (*ibid*:1653). Drucker endorses Ford II's compassionate actions in relocating the displaced executives on the grounds that Ford corporately were responsible for making the decisions that displaced them (*ibid*:146).

Drucker's chapter 'The Ford Story' recorded the metamorphosis of a business that outgrew its structure (*ibid*:109-118). His Chapter 'The Sears Story' was a record of the progress of Sears from a trading company managed by Richard Sears at the close of the 19th Century by Rosenwald, whom Drucker described as the "*father of distribution revolution*". Rosenwald transformed Sears into the most successful mail order business in the US by anticipating *"how the customer needed to buy"*. Drucker recorded again their team contribution by identifying Doering as predating Ford by five years in designing and installing the first mass production plant in 1903. Doering's design was for mail order. Drucker continued with Sears' successful mail order business, recording that Wood succeeded Rosenwald. Wood was identified as being as innovative as Rosenwald was in anticipating that many customers would want to shop in standardised out of town non-food supermarkets. Drucker's conclusion was that Sears was an outstanding application of the 'customer's wants'. Drucker acknowledged that he drew extensively on *Catalogues and Counters – A History of Sears Roebuck & Company* (Emmet & Jeuck 1950).

AT&T around 1905 under the leadership of Vail, was included as one of the earliest and most successful exponents of correctly answering the question *"What is our business"*. Recognising that as a natural monopoly it was a candidate for nationalisation, AT&T's management objectively decided that their business would be service. The object of this policy was to gain and keep customer's support (1954:46-47).

In general once the executive of the business had decided *"What is our business?"* then the most suitable structure could be selected. Drucker warned against imposing the wrong structure on the business, which could jeopardise its survival (*ibid*:190).

Drucker identified GM in *Concept* as having evolved its own form of Decentralisation. Historically du Pont preceded GM as the initiators of Decentralisation by a few years in the 1910s. But because du Pont's business was different from GM their model of Decentralisation was also different (Kennedy 2002:224). In *Practice* there was no further identification of fundamental change within GM from that recorded in *Concept*. Ford II was identified at Fords as a late convert to Decentralisation after succeeding his grandfather, Henry Ford in the mid-1940s. Ford II recruited from GM implanted Decentralisation. GE, an early convert, had commenced work on the implementation by 1929 (1954:202) as had Sears. Drucker recorded that there was a variation of details in the models adopted. Fords had moved from Vertical Integration and were buying-in components [Idea: later called

151

Outsourcing] (*ibid*:71). They were also changing over from old style mass production (*ibid*:96-99) to mechanising the assembly line to reduce manual effort (*ibid*:217 & 286). Management was reorganising the work from "*chain of command*" to "*task force*" production, thus making progress on job integration along similar lines to IBM (*ibid*:286).

GE's approach had similarities to GM with variations in patterns to adjust to the size and type of businesses within the Group (*ibid*:202 & 206). Sears' application of Decentralisation was a restricted form, with rigid head office policies and emphasis on central services and supplies. Sears concentrated on supply sources, which was a critical factor in their business. But as previously mentioned they pursued a policy of integrated Personnel Management (*ibid*:71, 1202, 206-212 & 270).

IBM was not mentioned because it was not Decentralised until after *Practice* was published. This was the only reason that Drucker classified IBM as transitional. Watson Jnr described how prior to the 1950s the business had been 'run' by the founder Watson Snr, who made all the decisions. A team of thirty reported to him directly. Later, a Decentralised organisation was introduced with independent divisions (Watson 1963:66-67). This would make it Drucker's model company, by adding the benefit of Decentralisation, which is "*unity by diversity*" (1954:221), to what IBM already had, - common citizenship (*ibid*:220). [Idea: Empowerment]. Drucker's help with management development at IBM was recorded later "*(They) were clients of mine. Friends of mine*" (2002:73) "*in the early 1960s when I was working with IBM…*" (2000:43).

For Crown-Zellerbach, a pulp and paper manufacturer, the concentration was on securing supplies of forestry fifty years hence. The problem was so different that it was organised as a major function including the related capital investment (1954:71, 81 & 191).

Chrysler was recorded as being forced into Decentralisation. It had previously been organised as a medium sized business for simplicity. It manufactured only the engines and bought in everything else. To a great extent Chrysler was exploiting its "*brand*". [Idea: 'brand-power' and 'value']. By simplifying its operation before World War II, Chrysler had become the world's third largest automobile producer and was managed by Walter Percy Chrysler (1875-1940) with two associates. In the Post-war era Chrysler was losing ground and had to restructure (*ibid*:68, 206, 227-228). But Drucker's criteria was that the size of a business was determined not by the number of employees or the size of its sales, but by its management structure and concluded that Fords under Ford was a small business (*ibid*:224).

Drucker identified that one of the greatest problems for a business resulted from its success and the related growth. The problem lay in recognising the need to restructure the business to match the change. Four sizes of business were identified: small; fair-sized; large; very large and maybe another size "*too big*". Despite the American belief that small businesses were the model, Drucker was generally contemptuous of them, identifying that they have more problems generally stemming from the dominant boss who "*plays it close to his chest*". He concluded that the large business had a definite advantage and was the preference. Small-sized businesses had many problems, but lack of an outside view could be corrected by appointment of a non-executive director(s) (*ibid*:224 & 237). Decades later Drucker would revise his position and question the very survival of large businesses that remained domestic rather than converting to global organisations. Also he would become a supporter of smaller dynamic businesses because in the economy of the future they were most likely to survive.

(c)   Delegation by: '*Span of Control* and *Span of Managerial Responsibility*'.

Drucker examined the merits of the traditionally accepted *Span of Control* as promoted by Hamilton and Urwick and *Span of Managerial Responsibility*, which Drucker identified in GE and attributed its title to Race (1954:137). The space that Drucker allocated to these methods of management was limited and they will benefit from further examination. An examination of the ideas of his references reveals the following. Hamilton's position as set out in his 1921 book *The Soul and Body of an Army* was "*the human brain cannot control more than five or six other brains*". Hamilton was making his comment in the context of a military organisation. His idea was connected to the need for close relationships

153

between the officer and his soldiers to display care and responsibility and to engender *esprit de corp* as implied by the title of his book and expressed in its contents. Drucker did not refer to Urwick's contribution on this aspect of management, which required examination. Urwick, in his 1933 book *Management of Tomorrow* referred to Hamilton's work and picked up on Hamilton's qualifier and concluded that he was referring to complex activity. Urwick wrote:

> "*Where the individuals supervised have no relationships with each other or perform substantially uniform functions, some increase in the numbers supervised is possible*"

(*Ibid* 1993:60).

Urwick reconfirmed his position:

> "*There has been much disputation about the principle of organisation known as "Span of Control": but all experience, and indeed ordinary common sense, support its validity*"

(Urwick 1957:9).

He also referred to his association with V A Graicunas (1898-1947) in defending Hamilton's "*three to six brains*" depending on the complexity of lateral relationships (Urwick 1956:59). Drucker's position was that both *Span of Control* and *Span of Managerial Responsibility* were valid when MbO had been affected. This was possible because MbO enabled managers' development whereas *Span of Control* "*stifle the development... and erode the meaning of the management job. ...by supervisors who "breathe down people's necks*"" (1954:136-137). *Span of Managerial Responsibility* was more relevant with mature managers and at levels nearer the top of the organisation. Junior managers needed more assistance and *Span of Control* is more appropriate. Race's conclusion was that the theoretical limit of *Span of Managerial Responsibility* for subordinates reporting is around one hundred (*ibid*:137). Race did not give calculations, as to how many relationships this would involve.

{Not referenced by Drucker but important to record is the work of V A Graicunas who published a detailed analysis on *Span of Control*

154

producing calculations that supported his ideas. He produced a table to which he applied two separate formulae. His calculations on 'Control' of one to twelve subordinates produced number of relationships that ranged from one to 4161. "*...if computed on (a) Minimum Basis*" for the range of one subordinate to twelve. But if indirect relationships within the group were considered, then the number increases to 24708 if "*computed on (a) Maximum Basis*" in *Papers on the Science of Administration* (Graicunas in Luther Gulick & Urwick *et al* 1933:181-187)}

Returning to Drucker's influences, how GE applied the principle was not recorded. However, Drucker referred to work that Worthy started when a manager at Sears and resulted in his paper *Organisation Structure and Employee Morale* (*American Sociological Review* April 1950). Worthy wrote, based upon twelve years research, that some highly successful organisations had gone counter to the prevalent "*modern management theory*" of *Span of Control*. Intentionally key executives were given so many subordinates that too close supervision was impossible. The subordinate had to "*sink or swim*" as his growth and development was not too severely restricted by detailed supervision. Not all individuals could operate in this environment but those that do "*require large measures of self confidence and personal capacity*". The survivors of this system were likely to survive and succeed by their skill in building employee teamwork and co-operation. The CEO who used fear as a driver could not operate in this type of organisation. Although not mentioned by Drucker at this time because of its later publication, Worthy wrote further on *The Behavioural Dimension of 'Span of Management' Theory* (Worthy in Zimet & Greenwood 1979:405-414). In this essay Worthy repeated what he had previously written with more emphasis on a flat structure with fewer levels of management, while repeating that not every type of person could survive in this demanding environment.

Drucker used Sears as a case study to support Worthy's ideas, writing that Sears' young male recruits were ready for management positions after five years working in stores. They had worked in a Decentralisation structure with only two levels of management between the lowest management job of store selection manager and the regional vice-president who may have up to a hundred stores under his authority, each

155

an autonomous unit responsible for marketing and profit. [Idea: Delayering and Re-engineering]. The young male recruits who worked in the mail order division, which was organised as a Functional Speciality, had not made the same appreciable progress in the company (1954:206-207).

What Drucker was joining together in his research was that Decentralisation was the preferred structure and that *Span of Managerial Responsibilities* develops managers and that it was essential to have as few levels of management as possible. GM was identified as another example of a flat organisation. Described as one of several examples, GM had only two levels of top management between the president and divisional heads. [Idea: Delayering and Re-engineering]. Drucker confirmed that one of the attractions of automation is that it promised to make the organisation flat (*ibid*:218). A sign of executive dropsy is layers and layers of management (*ibid*:169). Drucker wrote that he knew of no examples where excess levels of management were necessary and warned against confusing fat for growth (*ibid*:233). IBM, as previously noted had applied the principle of *Span of Managerial Responsibility* to the role of the foreman relating to forty-four workers. Worthy recorded that a support team was needed for the foreman at IBM to be able to span his management across the forty-four workers. What neither Drucker nor any other of his influences whose work related to the working of Sears record, was what the support team was for a Sears vice-president with his hundred stores.

Drucker concluded that *Span of Control* and *Span of Managerial Responsibility* both had applicability. Large organisations could attract high calibre management material with high levels of perception. If they were exposed to continuous training they quickly learnt what the company's 'end game' was and personal competition was stimulated while little direct supervision was needed. In this environment *Span of Managerial Responsibility* was applicable. However, where average calibre candidates were the base materials and little training had taken place then tight personal supervision was required. In this environment *Span of Control* was needed. However, if the supervising manager was of low calibre then he would only be able to apply *Span of Control*, even if his subordinates were of high quality.

156

(iii)   Managing Managers

The first person that a manager had to manage was himself. For Drucker the manager's job was becoming more complex and more demanding, and this applied to the managers that he had to manage. Managing managers commenced with The Second Function of management "*to make a productive enterprise out of human and material resources*" (1954:11-12). Drucker had already established in his previous books that the manager must bring to his job character, and morality. It was necessary to be realistic because no man is perfect but Drucker identified some disqualifying criteria for managers. If the candidate was more interested in "*who is right?*" rather than "*what is right?*" this was putting personality before the task of the work and corrupts. The 'who is right culture' encouraged a regime of covering-up mistakes rather than taking corrective action. Drucker advised never to promote a manager who was afraid of strong subordinates because this was weakness, nor a candidate who did not set high standards for his own work because this bred contempt for the work of management. Whatever abilities a person may have, it would be even more decisive in the future than in the past that a manager must have "*integrity of character*" (*ibid*:155-156 & 371). Lack of integrity was the overriding disqualifier. This was a practical interpretation of Drucker's essential ecumenical element to life.

What the manager had to bring to the job, which enabled him to lead, were knowledge, competence, skill, vision, courage, responsibility and integrity of character, for the new tasks and challenges required by the "*manager of tomorrow*" (*ibid*:371). Drucker had identified that in practical terms the one qualification a manager had to bring with him was not "*genius*" but "*character*". Drucker believed that a manager's work could be analysed systematically and learned ("*though perhaps not always taught*") (1954:343). The one unique contribution that a manager gave was the ability for others to have vision and the ability to perform. "*It is vision and moral responsibility that, in the last analysis defines the manager*" (*ibid*:344).

Managers were paid to make decisions, which Drucker advised should be based on analysis of as many facts as possible. It was regrettable, but

157

true, that the manager would never have all the facts, but this was not necessary to make sound decisions. What was necessary was to define the unknown, know where lack of information had caused him to guess and judge the risks. The worst and most common practice was to make precise decisions based upon incomplete information (*ibid*:345-353). Once made, a manager must take ownership of the decision when selling it to create motivation (*ibid*:359).

Drucker believed managers of tomorrow would have to prepare themselves for the new demands that were being brought about by automation. Marketing was being affected by the new technology and was becoming an integrated process within the business. Emphasis would be on product design and customer service. The creation of mass demand would be the pay-off. According to Drucker "*Television advertising is as much Automation*" as was production processing, and would be impacted by the new technologies in marketing, and distribution (*ibid*:364). Innovation and marketing would have to look at longer futures. New technology would produce greater opportunities by broadening markets, raising production, and increasing consumption. All these opportunities would require the manager to work considerably better. Managers would need new tools and yardsticks, some of which they would have to develop for themselves for the key business objectives of long range planning and decision-making (*ibid*:364- 365).

Drucker noted that the fact that more managers were going to be needed, (although they were the enterprise's most expensive resource (*ibid*:109) was becoming accepted. Few had identified this problem although Sears had fifteen years previously. Now there were hundreds of management plans (*ibid*:179). Management development was for all managers at all levels of the business not only those at the top (*ibid*:181-183). But management development is 'too important' to be considered as a special activity. It was absurd that the enterprise alone should become responsible for the manager's development. It could provide systematic challenges, but development must be self-development of the manager and those for whom they are responsible (*ibid*:184). For Drucker, what management development was not, was a promotion plan (*ibid*:180-181).

Drucker believed tomorrow's managers would need two perspectives, one based on the education of youth, the second adult education, which could be learnt only after they had managerial experience. Drucker was arguing for, not against, the importance of a general education as well as learning journeyman skills, which enable a manager to acquire respect for workmanship, which was a Rathenau idea. A young person, who only learnt specific business or engineering subjects, was prepared only for the first job. Drucker was against "*letting loose*" a young person who had learnt "*Personnel Management*" in a business school but believed themselves to be qualified to manage people, the reason being was that through their inexperience, they could only do harm and little good. "*The specific work of the manager makes sense only to men who have set objectives, organised, communicated and motivated, measured performance and developed people. Otherwise it is formal, abstract and lifeless*" (*ibid*:367-369).

The new demands on managers meant that existing managers would have to continue with advanced general education to gain greater insight as well as continuing their technical education. [Idea: Continual Learning Society]. Experienced and mature managers would need to access and take risks (*ibid*:368-369). The new managers of tomorrow would need to take on seven new tasks:

(i) Manage by Objectives – MbO

(ii) Accept that the risks would have greater futurity and that they would have to be examined to identify the best options, also decisions will have to be taken lower down in the organisation. The results of the decision would have to be monitored against expectations;

(iii) Be able to make strategic decisions;

(iv) Develop other managers for tomorrow and build an integrated team with each member capable of measuring their own performance in relationship to the common objectives;

(v) Communicate fast and efficiently as a motivator. To obtain responsible participation of other managers, professional specialists and all workers;

(vi)   Disregard the tradition of managers only knowing a few products or one industry together with the practice of only having knowledge one or two functions;

(vii) Now managers would have to relate to their place in the total environment in making their decisions. They must have to see the business as a whole and integrate their functions within it. Their visions would have to be outside their own markets and country, with economic, social and political developments regarded on a world-wide scale. These visions would have to be integrated into their own decisions (*ibid*:365- 366).

Although the manager's job would become more complicated, with an understanding of mathematical methods of analysis, the framework had been established as the basis to produce checklists to help to keep the job in focus by applying Drucker's philosophy of management. Exceptions could be separated from the routine and receive emphasis. This was Taylor's 'Management by Exception'. [Idea: The benefit of checklists was applying simple logic to work]. The benefits of "*check-lists*" were that rather than looking at each operation as a novel event they could be examined against established procedures. This reduced the prospect of error by omission through approaching each function of management and their elements as novel, rather than treating them as part routine. This was another example of Drucker's conversion of his ideas into practical advice and keeping them simple wherever possible. The other advantage of "*check- lists*" was that work could be divided amongst the team with each member being aware of his or her contribution in relation to each other.

When it came to decision making, for Drucker logic was the greatest tool. Fast decisions made without regard to the necessary information were wrong, although writings abound advising "*fast forceful and incisive decisions*". In Drucker's opinion one could not spend too much time on identifying a problem and defining it. Then analysis was needed but not the systematic diagnosis, which most managers used, that was based solely upon experience. Drucker's simple message was, gather all the facts available before deciding, but accept that, all the facts are not always available. A decision to do nothing was still a decision and might be the best decision (*ibid*:345 & 350).

There were five phases of decision making: (i) Define the problem; (ii) Analyse; (iii) Develop alternatives; (iv) Make the best decision by considering risk, economy, timing and resources; (v) Effective action that moved the balance between tactical and strategic decisions avoided time wasting.

In Drucker's opinion less and less reliance would be able to be placed on intuition in decision making. Preparation always had its rewards in the best results (*ibid*:347 & 362).

Drucker continued to compile his list of the manager's tasks, practices and responsibilities. In asking the question "*What it means to be a Manager?*" he answered with two specific tasks that nobody else could discharge, so that by definition anyone that performed these tasks was a manager: (i) Creating a true whole that was greater than the parts. As an analogy Drucker used the conductor of an orchestra who was doing exactly this. However, the manager performed as both the composer and conductor. To perform, the manager must utilise the strengths of his resources, especially human resources, while neutralising weaknesses. This was the way to create a genuine whole. But to achieve this, the manager must balance the three major functions of (a) managing the business, (b) managing managers and (c) managing workers. If a decision was not balanced then the whole enterprise was weakened. For Drucker the manager must continually ask two questions; "*What better performance is needed and what does this require of what activities?*" "*What better performance are the activities capable of and what improvement in business results will it make possible?*" (ii) To operate in two time dimensions, which were the present and the future, and not damage either for the sake of the other. By harmonising short and long term objectives he would fulfil his responsibilities for the performance of the whole enterprise (*ibid*:336-337).

While accepting that all managers spend time, and some most of their time, on things that are not managing, Drucker believed that the work of the manager could be systematically analysed by applying Scientific Management. By isolating the basic operations of the manager then the

161

manager's performance could be improved by enhancing each constituent part. There are five operations in the work of the manager, which together "*result in the integration of resources into a living and growing organism*" (*ibid*:337). The five are: (i) Set Objectives; (ii) Organise; (iii) Motivation and communication; (iv) Measure; (v) Develop people. Every one of these functions can be further sub-divided and discussed in books of their own. Drucker did not credit Fayol in *Administration industrielle et générale* 1908 (now titled *General and Industrial Management*) (Fayol 1949: 6) as the source of the first four functions as identified by Rosemary Stewart (Stewart 1963:4-6).

Drucker described information as the manager's specific tool. He later described information as only being data unless it was communicated. But without the ability to communicate by the written or spoken word, a manager could not succeed in producing results because he would fail to motivate his team. For Drucker communications were multidirectional, not as proposed by Given whose philosophy was that workers evolved ideas and initiatives communicating them from the bottom of the business to the top. This he described in his book *Bottom-Up Management* (Given 1949). Drucker rejected the idea not only on the grounds that initiatives should come primarily from the managers, but because communications that are "*bottom-up*" are as incomplete as those which are top down (1954:139, 339-340). Not noted by Drucker was Given's mission statement for Brake Shoe. It was the earliest identified in this research: -

OUR AIM

To build a company which gives greater security to its people
... employees and stockholders.
This means making our company.
A better place to work.
A better neighbour in the community.
A better company to sell to.
A better company to buy from.
A better company to invest in.

To achieve this Aim we must find for everything we do – a better way.

A plaque bearing this revised Aim hangs in every Brake Shoe plant, as well as on the walls of executive and sales offices".

(Given 1949:44).

In what was an exercise not only in instruction in part but a stimulus to cause managers to think and be adaptive, Drucker stated that responsibility and performance always started at the top of the business. The chief officer's team was preferred to a sole operator but the team was a performance organ not a committee. In addition to the responsibilities previously described there were other jobs that were unique to the top management role. Drucker devotes a chapter to the *"Chief Executive and Board"* (1954:158-179) and listed the jobs that only the CEO could perform. These included meeting investors, raising capital, visiting plants, and being the final decider on key reserved issues, as the final point of appeal, closing plants, sacking managers, and overriding local interests for the overall welfare of the business. A case study described the responsibility of a CEO taking charge in a crisis when a plant burnt down. In order to manage a CEO's time to the maximum then time had to be made to prepare for meetings to make them more effective. Drucker described an hour's conversation in which a CEO described a job list of forty-one different activities. Drucker's conclusion was that the majority of CEO's jobs were disorganised and needed to be defined. He referred to the only identified research conducted by the Swedish Professor Carlson, in his 1951 book *Executive Behaviour*, which Drucker briefly described (1954:162). The book was based upon a three years' study of twelve top executives in diverse Swedish organisations into how they performed their job. The results and conclusions were that 65%-90% of their time was consumed in contact with other people (1951:34). One CEO solved the problem of creating time for the primary purpose of his job of strategy by working at home before arriving at work. Another managed to work three hours a day on his strategic tasks by arriving at work two hours before anyone else. The average unallocated time for strategic work was half an hour per week despite their average working week being fifty-four hours (*Ibid* 1951:26-27). One of the dilemmas of the study was to define the question "*What is work? Is it a Sunday Walk while thinking about one's job?*" (*Ibid* 1951:42-43) Of the top executive team size, it varied from four to five, and up to fifteen or more, the larger numbers reflecting a Swedish practice (*Ibid* 1951:58). Carlson's conclusion was that the findings confirmed the need for further study.

Drucker also referred to a speech by the French industrialist Nordling on the CEO's job. Nordling's suggestion was that the CEO's job was the biggest and yet least explored of all the management tasks (1954:163). Drucker confirmed that a stopwatch study such as Carlson's was a start but it needed to be accompanied by hard thinking on topics such as "*What should the job be?*" "*What can he delegate and to whom?*" "*What jobs are first?*" "*How can he allocate time despite crisis pressures?*"

Drawing further upon Cordiner's work, Drucker identified the need for a CEO team. Also highlighted was Cordiner's belief that the CEO was failing if he had not identified, within three years of his appointment, at least three equal successors (*ibid*:166-167). Drucker offered advice on organising the CEO's team. It was essential that every member knew their role. If organised as tennis doubles they would have to have played together; if organised as a baseball team where there was a recognised format, strangers knew the team's predetermined roles (*ibid*:172-173). What was emerging was that Drucker was looking ahead beyond formal Decentralisation as the structural method of organisation. An emphasis of forming teams for projects and teamwork generally was included in Drucker's Chapter '*Managers Must Manage*' (*ibid*:135-144). Business team solutions were recognised and used, where different skills were required as in scientific papers where speciality contributions were required. Drucker saw this as becoming more common in business with professional employees. Inside an organisation business team solutions were regularly used for big jobs, as the work required more than can be achieved by one–man assignments. [Idea: Task force management]

Drucker continued throughout the book to add to the manager's jobs. In return for the essential authority to perform tasks every manager was

164

given three tasks which were his first duty: (i) Defining the objectives of his own job; (ii) Defining and contributing to the aims of the enterprise by his own performance and those of workers. This involved removing non-performers and promoting or ensuring those that contribute well receive extraordinary rewards. These are the heavy responsibilities of the manager that cannot be assumed by his subordinates. (iii) To help the managers, for whom he has responsibility, reach their objectives by acting as assistant to them, and providing all the resources they need. As IBM had defined it, the manager's job was to *"assist"* (*ibid*:140).

Of the worker initially there were three kinds by Drucker's count. There were managers, workers, and professionals. However, he had identified a fourth, the technician, as demonstrated in the previously identified case study of a telephone maintenance man whose job:

> "...*comprises a variety of operations.* ...*requires a good deal of thought and judgement.* ...*requires muscular as well as intellectual co-ordination*"

> (*ibid*:280).

Drucker devoted a Chapter 'The Professional Employee' to professionals, whom he identified as the fastest-growing group in the labour force (*ibid*:323-332). The trends identified by Drucker could only increase their numbers and range of specialities. Drucker's concern about the proper organisation of professionals appeared to be shared by almost all of his audiences. He recorded that after almost every talk he was asked, "*How can we manage the professional specialist?*" The problem appeared as acute in non-business organisation such as the Armed Forces. Even their title in the organisation was a problem. GE had coined a term "*individual professional contributor*" but as professionals regularly worked in teams this was of questionable use (*ibid*:324). Titles were required to convey standing, not only for professionals but also for divisional managers in large organisations who as "*General Manager*" would often have more responsibility than the "*President*" of a small business (*ibid*:151-152). Drucker reverted to the idea of *Practice* that there was no such thing as labour in sense of a resource but that all workers should have managerial

165

vision. The professional represented a distinct group of worker and we could only understand what a professional was *"if we can organise his job properly and manage him adequately"* (*ibid*:325). The professional was not a manual worker but neither in many instances was he a manager (of others) as he may work on his own. In Drucker's view his job should be organised on the basis of Functional Decentralisation. Basically the difference between the professional and the manager was that the professional was responsible for the results of his own work and his results would be measured against his professional standards, which are set outside the organisation. This distinguished his work from the manager and worker whose goals were set inside the enterprise. This only exacerbated the problem of determining the professional's place within the enterprise (*ibid*:327-332). Drucker further referred to his paper *Management and the Professional Employee* (HBR May/June 1952), which he recorded was the most demanding paper he had written. The paper was a very perceptive practical view of the situation. That Personnel Administration failed to follow their own principles did not help what was a difficult situation where professional groups would argue for weeks over details. The problems were compounded because a professional expected to be rewarded for his work regardless of the health of the business. Drucker argued that he should be rewarded for research rather than management skills. In Drucker's view the professional's job needed to be organised to relieve them of clerical duties, and to recognise that some outstanding contributors often want to work on their own. However, the professional did need to be exposed to business facts by being bought into long term policy debates. This would help to lessen his feeling of isolation. Rotation through various departments before placement was ineffective as the professional's only interest was to get on with his job.

Part of the problem in organising professional employees was the adoption of *"staff and line"*. Accepting that it may work for the military Drucker could find no justification for it in business. For Drucker, business was made up of two activities, business and supply functions. Drucker suggested that the supply functions, which some classify as *staff* should be attached to the business activities as an essential service rather than becoming a staff empire that attempted to exert control on the business activities. Drucker accepted that central office staff was needed but believed they should be rigidly controlled in scale otherwise they would seriously impede the performance of top management. It was an advantage of small businesses that they lacked the managers to allocate to service functions. The result was that one person managed all the work out of necessity of cost. The problems of staff empires were three-fold; they created work rather than assisted; they assumed responsibility that they should not have; and they controlled the destiny of people in business activities. As part of the '*staff empire* syndrome' Drucker was also against the "*assistant to*" mentality, where assistants assume authority, via that of their supervisor, above their own rank.

An ongoing problem was that those who manage staff did not have time to consider the business as a whole. GE was identified as the only business that had conspicuously tried to correct this problem. At GE Vice-Presidents in service functions had to allocate 20% of their time to being a member of the CEO team to ensure they focused on the business as a whole. The policy was contrasted with a case study where a services vice-president was engaged in all but full-time interviewing foremen for fifty-six plant managers (1954:237-242). As far as Drucker was concerned there should be no staff function, only management. As an example of the service functions integrated between Personnel Management and the foreman or supervisor's role, a case study in a large automobile company was described. In this 'firm' the method of selecting men for production work had changed from the Personnel Management department making the selection. While the employment office still carried out the screening, it was the foreman who made the decision. Two of the benefits were that the foreman could select the appropriate individual for the job, and the workers would know much better what was expected of them if selected by the foreman (*ibid*:320). The foreman's job had been described previously with reference to IBM. For Drucker management development started with the foreman (*ibid*:315).

(iv) Managing the Worker and Work

What had become clear in analysing *Practice* was Drucker's integrated approach to management. The book, by Drucker's declaration, has many major themes. In addition it contained ideas that would take on greater importance through progressive later development. As the theme of Drucker's work was people, much of what has gone before could justifiably have been incorporated into this chapter. Drucker stated *"that it is essential to realise first that everybody in the enterprise is a worker,..."* (*ibid*:325). Although management was charged with the responsibility of performance it could only achieve its objectives through the worker and through the worker's co-operation being integrated into the objectives of the enterprise. From this it followed that work had to be organised to make individuals productive and effective. People had a totally unique make-up when compared with other resources at the manager's disposal. Management must build on the strengths of the worker, individually and collectively, to eliminate or, at least, neutralise weaknesses. Only management could harness these faculties because *"management is the activity organ of the enterprise"* (*ibid*:12-13).

Drucker had already considered the worker's resistance to higher output, and their fears of loss of security. Not only was Drucker arguing that it was worthwhile and part of the new order to pay attention to managing all the workers, but that it was imperative. With the exception of the human resource the laws of mechanics govern all other resources. They could be inefficiently or efficiently managed *"but they can never have an output greater than the sum of the inputs. Man alone of all the resources available to man can grow and develop"*. Yet Drucker observed that we continually found that the rank and file worker was directed and did as he was told. He was managed as other resources, which was a fundamental misunderstanding of his capability. The failure was in not seeing that many *"rank and file jobs are in effect managerial, or would be more productive if made so"* (*ibid*:12).

For workers to make the maximum contribution, to be motivated, and assume responsibility, they needed to have the information to control themselves. Only then by managerial responsibility and *"through*

168

the experience of participation" would the worker achieve what was necessary "*managerial vision*" (*ibid*:301).

What the case studies and the references to the work of other management writers and practitioners had been accumulating was evidence of how management needed to project forward and that in some '*cases*' they had already progressed well into a model of the future. Conclusions could be drawn that Drucker had found enough evidence as to how the new order would work and had been working to achieve automation as a method of production. What he had demonstrated was that the rank and file worker wanted to work, wanted to contribute and be part of the enterprise. He had also established that there were certain working environments, which workers attend with reluctance.

Many of the practices required to motivate workers had already been identified in Drucker's previous description of model working conditions, mainly based upon the IBM practice. Drucker collected his ideas together in his chapter 'Motivating to Peak Performance' (1954:296-305). Drucker's conclusion was that we have no way of measuring what degree of satisfaction for the worker was satisfactory. {Walker & Guest in their *The Man on the Assembly Line* (1952), some people just choose to be dissatisfied but as they point out, just because "*soldiers moan out of habit*" it did not necessarily make them bad soldiers}. Drucker continued that as a motivator satisfaction was inadequate, it was passive acquiescence. What made a man '*want to do*' was personal involvement to give performance by internal self-motivation. Responsibility – not satisfaction – was the only thing that would serve (1954:297). Worker's performance was also dependent on manager's performance. The manager's performance had the greatest effect on worker's performance. What the worker required of the manager was to plan ahead on the basis that, the minimum disruption equated to the maximum performance. As IBM established, general standards were a disincentive to able workers, but even those less able to contribute could have objectives based upon their potential contribution.

Drucker advised that there were four ways that a manager could assist a worker to become a responsible worker: (i) By encouraging pride in the job, as the maximum not minimum performance; (ii) By keeping the worker informed to enable him to control himself; (iii) Enabling the worker to participate as a contributor to developing 'management vision'; (iv) Careful placement to which opportunities could be added. Drucker identified opportunity, or lack of it, as one of the major disincentives in worker's attitudes at all levels. What the manual worker saw was that opportunities for advancement were diminishing. While businesses complain about lack of suitable candidates to promote "*a criminal waste of Human Resources*" was perpetuated, as foremen were overlooked for promotion to management positions while in turn the rank and file worker was denied promotion to the foreman grade.

The easy and wrong way, according to Drucker, was for promotion to be confined to those who were college-educated. This was socially unacceptable and de-motivated both the rank and file workers and the supervisors who as a result "*play it safe*" (*ibid*:316-318). Drawing on IBM's practices opportunities and placements, should be seen as a continual process rather than GM's old policy of only analysing the first ninety days of employment (*ibid*:293). Financial rewards were important to workers but they are largely negative if worker demands for responsibility were not satisfied. Workers, like managers, also needed rewards of prestige and pride (*ibid*:297). [Idea: Continuation of the Hygiene Factors].

Drucker identified that promotion systems must be rational because promotion always loomed large. They must fully utilise all the managerial groups in the business, not only engineers, salesmen or clerks. Outside recruitment was also needed to create competition and correct balances of skills (*ibid*:153). The promotion system must be transparent and fair but even in the best organised business not everyone could be promoted, which may be through no fault of their own. What was important is that all received the proper treatment and recognition. Drucker drew upon Hawley's 1954 book *The Executive Suite*, which was later made into a film. The theme was the selection and appointment of the successor to the retiring CEO. It portrayed a drama of selection, with family intrigue and politics acting against what the reader was led to believe was the right decision. It also illustrated how imperfect the selection process could be and its limitations.

In what Drucker called *"The Management Charter"* every employee needed to know who had the power to make *"a life or death"* decision, which affected them personally. The policies were more complete in some companies than in others. In the Continental Can Company its policies were limited to the rights of appeal for managers only, but all of the members of the organisation including the workers needed to know as in IBM (1954:153-154). What the enterprise should never do was demand complete allegiance from its members because it could not promise immortality in return. Managers who lived for their company were too narrow and remained a *"perennial Boy Scout"*, which was something that the business should recognise. Brief examples were given of outside interests that helped to round people (*ibid*:237).

Of all the case studies that Drucker uses his most progressive inspirations regarding managing the worker came from IBM as previously identified. Drucker's acknowledgement of his information from Richardson & Walker, 1945 book *Human Relations in an Expanding Company* and also the more general information of Walker & Guest, 1952, that worker's performance was related to the informal relationships with their colleagues, was part of IBM culture. This was a reflection of its discovery by the Mayo led 1927-1932, Hawthorne study, which Drucker had recognised. Drucker returned to the problem of providing wage guarantees. IBM's staff conditions for workers he regarded as an exception. For Drucker business would have to change because work would change through technology and social pressures were demanding it. Managers would have to maintain employment "*as close to stability as possible*" as today's semi-skilled become tomorrow's highly skilled maintenance men. As today's skilled worker became the professional, labour would become a capital cost and its impact on the performance of the business would also compel the managers to aim for stability (1954:365). But Drucker warned that the pressures within business for a *"guaranteed annual wage"* were resulting in external pressures that were building up in government to do something. If businesses generally did not come up with some acceptable scheme that they could live with, then the government would be forced to impose something on them that would be unacceptable. It was one of Drucker's general

171

warnings that if businesses do not regulate themselves in response to the initial political pressure and put something in place that they could accept, then the governments would put something in place that they would find draconian. [Idea: Voluntary self-regulation was always better than government imposed sanctions]. On the practicality of who paid, Drucker quoted Heron whose message was that job security was linked to sales performance *No Sale No Job* (1954:310-311).

(v)   Time

Drucker recorded, although not strictly a function, the importance of TIME to the manager's job. Drucker used Carlson and Nordling to show how little control over time top management had in their working environment. He also used Dean to record how capital expenditure needed to be viewed as not just the purchase and running costs, but also the time span of the functionality of the equipment. That the manager's decisions were set-in two-time zones – today and the future, which had to be considered separately and then jointly, was another essential impact of time. If we had more time to gather more data then our decisions would be better. But the demands of today prevent us in practice from stopping the clock. To recognise the effect of time in the manner that Drucker had done was relevant and pertinent. It was an essential part of accurate measurement without which self-control was impossible.

The Impact of what was the Contribution of Drucker's Seven Key Ideas:

1   MbO

Drucker acknowledged that others before him such as Brown and Sloan had definitely practised a form of MbO some thirty - forty years before he identified it as a 'philosophy of management'. But it took Drucker to develop it intellectually into a practical application that could be used by others as credited by Odiorne and Greenwood. For Drucker MbO was different from how his predecessors had perceived it. It was not a function but the cement of all the functions. Drucker's brand of "*MbO*

172

and Self Control" was an enabler to make "*integration*" possible, which was the nucleus of Drucker's holistic ideas on management.

2   Decentralisation

Others before Drucker had recognised (Federal) Decentralisation as the preferred structure but again it took Drucker to present it to and describe it for managers in such a manner that it was set in a context that they could use and could become a common pattern for major commercial organisations. Decentralisation as 'the model' was the management discovery that Drucker made during his studies of GM, which resulted in *Concept*. By the time he wrote *Practice* he had become aware through his research and consultancy work that although the principles of management were applicable to all business organisations as preferable as Decentralisation was not all businesses could fit into one structure. What Drucker perceived was that there were organisations for which Decentralisation was not appropriate. With the advent of automation as the new concept of work, new structures would become appropriate for some where organisations would require task force teams and/or hybrid structures.

What Drucker was maintaining was one of his tenets of management that the structure must follow the organisation not the reverse. It was as a health warning that, in spite of Decentralisation being highly recommended, it was the manager who must decide which structure suited their particular enterprise.

3   Integration by Productivity, Automation and Profit

Although Drucker declared in *Concept* that he had no expertise in production, he accepted that he had to include the function in *Practice*; otherwise he would be in breach of his own standard advice that all functions occurred in enterprises and must be considered albeit with differing emphasis at different times. By using the work of Hurni and Diebold he was able to forecast where production techniques were heading. Drucker's own message was that automation had a wider implication than identified by others. For Drucker it was the new

173

method of working. It would not only replace mass production but it would be a new revolution in how all work would be executed. It was the application of applying logic to work and a new method of "*integration*" for the organisation. As with the MbO it took Drucker to interpret an existing idea and set it in context.

In examining 'what does profit mean?' Drucker adds his own work to existing research thus creating a new originality. He provided a contemporary composite picture for his readers who were unlikely to follow the writing of the other important contributors to the arguments that had been developed. By integrating the ideas of others with his own he had made the definitions of both automation and profit different.

4.   Managers Must Measure

For Drucker, this topic developed into a sub-history of the development of Scientific Management. Taylor made it possible, Brown created sophistication and many others as Kuznets, Knauth, Dean, McNair, Katona, Juran and the personnel specialists expanded it into other areas. Drucker's target was to ensure that all functions of management were made capable of measurement rather than having three separate camps: - Those that were measured - production workers, those that weren't measured - general advisors and those that measured other people's work -Accountants. Drucker was critical of accountants for their failure to deliver what was needed, which was comprehensive and appropriate methods of measurement that the manager can use as an effective tool. This criticism which would become a continual feature of Drucker's work was supported by examples. As with the analysis of profit, Drucker added originality to the function of measurement. He correctly concluded that it was a job that had been started but not finished.

5   Entrepreneurial Function

Drucker picked up from Schumpeter who in turn credited the influence of Richard Cantillon (c1680-1734) and Jean-Baptiste Say (1767-1832). For Drucker the entrepreneurial function was "*marketing and innovation*". This was the start of Drucker's work on this function of management.

He would eventually give it a new focus and place it at the centre of the business purpose. His would be identified as a unique contribution to this function of management as confirmed by Theodore Levitt the Harvard doyen of marketing.

6 People are Central to the Organisation

This was the function that Drucker devoted the most time and space to in his writing on management performance. People were the fundamental resource of the organisation. Without people there could be no organisation. They were its basic platform. For Drucker, people were the most wasted resource of an organisation as they were the least understood and most complex.

While being identified as a resource they could only be treated as individual and unique human beings. Of all of the resources they were potentially the most productive if they received the right treatment. Drucker was adding to the ideas of others all of who admitted the complexity of the situation and that so much more needed to be learnt. No-one was claiming that they had the answer but Drucker made a contribution by identifying the best practices that had a proven record of performance.

7 The Manager's Job is Total Integration

This is the essential identification by Drucker which he arrived at by elimination, having considered the following. Gillmor was included in Drucker's selected biography for his 1948 book *A Practical Manual of Organisation* but not the text. It is a pocket book that sets down the principles of organisation supported by a confirmation that he was aware of many of the influences that Drucker used together with others. Gillmor's message was that "*Organisation differed from the machine in that it is a living organism which must be continuously adapted to the changes in environment which will inevitably encounter*". For Gillmor management attitude had to be adaption.

For Drucker, this was only one of the manager's many necessary aptitudes, but it was not the encompassing essential.

Barnard, Follett, Lillian Gilbreth, Hopf, Moody, Urwick and Weber probably Fayol all identified that the management functions were welded together by co-ordination. For Drucker it was just part of a chain of management activities because the management of the organisation is more than co-ordination. What was required was the cementing of the mass. The cement was integration. As previously noted, Taylor may have seen the need. Hopf certainly had as Drucker had previously acknowledged and so had Urwick, who described the organisation and co-ordination principles as the task of the organiser - *"to secure the integration correlation of all functions"* (Urwick 1943:54). Urwick left the emphasis here as integration remained part of his definition of co-ordination. However, it took Drucker to emphasise it, make it central to management, and conceptualised it. Functions were isolated only for the purpose of practical and theoretical examination and to enable better understanding. It was for convenience of comprehension. It was not to establish that they could exist in isolation. For Drucker they could not because they were interdependent upon each other. The organisation's very survival depended on the fact that it was recognised that functions could only survive through their coexistence. This was integration. Drucker was the first to communicate so clearly this imperative followed closely by Smiddy.

Of managing workers and work by identifying that the manager had three tasks, Urwick believed that Drucker had given the manager's work a new concept (Urwick 1956:55). Finally of 'Time', it had been recognised by others previously as an essential for the manager to consider. But as with profit Drucker provided a new focus to quietly emphasis its imperative significance.

The Conclusion of *Practice*

Practice concluded by repeating management's responsibility. After placing so many demands upon the manager, and in return providing support but never sympathy Drucker suggested that the manager should resist the demands that were common in American big business of demanding managers' lives. *"The company is not and must never claim to be*

176

home, family, religion, life or fate for the individual. It must never interfere in his private life of his citizenship" (1954:381). Many of Drucker's ideas that he sets down in *Practice* were developed in his later work together with new ideas with which they were often integrated.

Drucker continues that managers must always support and never undermine what was the public good by acting only in the business's own self-interest. It was one of the businesses objectives (*ibid*:78-79 & 384). Drucker believed that in this area as in all of the others, managers had much to do. Capitalism was being attacked not because it was inefficient or misgoverned but because it was *"cynical"*. In his review of *Practice* Urwick 'highlighted' his agreement with this conclusion of Drucker's. On the last page of *Practice* Drucker suggested that the reason for the cynicism may have been identified by the English pamphleteer, Bernard de Manderville (1670-1773), who 250 years before wrote, in his famous epigram *"private vices become public benefits"* – *selfishness unwittingly turns into the common good"*.

Drucker suggested that the answer to the criticism was by adding further to the manager's tasks and telling them that they must *"make the public good.... the private good of the enterprise"* (*ibid*:386). The Contributions of Drucker's Seven Key Ideas have summarised Drucker proposals but the manager had still a long and challenging journey of further essential discovery of what his job was. Examined in the next chapter are the influences that Drucker considered to shape the way forward.

CHAPTER FIVE

REACTIONS TO DRUCKER'S WORK

This chapter is based upon *The Philosophical Influences that were available for Drucker to use*, (Starbuck 2005b) unpublished working paper OUBS (19,500 words) and *Quotations Regarding Drucker* (Starbuck 2005c) comprising one hundred and seventy seven quotations relating to Drucker's work, unpublished working papers OUBS (8,500 words). Volume III of this trilogy of Drucker work will include a more extensive citation review.

Introduction

This chapter highlights the whole of this sample to give a balanced and wide-ranging assessment to the reactions of Drucker's work. It helps to support the claim that Drucker is the most quoted management writer, and that the interest in his work ranges from academics, writers in general and achieving business practitioners. Of the academics that have considered his work, their attention has been examined in the most detail.

The range of this enquiry includes:-

1. Book Reviews of *Practice*.
2. Work of his Biographers
    (i)   Biographies about Peter F Drucker
3. Treatment of Drucker by Academics Introduction
    (i)   Non-contentious theses on Drucker's Work
    (ii)   Academic Reviews Summary
4. References to Drucker in other writings
5. Conclusions Drawn from the Reactions to Drucker's Work

1.   Book Reviews of *Practice*

Nine full reviews were considered - six British and three American. Of the British reviews Urwick stated that it is the best thing in American management literature since Mayo (1949), but the book was different because it deals with what it is to manage a business, and noted approvingly with support Drucker's use of *"integrity"* twenty times in his text.

Asa Briggs described Drucker as having *"acute perceptions, brilliant skill as a reporter and unlimited self confidence"*. Edward Francis Leopold Brech's review was more combative than those of the other reviewers as he inadvertently identifies the difference between British and American attitudes. He saw appeal in Drucker's challenge that Personnel Management should not be a separate function. He summarised that every British manager should read the book, which was dynamic, stimulating and challenging. The American reviewers all found, as Heron did, that the book was praiseworthy and had no similar predecessor, while only Taplow got Drucker's message of *integration*. All the reviews were complimentary to Drucker as for each reviewer there was a different area of appeal while they were unanimous regarding the need for the book.

2.   The Work of his Biographers

(i)   Biographies about Peter F Drucker

- Bonaparte & Flaherty (1970); this is the first full work on Drucker, which is a Festschrift with twenty-three contributors. As a selection of what has been written about Drucker, it is the most important work for its range, which includes glowing endorsements including Theordore Levitt, the HBS marketing doyen and Urwick, who terms Drucker as *"The Manager's Professor"*. Apart form the dominance of American contributors the contributions of the Germans, Freyberg and Gross widen the focus.

- Tarrant (1976) is an essential compliment to 1d and is accurately described as *"The first full scale study of this towering and original business thinker"*.
- Beatty (1998) is essential for Drucker's researchers but is poorly organised and is *"something of a missed opportunity"* (Wooldridge Wall Street Journal 21st January 1998).
- Flaherty (1999) after considering updating 1d he decided to write a new book, which makes Flaherty Drucker's most significant biographer.
- Heller (2000) is a pocket book for a focus in one-hour

(ii)   Chapters or Significant Entries on Peter F Drucker.

Although some of the compendiums of management thinkers are repetitious. The most important are Odiorne (1978), Greenwood (1981) and Wren & Greenwood (1998), because they show the greatest insight into Drucker work.

- Magnetta & Stone (2002) also shows great insight but in a more general manner.
- O'Toole (1995) is important both for the quality of his scholarship and for identifying the importance of Drucker's criticism in *Concept* being ignored by Sloan and GM, which he believes is the best book written about GM.
- Gabor (2004) is the most challenging of Drucker personally, while at the same time giving additional important information.
- Hoopes (2003) also gives additional information and counters Gabor's personal challenge of Drucker. Probably Hoopes most important contribution is in highlighting that *Concept* was the best book on management available for the GIs returning from World War II. It is important because it crystallises that *Concept* launched Drucker as a management writer.
- Kantrow (Jan/Feb 1980) *Why Read Peter Drucker?* explains the reasons why it should be read, such as mental stimulation,

because the reader is certain to find something which appeals and interests

3. Treatment of Drucker by Academics

Introduction

This section is in two parts. The first is non-contentious, as it considers the theses written about his work. The second is open to contention, as it is headed Academic Reviews, and should include reviews considered in general, previously by academics such as Barzun, Briggs, Hazlitt, Utley and others. However, the reviews chosen are because they are included in *Combined Retrospective Index to Book Review in Scholarly Journal (1886-1972)*.

(i) Non-contentious theses on Drucker's Work

- Nazergadeh for this research MbO is based on Theory 'Y', although MbO has its critics. The cessation of its use cannot be predicted.

- Olcese (1980) researches the effectiveness of the teachings of MbO in twelve school districts in Cook County Illinois in order to assess their teaching of management.

- Ormsby (1980) is in two parts. The first part is a response to the criticism of MbO in the preceding twenty-five years. The conclusion is that MbO is not a failed philosophy, but it does fail in practice if the objectives are only known to top management and not communicated down to middle management and the workers. The second part is a survey of eight hundred and fifty American State Banks and their application of MbO. Although the quantitative results are subjected to Likert Scaling and Statistical Coefficients the conclusion is that the research has been an ineffective measure of the bank's performance. The failure of MbO to be effective in part 1 and for the results not being contributory in part 2 is caused by lack of communication.

182

- Apfelroth (1983) ten books by others are selected to test Drucker's contribution to education in *introductory college management text books* in seventy-four locations. Apfelroth's conclusion is that Drucker does provide young students *"with some insights and tools to be applied against later experience"*, but for mature management students he provides an integrated body of management knowledge. This conclusion is consistent with Drucker's position that management education *"will only take if the recipient has experience to relate the ideas into practice"*. Of the other conclusions, MbO is considered not to be treated in sufficient depth.
- Colbourn (1988) her thesis is the typewriter is an agent of change in the business environment. Her study is an interplay between Drucker's five survival functions for business and Jacques Ellul's four rubrics for technological change. The time frame is from 1867 to 1954.

"The study addresses the major social economics, technological and educational impacts of the typewriter on the business environment in society but does not attempt to account for all concurrent influences. The study concludes that when the typewriter was introduced into the business environment it changed the way people structured, thought about, worked in and defined their environment. Many changes which occurred within the business environment had far-reaching, rippling effects on society. Moreover, once the typewriter was completely adapted to and rooted in the business environment it had long-range secondary, unforeseen effects not originally anticipated when it was invented and introduced into the business environment." (part Abstract)

(ii) Academic Reviews

'Economic Man'

Manheim describes Drucker as a *"hard boiled Christian socialist"*. His analysis of the German economy is described as *"shrewd"* although

Drucker's *"economic man"* never existed. However, the book covers a wide range, is uniformly interesting, informative and uniformly wise.

Manheim (1939) (Commonsense New York).

Mitray believes *"economic man"* did exist until Marx killed him off in the Soviet experiment. *"There are small blemishes in a highly intelligent book."* *"Mr Drucker has given us the kind of book we greatly need"*.

Mitray (1939) (International Affairs November London)

'Future'

Landman wrote that Drucker fails to tell us how to get to the new society, and that he frequently dissolves the facts:

> *"nevertheless his conclusions are very provocative."* *"...it is a stimulating book in that it explains why our industrial society must be a free society for the greatest good of mankind and why totalitarianism is empirical to those interests"*.

- (The Annuals of The American Academy of Political and Social Sciences 1941 Landman, College of the City of New York)
- Utley, as reported in Chapter 3, is totally supportive. (Commonsense 1942 Utley New York), Cook *"Mr Drucker does not balance"* which is a rejection of his arguments.
- (Political Science Quarterly 1943 Cook New York University of Washington)

In a collection of reviews of four books Gurian (Notre Dame University 1943) included Drucker's *Future* and Schumpeter's *Capitalism, Socialism and Democracy* (1942).

Of Schumpeter (his)

> *"...book is written by a very intelligent author, so intelligent that he sometimes overlooks the obvious"*. (Drucker) *"The author of the famous analysis of totalitarianism (Economic Man) has a much better understanding of political and social realities that the economist of*

184

Harvard". Although *"the book suffers from a continual change of direction it is full of wisdom and practical insight"*.

"Pure" practice is helpless without theory." *"It is a proof of Drucker's intelligent approach to political and social problems that for him this question is most important: What is the nature of Man?"*

"Schumpeter and Drucker have written books of a highly personal character; they present interpretations."

It is a credit to Drucker that he stands up to examination as well as Schumpeter. It is important that Gurian identifies Drucker as a bridge between political science and economics, because it identifies one of the unique cornerstones of Drucker's work that is often overlooked. It is also important that he should *"destroy the devastating overestimation of the purely "empirical""* because it anticipates the criticism of those who later accused Drucker's work of lacking, because it was not based upon *"empirical research"*. Drucker survives this rigorous examination, and comes out with credit from a reviewer whose performance is creditable.

'Concept'

It is a coincidence that the two reviewers from *The Review of Politics* (1947) (Notre Dame University, Indiana) should follow each other. Mann was the only academic reviewer of *Concept* that could be traced. Again the review was by a well-informed intellect. A representative selection of quotes will most accurately reflect the contrast and the spirit of the work and its conclusion, as in the previous review. As a preamble Mann identified that Drucker was *"drawing on a broad experience"*, he was promoting *"Decentralisation"* as the *"general model of organisation"*, which was correct.

For Mann, Drucker's definition of Decentralisation was confused and had different meanings. The chapter that identified the greatest weakness of the large corporation lay in its inability to see the need for status and function of the individual in society received Mann's support. The Corporation's analysis (monotony) the problem of it was flawed, because the problem was social or psychological one, and not a mechanical one. The problem could only be solved by evolving and establishing *"a new*

185

relationship between the worker and his product based on the purpose of his work rather than on his paycheck" (Pages 149-159). Mann confirmed that this was his specialist area and was in full agreement.

Mann raised some timely and important issues regarding Drucker's treatment of the relationship between the Corporation and society, many of which are dealt with satisfactorily. "*However he neglects modern development in economic theory*". Concept could be described as "*a sociology of the large corporation*". It discussed the appropriate questions.

The book:

> "*...adds to our knowledge of the political and social functions of the corporation. Combining the philosophical with the political and the technical approach and supporting theoretical deductions by the experience of a large organization, it demonstrates the complexity of its subject and encourages further studies in the field. Its forceful style and its many happy formulations will fascinate most readers from the preface to the end.*"
>
> "*Is Drucker's book an American publication of 1946 or Frédéric Bastiat's Harmonies Economiques of 1850*" (*Economic Patterns*).

This was yet another rigorous examination of Drucker's work. It got right to the root of the issue. It identified that Decentralisation was the obvious target of the book although its description was not concise, which it was not until *Society* (1950). Mann correctly identified that the main aim of *Concept* was to try to make sense of the organisation of a socio-economic unit, which had been previously identified in my text as the main content of *Concept*. Mann was correct when he wrote; "*It neglects modern development of economic theory*". Drucker corrected this omission in *Practice*, as well examined in my text, although in *Concept* he has examined the consequences on the worker of prolonged unemployment. Referring to Drucker's work, it is interesting that an academic of Mann's undoubted ability gave credit, and expressed that the need for this type of research should probably be supported "*by drawing on a broad experience*". Again this review is another positive outcome towards Drucker.

186

'Society'

Leob's work was not only a review, but also a conversation piece as he expressed his variations on Drucker's themes of the needs for full employment, status of the worker, and also the role of profit. Describing the work as a valuable study, the reviewer believed that the book "*will become increasingly influential with the passage of time as sometimes the importance of published work does not at first appear*". Similarly "*Mendel's study of genetics, which vitalised the science was ignored for decades*".

Leob (12th March 1951)
(Freedom Foundation for Economic Education)

Fainsod 's review identified that Drucker's new society "*bears a more than superficial resemblance to the old*". "*The major problems as Drucker visualised*" were the creation of a social system that would allow management to give full expression to the mass production economy. However, Drucker's ideas on mitigating labour fears of overproduction were "*an ingenious programme*". Regarding the construction of the book, there "*is the regrettable tendency when the going gets rough …to retreat into convenient vagueness*". While recording that Drucker's treatment of the role of government leaves a good deal to be desired, it was also acknowledged that Hayek was in a similar position. Yet the reviewer attributed this position to Drucker and Hayek's followers' "*profound pessimism or scepticism towards political action*". The reviewer concluded that he hoped that if Drucker's campaign was not successful then the future will not turn out "*quite as fearsome as he expects*" in this "*stimulating and provocative volume*".

Fainsod (1951)
(American Political Science Review Harvard University)

MJV's review was short in size but simply targeted on what the reviewer identified as the main topics of the book, including the "*autonomous self governing plant community*", while the Unions are ignored by the reviewer. The following extracts illustrate the spirit of the review.

187

"A disturbing theory emerges in this examination of the new industrial society envisaged by management consultant Peter F. Drucker". "The germ of this revolution was created in Detroit and evolved into mass-production technology, which is "is undermining and exploding societies and civilizations…""

"All things everywhere are being affected by it."

"What to do about it? Construct the "free industrial society." Politically, this must be a society in which responsible citizens are first developed through active participation in autonomous local self-government enterprise and plant communities."

"The new society would emphasize freedom of individual action, restore true competition, encourage good unions, and create capable managements."

For the reviewer it failed to deliver the promise of its *"Introduction"* - *"Somehow or other the assembly-line ideas, so well underscored in the Introduction get either lost or sidetracked as the book rolls along."*

M J V (1951)
(Sociology and Social Research University of Southern Californian Press, Los Angeles.)

Mitray recorded in a brief review that follows his review of *Economic Man*, that *"Drucker has laboured for some time to analyse the nature of the changes* (in)… *society"*. He did so again with *"much good sense"*, finding the solution for *"decentralisation of large industrial undertakings"*. Although in some of his arguments where the historical facts do not fit into the existing political beliefs Drucker ignored, but he could *"fairly retort that this is what is wrong with them"*. Mitray was incorrect when he contended that Drucker proposed that the Unions should be given a share in managing local units. He concluded that this could be their role if they ever found an essential constructive purpose. Only the Union could evolve a constructive role, which was not in prospect. Drucker concluded that the worker could manage these functions without the involvement of the Unions.

Mitray (1992) (International Affairs January Oxford).

188

JEF produced two reviews. The first was a compilation of reviews of recent literature on full employment. It appeared in the article "*Full Employment – A Discussion of some Recent Literature by Julius Gould*". Referring to *Society*, Gould recorded that we did not have to agree with everything that Drucker wrote, because it may only be applicable to America. However, there was much substance in his chapter on "*A Rational Wage Policy*", where he argued that "*it is not enough to "allow wages to be set by pure power play", and his emphatic distinction between "the wage burden on production" and the fixing of wage rates*". Drucker's idea that "*old labour*" attitudes had to change because they still need to have "*a stake in profit*" was referred to.

"*It stands to the credit of Mr Rehn, Mr Meidner and Mr Drucker that the twin problems of "corporative complacency" and "full employment profits" do emerge, or are suggested, from their work. It is all the more surprising that these problems come out less sharply in the relevant sections of New Fabian Essays.*"

By comparing Drucker's work with other contemporary contributors, he was subjected to an examination, and emerged with credit.

In the second review, JEF confirmed that he was familiar with Drucker's work by referring to *Concept*. It was a balanced critical review; "*Drucker's description of the classicists structure of the giant corporation adds nothing to Rathenau's classic of the 1920s. However where Drucker does add is in identifying that the power of the Board is withering away*".

The reviewer believed that Drucker wasted many words on the Union's position regarding management. This may be a reflection of the different perceptions of what was acceptable by the Union in America and Britain. A further criticism was that the reviewer could perceive that the transfer of shares for bonds *vis á vis* the Directors and shareholders would solve the problem of responsibility for power.

However, the foregoing can be regarded as a spirited debate. Drucker was credited with identifying the business organisation as an autonomous body with the capability to analyse the business enterprise in its own terms, while professional sociologists have failed to do so. The reviewer concludes that *Society* is a provocative book that is rich "*in insights*" into a very important problem, "*but maddeningly glib in proffered remedies*". The reviewer left the impression that Drucker was involved in another fight, and keeps his title on points.

JEF (1952 & 1953) (British Journal of Sociology)

Brissenden's review came as an afterthought in 1956. It is an important review, because it previously featured in Chapter 3 in the summaries from *The Book Review Digest*, where the review was summarised as "*penetrating social-economic analysis*". This short review epitomised the spirit of the full review. Much of its concentration was on the idea of the "*self-governing plant community*", connected with Drucker's search to find a constructive role for the Unions creating a form of Democratic Socialism (which is probably what Drucker expresses, in Continental European terms, as "*Old Conservative*").

The review concludes that:

> "*The touchstone of the success of democratic socialism, in Drucker's opinion, will be the ability of the government to maintain the autonomy of management and the plant community. The dilemma of the unions is left unresolved.*"

I regard his final sentence as accurate for the same reasons that Fainsod and Mitray's are not, when they concluded that Drucker found a constructive role for the Unions.

Brisssenden, (Political Science Quarterly, Columbia University)

'Practice'

Singh found that "*the book is of absorbing interest and thought provoking even though one may differ from the conclusions*". Restricted for space, the definition of management was highlighted as the creative creature of the economy. It was the "*most remarkable analysis of management problems on Production, Manager's Structures, the IBM Story and Human Organisation for Peak Performance.*" Referring to "*some of the minor faults of the book amongst many of its major virtues by which it will ultimately be judged*" he adds:

190

"Though recognising the value of profit-sharing schemes for increasing production, the author has failed to appreciate the significance of worker-management co-operation in planning production: he considers that the effectiveness of the worker is determined by the way he is managed".

I find the statement that begins *"…the author has failed…and concludes he is managed"* to be invalidated by Singh's previous reference to IBM, which in this writer's view is the hidden discovery in *Practice* for the most progressive integration of workers' and managers' efforts. Drucker's message was that it is the way that the worker was managed that cultivated the attitude to make possible worker-management co-operation. The example of appeal to the reviewer of Drucker's general excellence in dealing with 'production' in *Practice*, with which I agree, is interesting when set in the context that in *Concept* Drucker declared his lack of expert knowledge. In *Practice*, he displayed at least a competent understanding. As for the reviewer, he suggested rationally that the book *"should really have been called 'The Philosophy of Management'"*. The reviewer was appreciative and supportive of Drucker's work and, as with others who examine his work, found different and fundamental alternatives. I agree with the title that the reviewer suggested as one of several alternatives.

An interesting aside is that Singh's entry was followed by a review of *TEACHING MANAGEMENT – A Practical Handbook With Special Reference To The Case Study Method* (1955) Harry Newman and D.M. Sidney, which also featured in the previously considered joint review with *Practice* in the 1955 *Times Literary Supplement*.

Of particular interest is the following entry:

"The book (Teaching Management) has a foreword by Lt. Col. L F Urwick and the authors also reproduced, as an appendix, a letter written in 1951 by Lt. Col. Urwick as leader of the Anglo-American Productivity Team on Management Education, to the Dean of the Harvard Graduate School of Business Administration."

191

This entry was a further endorsement of the importance in management ideas of Urwick's active contribution running contemporaneously with Drucker's work.

Singh (1955) (Indian Journal of Public Administration)

The final academic review by Flanders was very brief, and again was split with a review of Newman & Sidney's work. For Flanders, the book was pretentious and dull, and did not add to Drucker's reputation. It was accepted that he was *"more of a journalist than a scholar"* and *"his previous work was an intellectual adventure"*. It was *"a rather indigestible sermon"*. Flanders found space to write a barbed compliment; *"To be fair, wrapped up in all the verbiage there is sensible advice which management might with advantage accept"*. The final sentence was probably the most consequential of the review: *"Yet, despite the book's title, it is not put in a very practical form, and it is doubtful whether those to whom it is addressed will find the method of presentation persuasive."* The history of the book has proved the review to be at least foolish, and even defamatory. That Drucker scored no points is obliterated by the gambler (the reviewer), who lost his bet.

Flanders (1956) (Sociological Review, Nuffield College Oxford)

Summary

This selection has produced the most diverse reactions to Drucker's work. These reviews have been collected together for his five books rather than being dispersed, as previously as his other reviews. Of these sixteen reviews, two were critical, while one was neutral or ambivalent.

Without necessarily agreeing with Cook's review, he rejected Drucker for not winning the balanced argument. The only other critical comment was from Landman, who was disappointed that Drucker did not explain the new society in *Future*. Flanders not only rejected Drucker for the wrong reason, but also forecast that *Practice* would fail. By making such a fundamental mistake, he cannot be regarded as a reliable critic, and should be eliminated from the conclusions of the reviews.

As for the other reviewers, JEF criticised Drucker for being *"glib in remedies"* when cornered, while at the same time seeing merit in his work. The review can be seen as a support to much of the content, but also as being critical of some of the quality of argument. However, JEF's criticism that Drucker spent too much time on the American Unions was a reflection that JEF failed to get into the "*American mind-set*". A more informal view of Drucker's treatment of the Unions was that he was objectively critical of them, while being protective of the behaviour of some of the major automobile manufacturers. On the whole, the reviewer was ambivalent. Fainsod was also ambivalent to Drucker's ideas and accuses him at times of "*retreating in vagueness*".

The conclusion from the examination of these reviews is that Cook's rejection was a valid criticism and that it opposes Drucker in a poll, as does Landman. Fainsod and JEF were neutral or ambivalent. To be linked with Mendel, Hayek and Schumpeter in a complimentary way by the reviewers is an endorsement of standing.

The conclusion from this sample is that Drucker received 80% of the support from the academics. Further evidence that Drucker has standing amongst academics, not only his work being worth reviewing, as well as worth quoting, is confirmed in the *International Encyclopaedia of the Social and Behavioural Sciences* Vol. 25 2001. As a general reference he had nine entry references, while most other people had one. There may have been some entries from other management writers, but these were not conspicuous.

4. Reference to Drucker in other writings

As part of this research; as noted in the heading of this chapter; one hundred and seventy-seven quotations about Drucker and his work have been scheduled. In addition a similar number of articles have been examined from The Financial Times Library collection from other sources about Drucker. They are from a cross section of contributors that include academics, writers and business leaders.

From all of this material, only one work was totally negative: *Requiem For A Heavyweight* (May 1993) Foster in *Canadian Business*. This was a review of Drucker's *Post Capitalist Society*.

Foster stated that the thesis is that Capitalism in its existing form needed to be replaced by pension fund capitalism and 'educated work'.

For Foster despite the fact that there was an almost universal belief that Capitalism needed a replacement (which 'is the greatest wealth generator the world has ever seen'), on this basis alone, Drucker's central thesis was decidedly shaky. Sometimes Drucker seemed to want to coin a glib phrase rather than provide a genuine insight. I believe that Foster was right and wrong. He was right that Drucker did sometimes switch or slip from intellectual mode into jingoistic mode while maintaining the reader's attention. However, if we believe that excerpts are representative of the quality reviewers from the dust cover of the book as reflecting the full reviews, then Foster was wrong because the book was well received by *The Wall Street Journal, The Economist, HBR*, and *The Financial Times*.

It was certainly well received by Adam Smith in the *New York Times Book Review* 11 April 1993, when he described the book:

> *"It is cheering… to find this one of a kind thinker still writing in his 80s. He is as a state university professor who makes notes." "We're in a new age with a lot of disparate elements, and we lack the organizing principles. We need a new Isaac Newton. But Peter Drucker is saying it isn't Peter Drucker. Then who is it? We want to write down the new principles, neatly. We wish he'd take the job."*

In the other articles from The Financial Times Collection, *Practice* received praise as the first and best book in general management, and the subjects covered include ethics, entrepreneurship, non-profit organization, computers, quality, the failure of the Unions, the international spreading of 'privatization,' extensive writing on Japan, and even *"whistle blowing"* as early as 1981. Drucker is described as the 'Dr Spock of Management' and as 'The Philosopher King of Management'. Kantrow, whose work is also included in the collection, reminded us that perhaps his two most famous contributions to the study of management as a professional discipline are: *Practice* and *Management*. With the considerable amount of material written by and about Drucker, something unexpected is likely to turn up, as in Inc October 1985. *"But while Peter Drucker may be the master of modern management, there are serious collectors and curators of Oriental art who have never heard of Drucker, the*

194

management expert. They know him only as the authority on certain periods of Japanese art." But then Kantrow wrote that you will always find something in Drucker's work of interest.

In the electronic publications indexes of the most 'hot' management writers, Drucker is usually recorded as No. 1 and never lower than No. 3. In a comprehensive summary of business guru placing, which accumulated Google hits, Media Mentions, and Social Sciences Citation Index accumulatively Drucker is No. 1; Tom Peters is No 2 with Michael Porter at No. 3, scoring forty percent of Drucker's total. Warren Bennis is further down the list, but ahead of Rosebeth Moss Kanter, who is just ahead of Charles Handy with twenty percent of Drucker's score (Davenport & Pruzah 2003:217).

5.   Conclusion drawn from the Reactions to Drucker's Work

Something with certainty has appeared from this examination of Drucker's work. He has provoked more reaction through his work than any other management writer. This conclusion is supported by the weight of material that has been identified. It includes five biographies, twenty- seven significant book entries, eight PhD Theses, fifty-nine book reviews listed in *The Book Review Digest*, which, as established is not a comprehensive listing that may be nearer double the amount. The one hundred and seventy-seven quotations that have been scheduled (now soon to be published) as the unpublished working paper and the similar number of articles from the collection of the Financial Times library of other sources by a range of specialists, do provide a representative sample. Admittedly they are not the exhaustive accumulation, nor do I consider it possible to identify all the material in this area. However the material has been utilised as found with attention being paid across the whole range of opinions rather than selectively to prejudice the outcome.

Not only has Drucker created more reaction to his work than any other living management writer, also his influence has had the most longevity of the living writers along with Juran. However as consequential as Juran's contribution in Quality Management has been, his range of influences had not been as holistic as Drucker's. Although there is a similarity in the time span of Juran's work of over sixty years, it is Drucker who has covered the most ground for ideas and aroused the most varied written interest. Tarrant was correct in 1976 when he wrote that following The Hawthorne Experiments *"As a source it began to wear thin. As the vein appeared close to being mined out, the pundits looked around for another Golconda. They found it in the thinking of Peter Drucker"* (Tarrant 1976:141).

Of the reactions to his work, only handfuls are negative. Very few are ambivalent while the others join a landslide of appreciation and acclamation, which includes a distinction that has not befallen any other management writer of being compared with Bastiat, Hayek Schumpeter and Shaw, but also Newton and Mendel. Not only is Drucker entered in every appropriate collection of management writers, he has also been the core of management books where he does not appear in the title as 29(e) and also 11(e) as in Micklethwaite & Wooldridge (1996) where he is used to explain what others mean or what their ideas are. To be used as a comparative to explain the work of others is a considerable compliment and distinction. Maybe the most important aspect of this chapter for academics is that the source of the accusation that (all) his work lacks academic vigour cannot be identified and also that those who have been identified for jumping on what appears to be a convenient bandwagon have failed to live by the demanded standard themselves.

CHAPTER SIX

DRUCKER'S CONTRIBUTION TO MANAGEMENT AS A PRACTICE

The themes that will be examined are – Was Drucker a synthesiser or an originator? Did *"he make a discipline"* of Management?

1. As a Synthesiser?
2. As an Originator?
3. Did *"he make a discipline"* of Management?

1.   As a Synthesiser?

This research has established that one of Drucker's many outstanding talents was that of a master synthesiser. It is difficult to recall any other writer on the discipline of management ideas who has been so industrious in examining the work of other management writers across such a range of disciplines within the context of what was available in their day, with the possible exception of Hopf and Urwick. However, while Drucker's search appeared the more eclectic than theirs, what was not in doubt was that his published written output exceeds Hopf by a magnitude and Urwick's considerably. Drucker had acknowledged the synergy of his and McGregor's ideas, together with his debt to the work of others such as Rathenau, Schumpeter, Hopf, Taylor, Sloan, Brown, Mayo, Urwick and Maslow. As established, he did not always *"fully footnote"* their credits, which probably contributed to what appears to be academically originated criticism that he is not a rigorous researcher, but an armchair philosopher. Rosemary Stewart recorded a notable example with regard to Fayol's ideas of lack of reference (1997:6) while acknowledging *Practice* as *"one of the best of his books"*. However, in *Practice* he produced an original 'biographical list' of further reading regarding the influences that he had considered without tying them all precisely into the text. This was a pattern of references that he would use again. Fayol was included in this list and also made it into the text for being one of the creative thinkers of management insights (1954:275). Regarding the use of footnotes neither Taylor, Rathenau nor Fayol, as the great shapers of management ideas used footnotes, and yet they escaped criticism. Similarly McGregor, Drucker's contemporary, (see *The Human Side of Enterprise* McGregor 1960), and Charles Handy, who credits Drucker as a strong influence, did not use footnotes. It is surprising that Drucker is criticised for an absence of footnotes as both of these contemporaries escaped a similar treatment. But probably of greatest significance was the fact that although Drucker did not fully footnote his work, he conforms to the precedent set by the HBR policy of occasional footnotes. The fact that Drucker was frugal with his use of footnotes was not concealed. In the Preface of *Practice*, it was his express policy that *"footnote(s) acknowledging the debt would be neither helpful nor meaningful"* (1954:viii). This may be the crux of the argument regarding Drucker and footnotes. What, I believe, he means is 'yes' my work is based upon extensive holistic research, and the result was a fusion of many ideas including his own. If this was so, how does one reference in the traditional manner? We are back to his argument that management was *"integration"* with the influences not ignored, but acknowledged in *Practice*, as previously identified.

However, there was some point at which synthesising is seen as plagiarism, which was an accusation that had not been levelled at him, even by his harshest critics. But synthesising was in Drucker's case, a two-way valve that not only takes, but also gives. Theodore Levitt recorded:

> *"Nobody is more qualified to attest to a man's genius than his plagiarizers. A man as productive, creative, and versatile as Drucker predictably has lots of them. I am proud to confess membership in the large and grateful body of Drucker plagiarizers. If imitation is the highest form of flattery, plagiarism must have God's special transcendental blessing. If He creates only an occasional genius. He has no choice but to condone Drucker's plagiarizers – unless God is willing to have the truths spoken by His genius degraded into unprepossessing copies"*

(Levitt in Bonaparte & Flaherty 1970:6-7).

Sometimes it is difficult to recall where ideas came from. In Drucker's case with his holistic approach, there may be a combination of sources. Even Sloan, whose undisputed talents included being personally highly organised, had doubts, "*I cannot, of course say for sure, how much of my thoughts on management came from contacts with my associates. Ideas, I imagine, are seldom, if ever, wholly original*" (Sloan 1964:47).

I believe that Sloan's quote is pertinent. Whenever someone is credited with inventing something, researchers working away will be trying to identify a predecessor. Taylor's "*work measurement*" was a conspicuous example.

Although the idea that work can be measured was defined as an idea long before Taylor, what has to be established is, who was the first to make it work as a practice? It was Taylor who first made it practical, which enabled others to apply it. Taylor made it possible to design and set times, not only for existing operations, but also for projected ones. In doing so, he conceptualised the measurement of work and so changed its concept by making it part of his complete management system – "*Scientific Management*", which Taylor started by synthesising what his predecessor had done. Drucker created originality in a similar manner by means of synthesis by completing the ideas of others and collating them in a manner that makes them different. What Taylor had done with his "*time measurement*" or "*time study*" was to turn a half concept into a full concept. Drucker does similarly with some of his work, as in *Concept*, when he described Sloan's Decentralisation to which he added the social dimension of his "*autonomous self-governing plant community*", which he further developed in *Society*. In an attempt to find the solution to the problem of the industrial society being lop-sided, through as previously identified, industrial workers not having a balanced social society to live within as they had had in their agricultural society, which they left behind.

Again, Drucker did similarly with MbO, by taking what was there, but changing and adding to it. Of the changes, the most essential were by making the setting of the objectives more exacting and the most fundamental of making *integration* the cement for all management functions. *Integration* was so important because it could stand along effectively as a philosophy of management in its own right and also because it was the essential of any other workable management philosophy. Later Drucker repeated his process of creating originality by synthesis when he took Schumpeter's entrepreneurship and innovation and turned them into a new function (1985).

I believe that my research has established that Drucker was a synthesiser, but also by making "*integration*" the cement of all of the management functions, his synthesis has created something original.

During the whole of this research, the only detail regarding Drucker's synthesising is that as a student of Schumpeter, Drucker incorrectly attributed the original meaning of the word 'entrepreneur' to Jean-Baptiste Say (1964:162). Schumpeter made several references to the Irish/Paris domicile Richard Cantillon who used the word 'entrepreneur' earlier and probably for the first time ever, in a limited manuscript circa 1730. He used the word again later in his book *Essai sur la Nature du Commerce en Généralé* (*The General Nature of Business*) (1755:15). As a student of Schumpeter, it was surprising that he did not pick up this line of credit. What made Drucker's conclusion more puzzling is that his understanding of Schumpeter will stand favourable comparisons with the attempts by others to do similarly. Also of the management writer his understanding and inclusion of the work of economists was the most comprehensive.

2. As an Originator?

The starting point for answering this question is to determine Drucker's standpoint. At the onset of this text, I stated that Drucker did not belong to any particular school of management thinkers but that he had sat in the same classroom as others. The evidence supports this contention, as did Bonaparte, when he described Drucker as being a member of all schools but not of any in particular, who "*is primarily a social scientist that utilizes knowledge from all fields*" (Bonaparte & Flaherty 1970:31). This analysis was supported by the study of Drucker's life and influences in

200

the earlier chapters of this research. In spite of the turmoil of Austria at war which coincided with him starting school, through to the consequence of Austria's defeat he still managed to keep on track his continual to learn and development intellectually. When school bored him he joined the adults at intellectual salons in Vienna in order to exploit what Austria had to offer him intellectually through its unique collection of outstanding intellectuals. The attendance at intellectual salons was also an earlier past-time of Rathenau in Berlin, which indicates a similarity between Austrian and German intellectuals. Drucker's transfer to Hamburg was a period of intense learning, rather than being taught. His move to Frankfurt not only replaced his job as a clerk, (which was one of Einstein's first jobs) but enabled him to work for one of the country's leading newspapers *Frankfurter Anzeiger*. Also, Drucker's move to Frankfurt led to an improvement in his prospects. In one of his parallel careers as a journalist, he had moved to a centre with a greater variety of activity together with a university that had a collection of internationally recognised academics such as Martin Buber (1878-1965), who had taught comparative religious beliefs between 1923 and 1933. This widening of experience and influences was a pattern that Drucker used over a long period of his development by always searching for people who were more knowledgeable in their field than he was. This search was illustrated in his first two books and subsequently as evidence of his eclectic search. This quest continued until he ran out of suitable people, resulting in him pursuing a pattern of asking himself questions, and then seeking the answers from the best possible sources. This approach resulted in him becoming an outstanding synthesiser. Drucker's distinction was that he did not stop there. When a synthesis did not provide the answer, he moved his position and became an originator, either with an extension to his synthesis, or by creating something new.

Of the ideas that Drucker conceptualised for which he never claimed originality were Decentralisation as he first described in *Concept*, or MbO as first described in *Practice*. Although as others had recognised he changed MbO to such an extent he could have claimed originality. Even with Decentralisation he also gave it a new originality in *Concept*, which was the first study of a mammoth-manufacturing organisation - a

201

Corporation - as a social organisation. Drucker took the GM model and added his own ideas. The main idea was based on Rathenau's society, which Drucker converted into his own "*autonomous self-governing plant community*", which he developed more fully and later described in *Society*. It differed fundamentally from Rathenau's ideas on two main principles. Rathenau's community was prescriptive rather than autonomous, and he anticipated that the Corporation would not remain shareholder owned, but would be converted into a co-operative.

Although IBM came very close, closer still have been the few democratic co-operatives. Though Drucker's ideas were never rolled out, what is important was that he was identifying the essentiality of a social balance to the industrialised process of work.

Drucker often took other people's ideas, redefined their meaning, extended their ideas and turned half concepts into completed concepts, or he amalgamated them with others to make them more complete or appropriate to contemporary needs. For example he redefined Taylor's ideas and made them contemporary, while with the ideas of Holden *et al*, that the top manager's job was different to the divisional or functional manager's, he developed their ideas and set them in a result-producing concept. He also extended one of their basic definitions that the structure must follow the objectives of the business, explained why it needed to happen and emphasised that it should not be a force-fit or more likely a misfit.

By the time Drucker wrote *Practice* he had answered the criticism that O'Donnells review levelled at Holden *et al* for the questions that they had left unanswered. For O'Donnell, they purported to tell the businessman "*how to do it*" and yet they only "*get close to the right issues*" with regard to the way in which the management of an enterprise occurs in practice. Again Drucker was creating originality by turning half concepts into completed concepts. Drucker also treated Schumpeter's innovation and entrepreneurship differently, by developing the ideas into a separate function, thus giving them originality. Drucker also created new concepts by amalgamation, as with the ideas of Diebold, Hurni and others, concerning automation and production, by extending their

202

meaning and giving them a new context by way of relating them to profit.

With *Practice*, Drucker created a new type of management book by aiming it not only at an audience of managers, but also at people who wanted to learn about management. In doing so, he set about making management a part of everyday life. It was popularisation without trivialisation. He achieved this objective by extensively using particular case studies in order to produce an understandable story, or by only taking as much detail as was necessary in order to illustrate one idea, as was the case with Crown-Zellerbach and Chrysler. Also, through his holistic approach to developers he conveyed the essential message that management had to be the integration of all the functions not just some of them.

What *Practice* primarily contributed in detail was that it conceptualised MbO, which had been one of the few philosophies of management from the second half of the 20^{th}c Drucker described it as a principle of management, meaning that it could be used to manage a whole organisation through the integration of all the manager's activities.

Drucker later said that his ideas were attractive because they only had one part, and without doubt some did. While MbO was based upon one idea, it consists of many parts for example, "*the purpose of a business is to create a customer*", "*what is our business*" and "*what should it be*". It was often this simplicity of his relevant and essential ideas that had clarity of purpose that others aspire to but fail to match.

Maybe if Drucker had stopped work after writing *Practice*, it could have been concluded that he was an outstanding synthesiser, as there was not enough convincing evidence to affirm his originality. A random examination of a handful of his thirty plus books that followed dispelled this doubt. Three of the most mentioned are *Landmarks of Tomorrow* (1959), *Managing for the Results* (1964) and *The Age of Discontinuity* (1969), which matches the message on the dust cover "*a road map to the next period of history.*" It was a masterly but readable work, which opens horizons that managers and others should scan to determine what was ahead. The contribution was encapsulated "*he is a brilliant and provocative thinker – one who refuses to be bound by standard assumption*" Leo Taplow *Management Review*

(October 1959), *The Book Review Digest* 1960. Taplow had also reviewed *Practice*.

Managing for Results (1964) told us that the only distinctive resource that a business has is knowledge. Drucker believed that it was the first book on *"strategy"*, which was its proposed title. However, this title was not used because the publishers believed that not enough people would understand its meaning. Another section of the book, on the subject of marketing, which I believe is the dominant feature of Drucker's proposals, was so demanding on the manager as *"today's breadwinners"* - became *"yesterday's breadwinners"* - which then led to the ever seeking *"tomorrow's breadwinners"*. My contention is that if this were compulsory reading for budding managers before embarking on their chosen career, then they would think again. This is a reminder of Schumpeter when he wrote that he could not perceive why anyone would want to be a manager in business – because it was too difficult.

The Age of Discontinuity (1969), like *Landmarks*, was a forecast of the future, which introduced 'Privatisation' and 'the knowledge worker' as his ideas are reflected. *"Of his strengths is that he is a geyser of original thought"* anonymous *Economist* 5th April 1969.

After *Practice*, Drucker wrote a consistently overlooked book, which his shortest up until this time at a mere thirty-two thousand words, *America's Next Twenty Years* (1957). It was an exercise in forecasting using demographics, a method that was overlooked by other contemporary management writers. The following is an expert opinion about the book. *"It's extraordinarily prescient over measures concerning pensions and retirement and surely one of the few forecasts over 20 years which has stood the test of time to any reasonable degree. Where it could not foresee is of course immigration, which thanks in part of legislation in 1965, took off in a most unexpected way in the US and now accounts for a high proportion of population and workforce growth"* - letter from David Coleman, Professor of Demography, Department of Social Policy and Social Work 6th January 2003/Starbuck. David is a world acknowledged specialist who writes, broadcasts and works for the UN, UNESCO, The World Bank, ECC and many governments, in addition to his ongoing teaching.

Also what did flow from *Practice* was what Drucker's major conspicuous influence was. The insights of this were recorded in the first book written about and entitled similarly as *Innovation and Entrepreneurship* (1985). Drucker described how his work for this book started *"in the mid-fifties"*. He recorded that it is based upon empirical research, as, week after week for two years, the ideas were examined and then *"tested, validated, refined and revised* (over) *twenty years"* (1985:x). His description of his research method was an answer to those who criticised him for a lack of rigour.

I believe that the foregoing examples confirmed that there was also significant originality in Drucker's work. While Theodore Levitt did attest to Drucker's inspiration he could have added that his work was contemporary with that of McGregor and that Drucker anticipated Herzberg in particular and Mintzberg and many others in general.

3.   Did he *"make a Discipline of Management?"*

The dictionary definition of 'discipline' is from the Latin *disciplina*, - instruction, knowledge, or training to engender self-control and an ordered way of life.

From the evidence examined it is seen that many of Drucker's influences whose work on management ideas either preceded him, such as Hopf or Urwick, whose work began before or spanned the time of Drucker's work during the period of this research. Both had made a considerable contribution to the development of management ideas in their own right. They were also accomplished researchers who by understanding the work of others incorporated it in their own work and ideas in order to produce original ideas as did Drucker. Hopf anticipated Drucker's ideas in general on *integrating* any contribution to management ideas from any discipline by holistic application in order, as he described *"to provide equilibrium"*. He named his ideas *"Management and the Optimum"* (Hopf paper 1935). Hopf as always, wrote in his other papers relevant material presented as acceptable common-sense. Urwick also outlined ideas regarding his solution to the need for a discipline of management in his 1929 book *The Meaning of Rationalisation*, which he supplemented

205

with his own extensive later writing and also through his collaborating with Edward Brech.

As for Drucker's claim that he made "*a discipline of management*", there were contradictions. His earlier claim that nothing existed was contradicted by Hopf, and then by Drucker in his book *The Frontiers of Management* (1986). When referring to *Practice* he claimed that he only invented the discipline of management in "*large part*", and that "*when you put the tools into one kit you invent*".

Flaherty believed that Drucker did make a discipline of management, because he answered for the first time the question, "*What is management?*" However, he did not "*invent a single modern function instead his originality* (was) *in merging the key specialities into holistic perspective*" (Flaherty 1999:112). Consequently Flaherty recognised "*Drucker as the father of modern management*".

I disagree with Flaherty's contention that Drucker "*made a discipline of management*", as references to the British quartet of Joseph Slater Lewis (1852-1901) *The Commercial Organisation of Factories* (1896); Edward Tregaskis Elbourne (1875-1935) *Fundamentals of Industrialist Administration* (1934); Urwick (1929) (1933) and Brech *Management, Its Nature and Significance* (1946), confirmed that it was known what management was before Drucker's *Practice*. However, Drucker with his holistic approach did fundamentally change the way that we perceive management. He widened the perspectives from which we review the management process. An obvious major addition was in the consolidation of the work of selected economists in the management process. Urwick stopped his examination of the financial aspects of the work at accounts with the contribution of Accountant of whom he was not complimentary.

I conclude that Drucker made the practice and theory of management homogeneous. As for Flaherty's quantification of Drucker's contribution, "*he didn't invent a single new management function*". I believe that there are two alternative responses. The first is that no one has done so since the work of the pioneers, had up until the first third of the 20[th]c except the Quality Movement. The second response is in three parts. Firstly, he changed the way we looked at existing functions by refocusing the meaning of profit and its measurement. Secondly, he redefined

206

marketing to include innovation and entrepreneurship by giving Schumpeter's ideas a practical relevance. Thirdly, Drucker did invent a new function by moving co-ordination to a function rather than the cement of the functions and replacing it and making *integration* the "*imperative cement*", whereas Smiddy gave this idea contemporary support and Hopf has earlier highlighted its importance as had Urwick. However, it was Drucker who clearly explained why it was a central and imperative need as he again conceptualised an idea.

It was Drucker who by applying Gestalt's holistic approach explained that there was an imperative need for "*integration*" in order for the business to survive. He also explained the benefits of the results being greater than the simple sum of the parts; illustrating his argument by using the analogy of the difference between the separate letters of C-A-T and its compounded meaning when it forms the word 'cat'. He continued by stating that 'Scientific Management' teaches us to separate each item of work, while automation demands that we join them together by "*integration*" {in effect by Gestalt via Wertheimer). What Drucker could have made clearer is the dire consequence when managers only concentrate on the function that they find enjoyable. If all the functions are not kept in balance, then the business will fail, which was Drucker's point. For example, if the organisation keeps building inventory and fails to sell in order to maintain liquidity to pay its bills, then it will simply run out of cash. The reality is that an organisation can only run out of cash once. It can incur losses, maybe for several years, and survive, providing it has a positive "*cash flow*".

Drucker's clear explanation is that:

> "*At first sight it might seem that different businesses would have entirely different key areas – so different as to make impossible any general theory. It is indeed true that different key areas require different emphasis in different businesses – and differing emphasis at different stages of the development of each business. But the areas are the same, whatever the business, whatever the economic conditions, whatever the business's size or stage of growth*" (1954:60). "*When it comes to the*

207

job itself, however, the problem is not to dissect it into parts or motions but to put together an integrated whole. This is the new task" (1954:289). And later from *"The Fallacy of the Dominant Dimension These dimensions of working – the physiological, the psychological, the social, the economic, and the power dimension – are separate. (and) indeed, (they) should – be analyzed separately and independently. But they always exist together in the worker's situation and in his relationship to work and job, fellow workers and management. They have to be managed together. Yet they do not pull in the same direction. The demands of one dimension are quite different from those of another."*

(1974:194)

Like many of Drucker's ideas, his strength is that he redefines, then adds to and improves on his initial messages. The need for *"integration"* could be Drucker's most important message to managers, especially when it is linked to his *"boundaryless"* search for applied knowledge.

Despite the fact that Drucker widened the boundaries of management he never lost sight of the central unique resource that managers must always utilise and consider. The resource was people. Drucker's approach to them was humane but realistic, as he admitted they were complex and often frustrating. However, they were not only worth the effort, but they were the imperative that could not be ignored because they were inside and outside the organisation. Reflecting the extent of Drucker's work regarding people has been a major element of this research.

However, despite Drucker's considerable unique contribution, I do not believe that he made a discipline of management because it was not a new invention or discovery in itself. Others had preceded him, as he admitted. *"Indeed, I myself have always insisted that the work in management and organization had largely been done before I began. I may have sharpened and clarified."* (but) *"…all I can claim to have done is a different approach"* (Drucker in Bonaparte & Flaherty 1970:363).

Reflecting in his 1995 book *Managing in a Time of Great Change* Drucker wrote:

208

"Management as a practice is very old. The most successful executive in all history was surely that Egyptian who, 4700 years or more ago, first conceived the pyramid – without any precedent – and designed and built it, and did so in record time. With a durability unlike that of any other human work that first pyramid still stands. But as a discipline, management is barely fifty years old. It was first dimly perceived around the time of the First World War. It did not emerge until the Second World War and then primarily in the United States. Since then, it has been the fastest- growing new function, and its study the fastest growing …".

I agree that, as a discipline, management is a relatively recent emergence, because it had emerged by or during the 1930s, following the work of the pioneers that Drucker rightly identifies.

However, I contend that it has become more generally recognised as a discipline in the last fifty years much to Drucker's credit because he got to the core of what the practice of management was about before making it into a complete philosophy. Not only by *integration*, but by also highlighting what *integration* was if it was to succeed. It had to be the integration of the complete functions of management, or as he termed it all *"the objectives"*, for it to succeed. It could never be to a selection of what a manager liked doing.

It is this ability of Drucker to identify the core issues that are consequential to the managers that has set him apart from other management writers. For Drucker, the manager has to have the ability to see the whole, while keeping all the targets in balance, regardless of personal or national prejudices or preferences. *Two illustrations of how Drucker has made management more important can be drawn from British and American attitudes and perceptions.*

When Urwick quoted the American F Plachy's *Britain's Economic Plight* (1926) that *"A tremendous drawback to effective business organisation in English is the habit of asking who you are, as opposed to the American inquiry as to what you are"* (Urwick 1933:184). Urwick could have continued by emphasising the difference between the American and English with regard to money,

209

as another drawback of British management performance as the differences in the British perception and the way the Americans regard money or profit. While Urwick wrote about profit, he never made it a central issue. Also, he never described what it was which Drucker did, and in doing so, made a further contribution. British management in this period was handicapped by its failure to place profit, as an essential, which was the result of the culture of *"it not being the done thing to talk about money"*. You either had it because you were entitled to it, or you didn't because you weren't entitled to it. A further illustration of the British sensitivity to money is in *The Principles and Practices of Management* (edited by Brech 1953). I have private correspondence relating to this book between Sir Hugh Beaver, a high achieving businessman and acknowledged promoter of management training and education, John Jewkes, and Professor H S Kirkaldy, Queens College Cambridge. Jewkes has produced a private review of *The Principles and Practices of Management*. Beaver despatched the review to Kirkaldy for his opinion. Beaver writes,

> *"I do not really want to impose upon you, but as Brech's book is likely to be for some time the most prominent in this world of management study. I feel it would be very helpful to me at the British Institute of Management to have the views of some competent and unbiased critics"*
>
> (7 August 1953).

Kirkaldy's brief response is disparaging, while admitting, *"when I am able to read some more of the book I shall write you again"* (5 August 1953).

On the dust cover of the book the claim is made, *"This is the first comprehensive textbook of management in the present generation"*. I believe this was a fact, as it was the target purpose as Brech's editor's Preface says; *"This volume is a textbook, offered as a further contribution to those who, at college courses or by private reading, are pursuing the systematic study of management in principle and practice"* (Brech 1953:v). I believe that the following extracts from Jewkes' review confirm the weakness in management thinking in Britain during this era. It highlights another of Drucker's contributions, this time to fill this gap in management by using his holistic contribution

210

on economics and the necessary profit, which is the essential result for survival and success of the business.

> *"The book left me with an impression of emptiness (despite its size); of lacking something vital. And I suddenly realized what it was. Business is fundamentally about profits. And yet the word 'profits' only seems to occur once in the book – and that when it is pointed out that sometimes it is worth while selling at a loss! That seems to me what a book on Economics, however abstract it might appear, is more real than this type of book on Management, for at least the Economics is about prices and costs and profits and losses, which institute the stuff of business management".*

Jewkes make a cricketing analogy and believes the book sets out how to learn to play, whereas a book is needed that "*assume(s) that Management is a strategy, the art of Management is that of taking decisions, the purpose of these decisions is to make a profit, and the decisions have to be taken within a framework of costs, prices and estimates about future markets and the worthwhileness of certain investments*" (Jewkes 27 July 1953).

What this correspondence does is support one of the agreements in my research, because Jewkes was anticipating Drucker's *Practice*. Where I disagree with Jewkes is that we needed both types of books. The first is the rule book which is one on how to learn to play — the textbook. The second is — what is the game and how to play it professionally by the rules to win as a professional. Brech provided the first and Drucker the second. Further evidence of the need for both and of the British perception with its absence of attention to economists is in a praise-worthy review of Brech's *The Evolution of Modern Management* (Wren August 2002). In an extensive review for the Academy of Management's History Division he wrote "*Britain and Scotland have produced a long line of excellent economists.... Yet no mention is made of the influences of economists on Management Education*". Or as previously noted – see my reference to Urwick, Brech was also following Urwick.

This leads to the second illustration of a further cultural difference between Britain and America, which affected management development in the period following World War II. When the British servicemen returned from World War II they were promised "*a land fit for heroes*" by the politicians. This was based upon the British socialist philosophy that there was a finite amount of wealth in any country. If the "*returning heroes*" were to be rewarded, then this finite pot would have to be more "*fairly*" shared out, which it was. This choked any progress on the essentiality of profit as illustrated by even the leading management literature, as previously indicated. The American attitude was quite different. They believed that there was an infinite supply of wealth and that there was plenty for everybody so go and find your share. Consequently, when the American GI's returned from World War II the ambitious availed themselves of their government's offer under the 'GI Bill of Rights' to continue their education. Many chose management. Drucker wrote:

> "*The GI Bill of Rights – and the enthusiastic response to it on the part of America's veterans – signalled the shift to the knowledge society. Future historians may well consider it the most important event of the twentieth century*"

(1993:2).

Flaherty refers to Drucker, and writes similarly:

> "*With over 2,332,000 veterans availing themselves of higher education; it was the largest and most successful single investment in human resources ever undertaken*" (Flaherty 1999:233). *Concept "became recognised as the best book on management available filled with insider information about General Motors the world's most successful company*"

(Hoopes 2003:252).

This leads to the third cultural difference between Britain and America. Managers had "*standing*" in America, whereas in Britain they did not, because they were not owners or professionals. It was a job you "*picked up*" or, if you were an owner manager, then your "*management skills could be taken for granted as naturally inborn*" (Brech Vol 1 2002:7). Although

Brech was writing about the late 19[th]c his analysis was still relevant. Others have also noted that Britain's decline as a *"world power"* started circa 1870-1880, when America and Germany - Britain's competitors in world trade - started to take management ideas and its training seriously. For the British it was not important. For Drucker, management was the only dynamic wealth creator for society and an organ of change. Retaining traditions or personal or natural predecessors could not compromise it, nor could it be compromised by selection of managers by privilege. Only managers with the ability to perform and produce effective results were good enough.

Conclusion

My contention is that Drucker did not *"make a discipline of management"* in that he did not invent or discover it, because it already existed, but he did make it more complete. However, I believe that he missed an important opportunity to make a further emphasis from his influence Gantt, who is mentioned in *Practice*, but his *"charts"* are not.

This omission is corrected in *Management* (1974:182) I believe he missed the point.

> *"The Gantt Chart, in which the steps necessary to obtain a final work result are worked out by projecting backward, step by step from end result to actions, their timing and their sequence, though developed during World War I is still the one tool we have to identify the process needed to accomplish a task, whether making a pair of shoes, landing a man on the moon, or producing an opera. Such recent innovations as PERT chart, critical path analysis, and network analysis are elaborations and extensions of Gantt's work.*
>
> *But the Gantt chart tells us very little about the logic that is appropriate to given kinds of processes. It is, so to speak, the multiplication table of work design. It does not even tell us when to multiply, let alone what the purpose of the calculation is".*

Although Drucker tells us how important the 'Chart' is and what it could not do, I believe he is not clear. What the 'Gantt Chart' or 'Bar Chart' did for the first time was to enable the operation and its time to be plotted together as PERT, the critical path analysis. Once the 'programme' has been compiled into a 'chart' it is a fixed record of the intention. Drucker said that the skill needed to compile the 'chart' was missing. It was not missing because it was part of the thought processes, which were applied to the basic calculations that are needed to assemble the 'programme'. It is a regular oversight by people who have never compiled a chart that because they do not know how they work in practice they are unaware of the first essential basic steps. Firstly, the designer of the chart has to have had experience in the practical application of what was being programmed. Only then can he produce the first basic step of the *"sequence study"*. The *"sequence study"* was a chronological schedule of the operation needed to complete the task (the programme). Once the schedule was complete then the time needed for each operation had to be calculated. The ability to produce the 'chart' exposed if the creator had the knowledge to perform his job. When this has been calculated, the skill is to arrange each activity in its production sequence. In compiling the chart the designer will have had to calculate and determine the *"resources"* required, which can be appended to the chart. The systematic approach of the *"sequence study"* is compatible with Drucker's end of the intuitive manager. In the context of what Drucker wrote, the 'charts' are simply a production or operation programme (although they can be used for many other purposes as stock control) (Clark 1923). My main point that Drucker omitted was not only does he make this basic mistake but that in his pioneering search for 'methods of measurement', he missed one of the least corruptible tools. This writer has used Gantt's 'charts' in the construction industry. They are part of The Contract Documents that commit the contractor to the contract period. Once it was plotted at say forty-weeks an educated child could tell if the work was on schedule. However, when people are allowed to report in writing then the indelible record base of the 'chart' has been compromised. In *Concept* Drucker declared that he had no expertise in production. I believe that this is evident in this example. Encouraging people to write reports may be Drucker's weakness. The purpose of Gantt's charts are explained and their use to counter *"bad accounting"* are

214

well described and the attraction of managers writing "*what they had done rather than compare it too closely with what might have been done*" (Hoopes 2003:75-89). The 'Gantt Chart' or 'Bar Chart' was in reality a series of different charts for different activities. Drucker was writing about the progress chart, or programme chart in which '*time*' was the priority (Clark 1923:83).

In my opinion, Drucker's treatment of the 'Gantt Chart' illustrated one of his few limitations. It was an example that practical applications needed to be examined from the inside from the experience of the practitioners which incidentally Drucker advocated, as well as, from the outside for it to make complete sense.

However, important the Gantt charts are to the discipline of management, this argument should not deflect what Drucker did although he never claimed it, in *Practice* he made "*management into a philosophy*". He achieved this by proposing that the managers needed to approach their job holistically and view their tasks as part of an "*integrated whole*".

For further clarification of Drucker and Gantt Charts, we are indebted to long-term Drucker scholar Joseph A. Maciarello, Professor of Management at Claremont University's Peter F. Drucker and Masatoshi Ito Graduate School of management (Management Revised Edition 2008).

CHAPTER SEVEN

EVALUATION OF THIS RESEARCH

This research has tracked the life of Drucker from his birth in 1909 through to the publication of his book *Practice* (1954). The work of his influences has been analysed and their relationship to Drucker's work has been identified. This has enabled the evolution of his ideas to be followed and their eventual emergence as his consequential messages and their impact has been recorded. This chapter explains in four sections: -

1.   Personal Reflections on Drucker's Work
2.   What is My Contribution?
3.   What Is My Research?
4.   The Arguments and Evidence that Support this Research

1.   Personal Reflections on Drucker's Work

My first introduction to formal management ideas as recorded, were those of the Urwick, Orr Partnership. That there was continuity in what Urwick and Drucker were trying to achieve is of personal significance. If Urwick had been alive today, such was his contribution that he would have been amongst the score or so who deserved to be entitled '*Guru*', despite Drucker's contempt for the title, which he regarded as being akin to '*charlatan*'. That both had profound respect for each other's contribution to their profession should not be a surprise. Drucker gave Urwick credit for making management consulting possible, and also as one of the founding generations of management studies, "*how deeply indebted my own work in the management field has been to the foundation he and his generation had bequeathed us*" (Drucker in Bonaparte & Flaherty 1970:363). For Urwick, Drucker was "*The Manager's Professor*" (Urwick in Bonaparte & Flaherty 1970:67), because he saw the issues and expressed them clearly. A consequence of this research was that it has established the significance of Urwick not only to Western management in general, but to Britain in particular. From the evidence Urwick's work was much more related with Drucker's earlier work than Charles Handy's contemporary work, which was in contrast to Drucker's management ideas. Drucker demanded change, while Handy chronicled it. Despite Urwick's military service in World War I which interrupted his academic training, he was always working from a more practical base than Drucker. Fortunately, Edward Brech's biography of Urwick, (*Lyndall Urwick Management Pioneer A Biography* Brech, Thomson & Wilson 2010) provides an essential accessible record of Urwick's contribution. Brech's own contribution was also acknowledged by Drucker who wrote "*you and I are probably the only survivors of pioneering generations of management*" (letter Drucker/Brech 8 February 2002). {Drucker also believed that Juran also qualified (1954:281) and his comments made as celebrations were being made for Juran's one-hundredth birthday on 24 December 2004}.

Continuing with the comparison between Drucker's and British ideas, I refer to Child, in his 1969 book *British Management Thought - A Critical Analysis* (Child 1969:237), when he wrote that in Britain there was a reluctance for managers to accept the ideas of intellectuals, as they preferred trade to conceptual training. I believe he was correct and that this was one of Drucker's aims in *Practice*, to launch the idea of conceptual training and, in so doing, solve Child's problem.

Huczynski expressed another British focus when he answered his question, "*What makes a management guru?*" with five requirements, which in reality amounted to four. They were, timing, visibility, relevance and to be presentationally engaging. I believe that this research has also identified a further requirement, the need for intellectual rigour of enquiring, which was present in Drucker's work. An illustration is that Jonathan Hall, who proof-read the earlier part of my script perceived that what Drucker did, was turn half-concepts into concepts. While agreeing with this idea, I also believe that he formed new half-concepts as if he were writing titles for someone else's thesis. This setting of tasks for others does give some justification to his critics who accuse him of having some partly formed ideas. But then, this is the burden of managers, who must look forward into the evolving future for their staple "*of results*".

As previously noted, one of Drucker's appeals had been his consistently 'high sure-touch'. However his readers will occasionally find

218

areas of disagreement. Similarly I have two areas of difference with Drucker. The first is his crediting Say as using the word *entrepreneur* before Cantillon and more importantly regarding his interpretation of the preparation and purpose of Gantt's *charts*. Accepting that Drucker understood the conceptual aspects of the requirement of production as organisation research, logic analysis and automation I contend that the one weakness in his analysis is the omission of the Gantt *chart* as both a measuring and planning instrument. However, as Urwick, "*I* (still) *find myself applauding Drucker*".

Of *Practice* I believe that the only aspect that is dated "*to some extent*" is Drucker believed that he could convert everyone to a Protestant-based ethical management philosophy, although it has been the overwhelming policy in Western Society for many years both before and after the publication of *Practice*. Barnard, as one of Drucker's influences and later Odiorne more clearly as a commentator, both reflected that people's faiths across the world varied. Later, by the 1980s, the Netherlander management academic Geert Hofstede had developed ideas that even nations in close proximity with the same ethical religious bases, showed discernible variations (Pugh & Hickson 1989). Hofstede was then followed in the 1990s by fellow countryman Fons Trompenaars, who added to the ideas of individuality by his research into cultural diversity, which affected how we behave, how we think, how we resolve differences, and how we manage (Trompenaars 1993).

Subsequently, there has been a general awareness of the greater variation in cultural values and ethics, where the same words spoken to different people do not mean the same thing. We now talk about "*winning hearts and minds*" in response to some of the enormous cultural and ethical gulfs that exist. I qualify my comment with "*to some extent*" because the business ethics that Drucker promoted are needed to a greater extent today than ever before. Also Drucker's Protestant Christian adoption of Roman Law is still the basis for the "*commercial contracts*" used for conducting half of the world's commerce. This brings us back to Drucker's current position and yet again his ideas are still relevant and central to the issues of today. This time it is his ethical standards that are the best of the alternatives and are the most utilised internationally.

However what I find surprising about *Practice* is not only the proven relevance of its messages, but that Drucker found the time and energy, with his other ongoing commitments, to create a different type of management book. It was a book that was as near to being "*all embracing*" as anything, before or since, on "*What is the manager's job?*" So many of the references that were contemporaneous with Drucker were also pushing out the boundaries of management ideas, and those whom he selected still have relevance today. Examples are Knauth and Dean whom Drucker identified as writing on "*what the manager is supposed to do*", which was the objective of *Practice*. As Jewkes identified in his interchange of letters regarding Brech's book, what was needed was "*how to play the game*", whereas the market was being serviced with books that only set down the rules. It had been established that a few others had identified Jewkes need, some of Drucker's pioneers in particular saw the need for management to be a homogenous concept and practice - a "*philosophy of management*". Hopf, one of his immediate predecessors, Smiddy as a contemporary and colleague on the GE project, and Urwick, as both a predecessor and a contemporary all did. However they failed to deliver the solution because they all lacked the compelling vibrancy and vision that many have found in Drucker's work.

Maybe, above all, the appeal of *Practice* was that it was a treasure-trove for discovering it was written with GE as the inspirational base. I believe that IBM was the hidden find, confirmed by linking the work of Richardson & Walker and Juran followed by Thomas Watson Jnr though to "*Kaizen*", MbO, and then to Tennant and Roberts' of Warwick University identification of "*Hoshin Kanri*". What Tennant & Roberts' work has established is an important linkage between Drucker's works up to *Practice* and his later work in Japan. However this development has not been pursued in this research through space restriction and the work being outside the time zone of this research. It will be included in Volume III of this trilogy of Drucker research, including a research paper on these developments (*A View on the evaluation and outcome of Peter*

F Drucker's Management by Objectives and Self Control, was presented to the Management History Research Group, Starbuck 14 June, 2005).

A by-product of the examination of IBM is that although Watson Snr and Ford could be described as *"Caesar Managers"*, as both were proprietor managers, the contrast between the two, places them years apart. As Drucker noted, Ford's management was that of the past, while Watson Snr was so far ahead of this time, but was unaware of it because he was so focused and committed to his own organisation that he did not research what others were doing (1993:48).

But even Drucker could not cover every aspect of impacts on management. Throughout my search through his range of ideas, the only omission that was not conspicuous in his writing that I would have expected to find, was the French psychologist sociologist Gustave LeBon (1841-1931) for his work on crowd theory *Pyschologie de joules* (LeBon 1895) translated as *The Crowd: A Study of the Popular Mind* (LeBon 1897). I was anticipating that his work would have been linked to Hitler's manipulation of the masses and also Fords and GM's problems with the Unions. Smiddy and Naum referenced him in their 1954 book *Evolution of a Science of Management in America 1912-1956*. In Drucker (1986) he referenced Elias Canetti (1905-1994) as his first reference to crowd study.

The fact that Drucker has critics may have been in part brought about because of his critical attacks on sections of management. Three of his favourites are the *"old time economists"*, accountants and HR as the following examples illustrate. The first also illustrates his purposeful journalistic skills when interviewed about some of the current successors to the *"old time economists"* where he accused them of knowing nothing until twenty years after the events. For Drucker when they did come out of their wilderness for a time, the result was disastrous when:

> *"...after 1929, government took charge of the economy and economists were forced to become dogmatic, because suddenly they were policy makers. They began asserting, Keynes first, that they had the answers, and what's more the answers were pleasant. It was like a doctor telling you that you have inoperable liver cancer, but it will be cured if you go*

to bed with a beautiful 17- year-old. Keynes said there's no problem that can't be cured if only you keep purchasing power high. What could be nicer? The monetarist treatment is even easier:..."

(Inc October 1985).

The quotation is a good illustration of his skill to emphasise the seriousness by entertaining and educating simultaneously. In the process he had created a *"memory hook"* to aid retention of his messages. Earlier, when writing about economists in a traditional, serious manner, he links them with accountants and considered that it was their bad luck that people do not readily submit to 'quantification' and mathematical treatment. Consequently they *"consider these areas impractical* (but) *the enterprise is a community of human beings.... Otherwise it becomes paralyzed,* (and) *unable to act..."* (1954:61). Not only had Drucker made a predictable link between economists and accountants, but also by his holistic approach he had integrated their problems with society.

In support of Drucker's attack on accountants, they do not appear to have learnt from Drucker's criticism, as their major misdemeanours in performance are reported regularly in international scandals that beset all the major, and not so major, economies. Opinions from two heavyweight supporters of Drucker's criticism are from the British Accounting Standards Board. It proposes changes to separate the trading activities, so that, in the words of the board's chairman Sir David Tweedie when Accountants report, *"No longer will the profit and loss account look like a dogs dinner"* (*Profit and Loss; Accountants Should be Clearer* J Kelly *Financial Times* 17 June 1999). The American investment ace Warren Buffett believes that America Accounting is a business disgraced as they are actually proposing accounting tricks in order to flatter a company's earnings. *Warren Buffett The Man Who Made Billions With a Unique Investment Strategy* (Heller 2000:53). I align myself with Drucker and {add that company accounts should also show the organisations redundancy liability. This is because the purpose of accounts is to allow creditors to assess the risk of their activities with whom they trade. Without knowing the amount of redundancy liability the creditor is unable to determine, in times of change, whether the company can afford an essential restructuring to survive}.

The other function of management that had attracted much ire from Drucker was the now termed 'HR' Function. An intended move was afoot, which would cause a *"turf war"* as the accountants were plotting to have greater control over the HR function as was shown in *Moneymen see beauty in human capital* (Richard Donkin *Financial Times* 16 March 2003 from *Human Capital Management – The CEO's Perspective*). It was doubtful that Drucker would have considered this as progress, as his recorded view was that amalgamation weakness does not result in strength.

A more positive and recent development was the idea of measuring human capital and its relationship with other measures of business performance. The requirement of *"Accounting for People"* will become a legal requirement in the annual reports of publicly listed companies from the financial years commencing 1 January 2005. Also, Richard Donkin, in a report *Accounting for people does not add up* (*Financial Times* 2 September 2004) describes that progressive businesses were already turning in improved results, as did Sears in America by measuring employee and customer performance and satisfaction. Donkin recommended that businesses should not wait for legislation to make them act, as the advantages are evident. While endorsing the idea, he reported that there was *"dismay"* within.

The Chartered Institute of Personnel at the interpretation and recommendations of the Department of Trade and Industry. Maybe the HR Section was listening to Drucker's fifty-year-old messages of the primacy of enabling people to perform, but also that all functions need to be measured. However, it does appear to have received his messages that governments cannot manage.

As Drucker's work and standing continued to be discussed, how he was recognised in America was important. Not only was he *"the"* management guru, he was also the nation's responsible consumer's champion with his persuasive messages to organisations, as highlighted in *The Sage of Value and Services. At 90 Drucker still preaches Customers over Profits* (Fred Andrews *The New York Times* 17 November 1999). In a society that had a stronger consumer lobby than the UK, Drucker was seen as a rational counter-force to Ralph Nader, who was recognised, as the *"gadfly"* of organisations through his strident approach. An illustration of Nader's method is in his 1965 book *Unsafe at any Speed* which is an assault on GM and Chevrolet.

In Britain, we do not have anyone like Drucker, and therefore have difficulty in appreciating him in full. We neither have an all embracing national management guru nor anyone in the management movement who is recognised as championing the consumer's interests. Edward Brech, who accompanied Drucker when he visited The British Institute of Management in the 1960's, said that Drucker never had as great an impact on British managers as he did with their American counterparts, despite the fact that those who attended his lectures in Britain received his ideas with great acclaim. Maybe it was a matter of being in tune, or in time with your audience. Drucker could be said to have left Europe behind by rejecting Rathenau's cartelisation, Weber's monopolies and Schumpeter's intelligent monopolies, as he passed through Britain without finding any great compulsion to stay, after having examined and rejected Keynes economics, before departing for America, where he conceptualised for them, their belief in the entrepreneur.

Despite Drucker's popularity, he does have a small hard-core of critics. Maybe they would have been happier if he had been a hedgehog who does one thing well rather than a fox who does many things (*The Hedgehog and The Fox* [Berlin 1953]). Drucker concluded that those with a simple mission have impact while *"the rest of us with multiple interests instead of a simple mission, are certain to fail and have not impact at all"* (1979:255) – but we enjoy ourselves. I believe that not only has Drucker enjoyed himself but he also has, and will to continue to have impact.

Drucker up to his death continued with a reduced workload that reflects his age. His active interest still included the works of 'The Peter Drucker Foundation for Non Profit Management', which was probably influenced again by Schumpeter.

"On New Year's Day 1950, Peter drove his father Adolph Drucker to visit Joseph Schumpeter, then in his last year of teaching at Harvard and in rapidly failing health (he died eight days later). He and Adolph

reminisced about their young days in Vienna…. The conversation took a more serious turn when Schumpeter, answering a question from Adolph, said: "You know, Adolph, I have now reached the age where I know that it is not enough to be remembered for books and theories. One does not make a difference unless it is a difference in people's lives." Drucker says he has "never forgotten that conversation." It gave him the measure of his achievement"

(Beatty 1998:187-188).

2. What is My Contribution?

I believe that my contribution widens the consideration of Drucker's work because it is the first full-scale research effort by a Briton and also by a practising businessman. As a consequence of these different foci I have added to the scholarship on Drucker by increasing the understanding of his contribution by continuing the work of his previous biographers, to whom I record my debt. I have not intentionally looked for gaps that needed to be filled, because my route has been determined tracing the evolution of Drucker's ideas. However, the outcome is that some of the gaps have been closed, which has contributed to the picture of Drucker.

Through these two foci I believe the research has benefited. Firstly by focusing on the British perspective, which has helped to add to the continuity of tracking Drucker's early development, first in Austria then in Germany and into Britain at the time when the forces of change appeared to be driven by their own dynamic energy. What has been highlighted, against this background of apprehension and the threatened annihilation of Britain and the destruction of Europe is that Drucker endeavoured to produce a new society after the assassination of the Archduke Franz Ferdinand (1863-1914) on 28 June 1914 signalled the end of old Europe. It is from this event, which gives Drucker's passage through Europe a logical sequence from his native Austria to a Germany converting to Nazism and into Britain, which was at the mercy of the events of change rather than shaping them. That Drucker would gather his thoughts and develop his management ideas in America was not surprising because attitudes towards management were more accommodating and the immediate pressures of war was not as critical as they were in Europe. I also believe that the British focus by its close association with Europe has heightened the reliance of the European contribution to Drucker's management ideas, in particular and to management in general.

Of the second focus, which has added to the perspective of Drucker's contribution, is my experience as a businessman. This is a world where survival depends upon a dominance of result producing activities and outcomes, not just to win the business game but also to ensure the very survival of the enterprise. Simplistically it has to be a game of consistently winning, which cannot be achieved by speculation, but only by systematic dynamic process, and the evolution, examination and re-examination of ideas. This is the process that Drucker has used in his practical-based theoretic work. This is also why his work is relevant and by the evidence the most relevant to managers in general but to business managers in particular. What the research has done is systematically and sequentially tracked the developments of Drucker's ideas that lead from his search for a shaping force for his new society to the discovery of that force as management. His experience and his influences here have been recorded, discussed and examined as he progressed his research to the evolution of his answers to the manager's requirement to perform successfully and responsibly by his *integrated* MbO. As a testing template of Drucker's evolution of those ideas Appendix 1 Peter Ferdinand Drucker Time Line for the Period 1909-1954 not only provides and audit for the evolution but is also the first identified time-line of Drucker and his ideas. Of Drucker's MbO it fits the criterion of Kurt Lewin's (1890-1947) adage *"Nothing is as practical as a good theory"*. What this time-line has also done is remind followers of Drucker and of his unique contributions and act as a convenient starting point for those who are not familiar with his work.

The practical outcome of my research and analysis is that I have identified some of Drucker's imperative messages, hopefully given them a greater emphasis, and maybe set them in a different context. I have also identified Drucker's *"new economists"* who are absent except for some

226

referencing to Schumpeter in the work of his other commentators, and in so doing I have highlighted another strength in Drucker's work. Also identified has been the disregard of economists as contributors to management ideas by the prominent British management writer in the same period of Drucker. The research outcome of my book is that it has reviewed Drucker's contribution and confirmed that fifty years after the publication of *Practice* the ideas that flowed from it are still relevant to practitioners and students of management.

To summarise, I believe I have extended the research into Drucker's contribution to management. Through the work of Greenwood and Odiorne, who complimented each other with their different sensitivities, I have refocused MbO and hopefully added to the clarity of its messages, rather than add to the confusion.

3.   What is My Research?

Drucker has made a philosophy out of management by extending its boundaries. He has achieved this by utilising his considerable intellectual ability, continued research, acute awareness of the ongoing events and his experience. In doing so, he has added the idea of it being an intellectual challenge to the original idea of it being merely a process. His ideas have been generated by synthesising the best ideas of others, evolving them, and by adding his own original contributions. Although the general contention that he sits in nobody's school has been confirmed, I do believe that it has been established that he does sit in other's classrooms. The outcome of his contribution is that he has been the most consequential contributor to management ideas and their integration during the greater part of the second half of the 20thc. This contribution has been recognised in America and, although from less detailed evidence, in Japan. Yet in Britain, while he was the most quoted management writer in the quality press, he features only nominally in academic writing and contemporary management publications, although the evidence was that many of their ideas are rooted in his writing. An illustration can be provided by analysing twenty-four volumes of *The British Journal of Management* (March 2000 to June 2004). Although he was mentioned more often than his other *"influences"* of Berle & Means, Schumpeter, Fayol, GM, Barnard and Weber he was still only referenced five times. The topics were new organisations, the survival of universities, Marks and Spencer and, entrepreneurship twice. There were also several other papers that were central to Drucker's ideas, where consideration of his contribution would have been appropriate. This begs the question; are we missing out by not examining his work and repeating the cliché that *"he is an armchair philosopher"*, without carrying out the rigorous research that his critics demand of others? Or, by classifying him as a *"popularist management writer"*, are we relying on what has become conventional *"folklore"*, rather than examining the evidence regarding this most acknowledged management writer?

I believe that this raises the question; had he become a victim of a pattern in management academia where the methodology is more important than the practical utility of the research? However, I can only claim to be a supporter of the ongoing argument into the practicality of management research. In this respect, I am following Drucker, who had never lost touch with the needs of his primary audience, the managers and the students of management and their need to make ideas work in practice. They needed a *"lode star"* to follow to obtain results, which was not only the *raison d'etat* for their existence, but also the facilitator of their very survival. Inconclusive hypotheses are not only irrelevant to their needs; they are also an unwelcome and unnecessary distraction. It was because Drucker has serviced these requirements that he has remained relevant and maintained his following while so many of his 'pretenders' have failed. It is these reasons that Drucker is placed centrally with his argument that managers can only be taught how to learn the practice of management because management is a job that can only be effectively learnt by the experience of managers who have also learnt by practise. Drucker emphasises his position when he writes, that managers must always be prepared for things going wrong because they always will. However, by then the managers must have learned what they cannot be taught, not only that they have to act, but know how to act effectively.

What this research has not done during the period of this research regarding Drucker, minor exceptions excluded, is examine his papers, articles and lecture notes. Nor has the development of his identified ideas been examined as they were further evolved in his later works.

This leaves opportunities to link *Practice*, his *"how to do"* book, with his later *"what to do"* books, thus collating all of his ideas on management dynamics together.

Further questions that remain unanswered, besides Drucker's position in Britain, are his reception and impacts in the other countries affected by the thirty plus different language translations of his work, and in particular Japan as the world's second biggest economy. Of his influences, many deserve further examination in their own right and also in relation to Drucker's work. A project of this nature would benefit from being conducted in the countries where the work was published for accessibility.

If the foregoing conclusion of this research is treated as a *"shopping list"*, then a similar process could be applied to his later work and also research his ideas on society and politics. It is only if these tasks are concluded that we can move nearer to being able to appreciate the last words on the contributions of Peter Drucker.

As Kantrow wrote, there are plenty of ideas for everyone. For researchers there is much material still to be examined, even including his work as a scholar of Japanese Art.

4. The Arguments and Evidence that Support this Research

I have established that Drucker was not only a most competent synthesiser, but also a creator of original ideas. He had approached management with the minimum of preconceived ideas as he set out on a journey of discovery as a *"free spirit"*. He has shown a willingness to examine and be influenced by a wider range of ideas than any other identified management writer. His starting position for this examination is described as follows, he is *"primarily a social scientist that utilised knowledge for all fields"* (Bonaparte & Flaherty 1970:29-31). Odiorne adds similarly that the fact that *"he is a political scientist at heart and a management scientist by request only is often overlooked. Also he is probably nearer to his fellow Austrians*

Hayek and Mises than to McGregor, Maslow or Likert". Here I disagree with Odiorne; I believe that Drucker spans all five and that his work with McGregor on Personnel Management was synergetic. Odiorne then continues by saying that Drucker was forced to pay attention to MbO as a natural product of Decentralisation. Here I agree with Odiorne, and concur with his conclusion. For Odiorne, MbO was the logical result of the "*response of his audience in lectures and books*". His motive came not from engineering efficiency but from "*the strong belief that the preservation of the capitalist system required some basic structural changes in the corporate system and preferably from within*" (Odiorne in *Business Horizons* October 1978). The result of these and Drucker's other holistic examination has, in my opinion, produced the most eclectic range of management ideas to date by any one writer, and also in my previously noted personal experience, the most practical ideas that managers should consider adapting. For those who rejected Drucker's ideas out of hand there is evidence of the result: "*Agha Hasan Abedi, founder of BCCI, once boasted to his employees that he understood management far better than Peter Drucker, …whom he dismissed as an apprentice. Hasan Abedi of course was responsible for one of the biggest bank failures in history*" (Flaherty 1999:2). (As this document goes to print, the liquidator is now concluding his work and arranging to make the final distribution to the claimants).

The three primary ideas of Drucker that have emerged during the period under examination are:

- Decentralisation, which is a practice of management,
- MbO, which is also the all-embracing management philosophy;
- Managing People, where Drucker advocates empowerment and persuasion in order to obtain long-term results, rather than pressure applied for short-term gain.

Decentralisation is still in use in Britain, America, and Japan. In relative terms this was a simple first step that emerged in *Concept*. It led into the more intellectually challenging MbO, which is a refinement to the application of Decentralisation, or an independent stand-alone philosophy. Integrated into these two primary management ideas was the

230

ever present and most complex issue of people, which was impossible to avoid in any evolution of management ideas that are going to have any use. This was why Drucker correctly puts the most emphasis on people in his work.

Regarding the totality of Drucker's ideas and those of his acknowledged influences, what has been illustrated is how few "*totally new*" 'major' management ideas have been discovered in the last fifty years. My research has emphasised that it is because Drucker so comprehensively "*discovered management*" that it has resulted in him being established as the most consequential management writer since the late 1950's. This conclusion is supported by the overwhelming majority of people of quality who commented favourably on his work contemporaneously, and who continues to do so to the present day.

With regard to my own effort, in concluding this research I am reminded that Manfred Eigen, the German Nobel Chemist, wrote, "*work is only one PhD thesis*" (Kauffman 1993:464). But what Eigen did not consider was the proverb "*that a workman's work is never done*". I accepted some time ago that I had "*bought into*" not a management course by Peter Drucker, but a new education on the lines of Desiderius Erasmus' (1466-1536) objective "*When I get a little money I buy books*", and continue working, which Drucker promised himself when examining Verdi's efforts. So has the other European born octogenarian, American Jacques Barzun, whose perceptive review of *Future* also compliments *Economic Man*. There do seem to be many similarities between Barzun and Drucker, both as polymaths and as leaders in their fields; Barzun as the conscience of American Culture and Drucker as the conscience of American Management.

As for my own achievement with this research, my primary aim, when I conceived the idea of research into Drucker's work, was to make a contribution by identifying clear management messages that can be communicated clearly to younger managers to help them avoid making the old mistakes repetitively and focus on the priority areas. This is a step in the right direction. I also believe that, although my research is based on only a relatively small sample of Drucker's work, it has its own homogeneity because it covers the period when he was discovering

231

management for himself. He describes it as being out there and waiting to be discovered. This is the work for younger Drucker scholars to join in.

However it is appropriate and relevant that Drucker gets the last word *"The World's greatest management writer Peter Drucker turns 95"* is the banner above the front-page title of the *Financial Times* (16 November 2004). The back-up article is *"Drucker managed to do it first. Simon London meets the 95-year-old who first identified the subject as being worth serious study and whose ideas are yet to be usurped"*.

PETER FERDINAND DRUCKER TIMELINE FOR THE PERIOD 1909 – 1954

Highlighting the consequential events in his life and the management ideas that he identified.

Austria

1909
- Peter Ferdinand Drucker was born in Vienna 19th November 1909.

Childhood spent in Vienna
- Meets Freud, Hayek, Mises, Schumpeter and a wide range of intellectuals and artists.

Is influenced by Gestalt's philosophy of holistic thought.
- Receives Classics education.

1923 - Summer 1927
- Abandons Young Socialist Rally and decides to become a 'Bystander'.
- Leaves Vienna

Germany

Autumn 1927 - Hamburg
- Commences work as a clerk in an export business in Hamburg, Germany.
- Enrols as a part-time Law student at Hamburg University.
- First published work 'The Impact of the Panama Canal on World Trade'.

1928 - Influenced by:-
- Verdi's life-long quest for perfection in his work.

- Kierkegaard's writing on Protestant Christianity. It resulted in Drucker regarding an ecumenical element to his life as essential; it is the moral foundation for his work.

1929 - Frankfurt
- Transfers his part-time studies in Law to Frankfurt University while working as a Foreign and Economics News journalist.
- Joins the German Young Conservatives.
- Attends Schumpeter's lectures at Bonn University.
- Commences part-time lecturing at Frankfurt University.

1931
- Completes his doctorate in International and Public Law 'Die Rechfertigungdes Vokerrechts aus dem Staatswillen' (The Justification of International Law and the Will of the State)

1933
- Produces his monograph on Stahl 'Fr J Stahl: Konservative Staatslehre ünd Geschichtliche Entwiclung Motrtueringan' (Friedrich Julius Stahl: Conservative Theory of the State and Historical Development). A career shaping work; Stahl aligns with Kierkegaard Christianity, and adds the need for a constitutional Head of State to provide a robust democracy that will allow changes (Drucker's Discontinuities) without the breakdown of society or the need for revolution.
- Nazi's burn the Stahl monograph for two reasons, because he is a Jew by birth, and that his political philosophy is for democracy.
- Drucker providentially leaves for London via Vienna.

England

Summer 1933
- Works in England including a trainee in an insurance organisation.

January 1934
- Joins a small merchant bank in London, as an economist report-writer and secretary and remains with the company until he leaves England.
- Attends John Maynard Keynes' lectures at Kings College Cambridge University.
- Introduced to Japanese 14-19th Century Painting, and would later become an expert in the Zen period.
- Commences writing for British Newspapers.

1935
- Commenced writing for the American Press.

1936
- Published paper Die Judenfrage in Deutschland (The Jewish Question).

January 1937
- Contributes to an English language book on the German economy 'Germany the Last Four Years'.
- Marries German, Doris Schmitz at Hampstead Registry office, London 16th January 1937.
- Although now a banker and offered a partnership with the bank, he leaves for America via Vienna.

United States of America

1937
- Continues working as a journalist for the American and British quality markets.

May 1939
- End of Economic Man published.
  An analysis of the collapse of European Europe: a social and political study with wide ranging references, which attests to Drucker's eclectic

235

search for the *"new society"* that is desperately needed. The American model is the *"hope"* as identified by Alexis De Tocqueville.

- Of the wide ranging references Kierkegaard and Stahl are mentioned confirming their previous impact.
- New influences added including Walther Rathenau the German polymath, businessman, diplomat, politician, and writer.
- Robert Owen for advocating industrial democracy and as the almost saintly figure of early Capitalism
- Hitler is the most dominant character in the book whose destructive policies are catalogued factually. Hitler's only positive influence is his reprivatisation of the German Banks. This would eventually become Privatisation in 1969, which inspired the privatisation movement that was founded in Britain and then spread internationally.
- Drucker states that economists in general are, responsible for the social consequences of their work but that, economists cannot solve society's problems. Maynard Keynes and Adam Smith receive specific mention.
- Henry Ford is credited with destroying the classic economist's theory, by dominating the market without monopoly.
- Churchill is among the reviewers, subjecting the book to a vigorous examination.
- Establishes a political economic consultancy.

1940
- Returns to lecturing with a part-time appointment at Sarah Lawrence College, Bronxville, New York.

1942
- Moves to Bennington College Vermont as a full-time lecturer.

- Re-establishes an earlier contact with Karl Polanyi, which confirms Drucker's willingness to consider in detail other socially based intellectual ideas without necessarily agreeing with them.
- Embarks on an extensive lecture programme throughout American colleges

236

- Work as a serious journalist continues to expand.
- Future of Industrial Man published.
  Sets out Drucker's society of Christian individuality with status and function, and Rathenau's inspired autonomous self-governing plant community. This is Drucker's answer to correcting the shortcoming of the lack of progress in developing the society of economic man, which had failed to progress at a complimentary pace with the mass production industrial order.
- Future's wide ranging references records an emerging development and interest in management.
- Berle & Means (1933), and Marshall Dimock are credited with identifying that in the Corporation the shareholders have lost owner control, which is now in the power of the manager (Rathenau identified this earlier in1919).
- Owen D Young is identified as having had the solution for ten years by accepting the 'status quo' by converting Ordinary Shares into Interest Bearing Bonds.
- Frederick Winslow Taylor is credited for making the worker an efficient standardised machine.
- Ford is linked with Taylor for the innovation *"of the worker as an efficient automatic standardised machine"*.

1942
- Adam Smith receives further credit.
- Karl Marx as an economist is described as pre-industrial.
- Schumpeter receives positive attention.
- The American system is the basis for the new industrial society because of its advanced political system, although its social patterns are the most promising they need changes.
- Trotskyist James Burnham's well-argued ideas for a manager-dominated society are considered but rejected.
- Management identified as the life-giving element.
- Future's American reviews identify Drucker as a brilliant intellectual with an outstanding range of enquiry. British reviewers appear to be

237

depressed by the nearness of war to see any cause for an optimistic future.

1943
- Drucker became an American Citizen

Late 1943/1944
- An examination of General Motors is commissioned.
- Drucker meets Harry Hopf to obtain a *"quickies course in management"*. *"Only a handful of books on General Management exist"*. The following are indexed for their general management ideas: - Chester I Barnard, Burnham, Frank Knight, James Mooney, Schumpeter, Alfred P Sloan Jnr, Taylor and Ordway Tead.

1946
- Concept of the Corporation published.
  It is the first book to examine the Corporation as a social organisation. Regularly regarded as a study of General Motors as a management organisation, which it is, but two thirds of the book is about society and many of Drucker's social ideas based upon his *"self-governing plant community"*. The book sets out Drucker's manifesto for:

Society
- The Corporation is central in society.
- The dynamic force within the Corporation is management.
- It is a pluralistic society with Government only undertaking projects that business cannot, as the giant public works of the Tennessee Valley Authority Scheme (TVA).
- Drucker's society rejects *laissez-faire* economics for a democratically based free-market model with markets managed to act responsibly towards the citizen.
- That it is in the Corporation's interest to provide security for the workers with wage guarantees for those with the greatest personal responsibilities.
- Labour's greatest fear is redundancy, which could be negated by developing an employment fund within the Corporation.

- GM has provides for *"character loans"* (Venture Capital), which helps their small business partners.
- Of the Union's, their role fails socially, through concentrating on economic issues but at the worst John Llewellyn Lewis the Mine Workers Union leader is identified for promoting major anti-social practices.
- Federal tax requirement is criticised for being anti-business start- ups, by taxing them the same as mature businesses.

Management:

- The Primacy of Management is identified. That it can be analysed and planned is credited to Ordway Tead.
- Top management's job is strategic and is different to operations managers, which is result focused.
- Management's first responsibility is the survival of the business.
- Decentralisation (Federal) is launched as the preferred structure for the Corporations. It is the first detailed description of Decentralisation and its components.
- Functional Decentralisation is also recognised, as a structure but should be substituted by Decentralisation.
- Decisions are management's responsibility and should be based upon fact and agreement.
- Motivation is essential throughout the organisation.
- Leadership is essential in management: Drucker notes that Chester I Barnard at AT&T uses assimilated testing but he advocates actual experience.
- Training is needed to provide managers of the future and develop opportunities for all.
- GM is winning its competition battle with Fords by Decentralisation and annual models.
- Fords are losing because it is too big for centralised control and also it is retaining basic rather than annual models.
- The power of the market is recognised through the GM annual models, which illustrates the customer power by choice. The customer's decision may seem illogical to the manager but it is the

239

customer's prerogative to make a decision. It is the practical working of the essential *"market check"*. The essentiality of the Market, Innovation, and Entrepreneurship: - Will become a major area of Drucker's work.

- The foundation of Drucker's business management and many other people's management ideas through Drucker can be traced back to Concepts. The management part of the book is a large *"case study of GM"*. GM is *"a well"* that Drucker will return to continually for his ideas.
- Alfred Sloan Jnr, Chairman of the Board, is established as Drucker's management mentor. Sloan and GM being the formative influence on his management ideas.
- Amongst the other influences at GM is Donaldson Brown, who was responsible for developing the most Advanced Cost Systems, which provides the basis for Impartial Measurement. This will become a major area of Drucker's work
- And also Charles Erwin Wilson the president who developed progressive worker benefit systems. However Drucker is cautious about business making long-term promises that they will not eventually be able to deliver.
- Drucker concludes that accountants are not making the contribution that they should. They aren't measuring the right things except for Donaldson Brown who is using statistics and apply *"Return on Investment"* (ROI) as a measure. Accountants generally are meeting statutory requirements but not making a sufficient contribution to management. Drucker extends Donaldson Brown's ideas and asks: *"How can we Measure?"*

Other ideas not identified as GMs:
- That the organisation is a social organisation is credited to Mooney & Reiley. Drucker would adjust this in his later work and attribute Rathenau's earlier identification of the 20[th]c and the 18th & 19[th]c work of François Fourier and Comte de-Saint-Simon.
- Industry's workers are its greatest asset, yet people and the Primacy of Human Relations within the organisation is not being effectively

implemented. This is because Personnel Management is failing in its commitment; they are not in general focusing on the management of the workers. This will become a major area of Drucker's work.

- The use of psychological tests is rejected, as they only establish what people cannot do. Drucker describes them as gadgets of Personnel Management. This introduces the word gadgets as Drucker's term for fads or ill-conceived theories.
- The Hawthorne experiments of the 1930s proved the worker's need for job satisfaction and colleague relationships at work.
- Taylor is credited for his contribution, of new theories of mass production technology and also for his contribution of industrial manipulation.
- Communications are recorded as non-existent, creating a major problem.
- Rejected is aping the military organisation with Staff and Line services. There should only be "*Line*" with the support of specialist services.
- Foreman are an enigma, they are essential but are neither labour nor management. They need one place. (Tead, Urwick and IBM have already resolved their position in management)
- Drucker examines the question "*What is profit and how can it be measured?*" The correct answer is essential for the survival of the enterprise. This will become a major area of Drucker's work.
- Game theory and risk assessments.
- 'Gadgets' Drucker's term for superficial management ideas.
- Concept is identified as a retrograde step for Drucker's promising career. Management and corporations are not regarded as academically acceptable.
- The 'reviews' regard the book as having brilliant flashes of insights and the first effort of its time, but Drucker had still to prove his theories. There is also some recognition that profits are too low.
- Concept launches Drucker's management career; his management consultancy commences adding to his existing activities.

1947

- British edition of Concept published as 'Big Business'. The title was changed because the publishers believed that the British would not understand the meaning of 'Corporation'.

1949

- Drucker moves back to New York to become Professor of Management at the Graduate Business School of New York University.

March 1950

- Commences writing for the Harvard Business Review with Management Must Manage which is a review of 'The New Society'. He will contribute more articles than any other outside contributor and of all the active contributors will contribute over the longest time span.

April 1950

- The New Society is published.
- Society covers three areas. The first is confirmation of Drucker's original ideas, the second are refinements, and the third are basically new ideas.
  Existing and Refinement of Ideas:
- Society must be Christian based and is central to American pluralism, which is working.
- Management is spreading to other parts of society. The clamour for it is the result of disorganisation.
- Mass production is the method of production and is being widely used not only in industry but also in other branches of commerce.
- Divorce of ownership and control is repeated with Owen D Young's ideas having become practice for Fords' "*Trust*" shares.
- Functional Decentralisation is now accepted as an alternative structure where there is no market-test.
- The self-governing plant community has now become "*The Autonomous Self-Governing Plant Community*", which is essential within the plant to give the workers management vision. It has now been

242

extended to become essential beyond the enterprise and be central to a free industrial society, which provides "*welfare*" but not "*hand-outs*".

- "*Hawthorne*" is carried forward with the team including Mayo recognised for establishing the existence of "*informal relationships*" regardless for those formally imposed.

1950

- Workers want to work.
- Work has to an act of integration
- Wages should be based upon the ability of the organisation to pay and will then vary depending on cost of living, efficiency and profitability.
- Opportunities for advancement are reducing for manual workers and need to be increased.
- Unions receive more detailed examination that further confirms that they are still a negative force. Their right to strike where it endangers society is unacceptable and should be illegal in a democracy.
- Schumpeter is credited with recognising the importance of the "*innovator*" rather than the capitalist. Keynes is receiving further attention most is adverse.
- "*Entrepreneurs, innovators and risk takers*" should not be excluded by lacking a college education as a passport as schoolteachers would not select "*the entrepreneurs, the innovators and risk takers*".
- Communications without which the enterprise will not survive needs to be the "*ears*" for the workers with management supplying more information.
- Profit has now moved to - The first law of the enterprise – The law of Loss Avoidance.
- The "*profit*" motive is irrelevant. Drucker's four reasons for profit are:

  (1)   cost of doing business;
  (2)   cost of staying in business;
  (3)   contribution for other business features;
  (4)   payment for society's non-economic needs.

- Profit is still too low as it is the only source of capital for new equipment needed for productivity.

243

- Profit is needed for society to survive but there is hostility to profit within the plant, and outside in society.
- The worker's resistance to profit is caused by the high salaries paid to managers, not by high profit. The focus should be on the net after tax payment.
- However when the public were surveyed they agreed that 8-10% was a *"fair return"*. When it accumulated to $2million is was considered excessive. There is a communications gap - nobody wants to listen.

The second law of the enterprise – The law of Higher Output.
- Society demands that managers produce better products at lower prices.
- Workers are resisting the challenge as they see profit as a charge on wages and incorrectly believing that higher output is jeopardising their jobs while the converse is true.
- To add security of employment, labour should be treated as a capital cost that rises and falls with the market. This would result in a guaranteed minimum wage, which is not a Guaranteed Annual Wage, which is not possible.
- The Labour Force is the major productive resource of any enterprise. The root of the problem is the conflicting view between labour as a commodity, and as a capital resource.
- Personnel Management has become Human Resources. Drucker has now become more constructive and recommends that top management should develop the function, bridging across departments and embracing the whole enterprise.
- The need for the competitive market as the performance measure is confirmed.
- The relationship between profit and productivity is developing.
- Big business is the preferred model but it must act ethically to its smaller associates.
- Business is too big when layers of bureaucratic support is necessary.
- In the society that is largely pre-industrial, managers aren't doing their jobs because they aren't seeing the big picture. They are performing primarily as specialist rather than as generalist.

- The new industrial middle class of middle managers, technicians and supervisors are the *"nerve and circulation system of the enterprise"*.
- Management's attitudes are spreading within the organisations. But there must always be clear boundaries as managers must always be the managers. Regrettably they have to play it by ear because the tools of measurement are primitive.
- American capital markets are handicapped because they are still 'carriage trade'. The tax and banking systems are debarring *"access to risk capital"*.

New Ideas
- American capitalisation, which is market competitive free trade, still has to evolve into a functioning and free society. The previous idea that Europe could adopt the American model is no longer considered possible. The cultural and political differences are too great. Europe will have to find its own model.
- The American Cast Iron Pipe Company is examined as a case study of a worker's co-operative. It is a working model for the self-governing plant community and also that workers have developed the essential management vision. Although Drucker sees merit in their achievement it could not be a national model.
- Drucker continues developing his management milestones.
- Identifies The Knowledge Society.
- That people are our greatest assets.
- That big business must treat small businesses particularly partners ethically otherwise the government will introduce punitive measures.
- The book is reviewed favourably with comments as, setting down a solution of our modern time, which includes a society between Communism and Capitalism. Drucker is described as one of America's experts across a wide ranging of specialised knowledge supported by his experience
- Society is a *"first"* in attempting to integrate the enterprise into a free-market democratic society and have regard for people within and outside the organisation. This identifies coherently what will become the *"Stakeholders"*.

245

- Drucker's work on Practice commenced while working as part of the team of consultants during the massive reorganisation of GE, which started in the early 1950s. Drucker eventually became the principle consultant.

1954
- The Practice of Management is published.
- Practice is written as a handbook for his consultancy clients and for people who want to understand the newly recognised force in society – management.
- Practice is about business management. The vital principle that determines its nature is economic performance.
- But it is the manager who is "*the dynamic life giving element in every business*".
- Foremen are now part of management with IBM's ideas being the most progressive. But foremen should no longer be called foremen or supervisors but managers to reflect their new role.
- Drucker claims that with the book he discovered and made a discipline out of 'the practice of management, which was waiting to be discovered'.
- The days of management by intuition only are over.
- As Economic Man and Future, which considered the influences and ideas to evolve a new and working society as the foundations for his work, Practice reflects Drucker's development from other management thinkers and shapers, and records that he is making his own unique contribution.
- Concept was based upon GM as the lead case study with Fords used as a contrast.
- Practice was written while Drucker was a management consultant at GE and uses over one hundred case studies as the book is written out of many years' experience of working with managements of all sizes of businesses.
- An extensive range of credits is given for those who have helped make the book possible including consultancy clients.

- His search for *"management ideas"* is as extensive as for his society in his earlier works. His *"quickie list"* in Concepts has now been expanded to a hundred or so writers on management. Some on the new list are writers on general management. Many as Schumpeter and Knight as economists write extensively on related functions of management as do many other specialists.
- Drucker has considerably developed his ideas and has established that management is an Integrated Discipline that must draw from as wide a range of ideas that can make a contribution. His message is that the objectives and functions of management will in general terms be similar in any business. Although the particular emphasis will vary, no necessary objectives or functions can be ignored.
- Drucker sets the manager many tasks, including:
- The First Duty of the Manager:

    (i) Define the objectives of his own job;
    (ii) Define his own job and his workers with regard to the aims of the organisation including removing non-performers;
    (iii) Help those for whom he has responsibility to reach their objectives by providing the necessary resources and also by acting as an assistant to them.

- The First Responsibility of the Enterprise to society is to operate at a profit because it is the 'wealth creating' and 'wealth producing' organ of society. Only slightly less important than profit is growth by productivity.
- Management's First Responsibility in Society was to ask and give the answer to *"What is our Business?"* followed by the supplementary question *"What should it be?"*
- One of the Manager's Responsibilities is, to never undermine the public good by only acting in the businesses own self-interest.
- The First Principle of an Organisation is that the individual's strength becomes part of the groups.
- The First Function of Management is Economic Performance.

247

- The Second Function of Management is "*to make productive enterprise out of human and material resources*".
- The Five Operations in the works of the Manager are

    (i)   Set Objectives;
    (ii)   Organise;
    (iii) Motivate and Communicate
    (iv)   Measure, all as Henri Fayol and
    (v)   Developing People. Drucker noted that every operation are subjects on their own and can be further subdivided

Practice identifies seven major integrated ideas for managers.

1 Management by Objectives and Self-Control — MbO is a complete principle of management.
2 Decentralisation (Federal) as the preferred structure. Although others, as task force, and team working are becoming necessary as an integrated part of Decentralisation. Hybrid structures and project management are being anticipated.
3 The Integration of Productivity by Automation and Profit. Profit serves three functions:

    (i)   the ultimate test of business performance;
    (ii)   risk premium for staying and being in business;
    (iii) source of future capital.

The two functions of work – planning and work, now need to be integrated.
4. Automation is the new method of working, which for Juran includes Total Quality. Drucker acknowledges Joseph Moses Juran's importance but does not attribute Total Quality to Juran or identify it as a separate function or philosophy.
5 Essentiality of meaningful measurement for all functions.

248

6 The Entrepreneurial functions of marketing and innovation are the purpose of a business - "*to create a customer*". To which was later added "*and get paid*".

7 People are central to the organisation and its greatest asset.
The Manager's Job - is total integration. Only the manager is responsible for setting objectives, making decisions, and producing results. It is not a problem solving activity because problem solving presupposes that the problem is known. The manager must first discover - what is the right question!

Other ideas that have emerged

- The law of the one-man CEO is rejected. It is a team job
- Delayering or Re-engineering
- Brain power is replacing muscle power
- Added Value or Value Added
- Outsourcing –v- Vertical Integration
- Danger of Short-termism
- Return on Invested Capital
- The growth of the professional worker and the need to establish their place in management.
- The Emergence of the Technical Worker
- Empowerment
- Power and Value of "*Brands*"
- Voluntary regulation is better than those imposed by Government
- Span of Control –v- Span of Managerial Responsibility
- The use of "*check lists*" to confirm predicable parameters and identify exceptions.
- The Continual Learning Society and that people are to be responsible for their own self-development.
- Benchmarking
- Identifies the Hygiene factors, which predates Herzberg's work. The prime motivator is proper pay before profit sharing and bonuses. For Mayo relationships at work were more satisfied than pay. However for Drucker the worker's first priority is security of income.

- Drucker's Theory 'X' and Theory 'Y' ideas were at least parallel and may be been in advance of McGregor's.
- The structure of the business must follow the business not the business follow the structure. This predates the credit given to Chandler for being the first to draw this conclusion in 1962.
- No business can do everything. They all have strengths that they should play to. Later would be repackaged by Tom Peter & Robert Waterman; Hamel & Prahalad
- MbO would be extrapolated into Kaplan & Norton's Balanced Scorecard in 1996.
- Operational Research is identified as a decision making tool. It has now been subsumed into general good practice for decision making. Other analytical methods are also identified. The advice is that methods are to be used in combination to obtain safest results.
- Attention is drawn to a survey conducted by a successful American bank that followed the results of their survey. They asked their head of research *"Are there any earmarks, which will tell us whether the management of a corporation is good or bad?"* The question was tougher than it looked. The answer was *"If the top executive in a company gets a salary several times as large as the salaries paid to Number Two, Three, Four men, you can be pretty sure the firm is badly managed"*. (Harpers April 1954)
- Many people will want to work beyond normal retirement age.
- Management should not burden their success with unsustainable promises – as today's under-funded pension commitments confirm.
- IBM are identified, as practising 'Kaizen' but it is not termed as such. Worker's progress and development is regularly examined usually in them being placed where they can contribute best. Workers are also members of the task teams that improve and develop the products from design concepts by engineering the product.
- Drucker does not claim that all the ideas are his own or that they are all contemporary. As Management by Exception, which was a Taylor idea from the turn of the 19th/20thc. But many change their meaning when given his holistic treatment.
- Practice has drawn together into one book a wider range of management ideas differently than previously.

250

- It records that a new breed of economists has been identified to contribute to management with Schumpeter.
- Drucker has set a life task for himself and others of discoveries and progress that management needs to make.
- Respective contemporaries confirmed that he is - one of the leading if not "*the*" management thinker of his time.
- His positioning of people as central for the manager's task, management has confirmed management as a social science more extensively than previously.
- Management cannot be taught but can be learnt.
- Management training will not 'take' until people have experience, which can never be taught only learnt through experience.
- Managers can only learn their job by the experience of practice. They must be allowed to make mistakes to learn how to correct the big mistakes that always occur later.
- All members of the organisation are workers.
- Of people first they must be responsible for their own performance. Then they can and must contribute for the team's performance.
- Members of the organisation must receive freedom, status, function and what they must bring with them is integrity. If all are present then the spirit of motivation should ensue.
- Of managers they have human frailties like us all but what can never be missing is integrity or morality, which has to be brought to the job.
- Despite all the promises that managers make they must always retain 'a welfare claims' to protect the corporate body at the cost of some of its members.
- His reviews describe the work as a book that should be compulsory reading for "*career master sixth formers and undergraduates including those who are lost to business because of the sordid scramble for profit*". This is an integrated whole "*of a single underlying philosophy*" and not a chopped up set of isolated functions. The case histories chosen are effective illustrations. A thought provoking work which may be a little harsh on "*personnel management*" in a world dependent on the striving of man if our society is to survive. But a book that was desperately needed (Management Institute Library), and also as an outstanding

contribution to the literature of management, one that will rank with the works of the Gilbreths, Harry A Hopf and Frederick Taylor. (R L Vormelker Library Journal December 1954).

- Alan M Kantrow summarised Drucker's contribution when he wrote Why Read Peter Drucker "Because a manager can profit from the ideas and from the discipline of mind by which they are formulated" (HBR Jan/Feb 1980).

- Subsequently management writers acknowledged Drucker's original contributions by quoting and referring to his pioneering work across his wide range of management related topics as confirmed by him being the leading reference in the Citation Index.

To the question: -

Did he discover the practice of management?

Drucker claimed that with Practice he made *"a discipline of management"*. A dictionary definition of a discipline is *"being under control by knowledge"*.

I believe that what he did was to make a *"philosophy out of management"* by emphasising that all of the functions of management need to be integrated and managers to think before acting.

In the fifty years since the publication of Practice as an "how managers do their jobs" book, an alternative has not become conspicuous excepting in a collection of some of Drucker's other work.

Drucker's development of MbO and Juran and Deming's Total Quality are ones of the very few philosophies of management to have emerged in the second half of the 20thc following the first half's ideas of the Taylor School of 'Scientific Management', Weber's 'Bureaucracy', Rathenau's 'Rationalisation' and Fayol's 'Theory of Management'.

2004.

As I conclude this *"Time Line"*, London Metropolitan University, UK, islaunching a series of books on Corporate Social Responsibility, which is yet another Drucker idea from the 1950s.

BIBLIOGRAPHY

Barzun, Jacques (1932) *The French Race: Theories of Its Origins and their social and political implications prior to the revolution,* New York, Columbia University Press, London, P S King & Sons Ltd

Barzun, Jacques (1937) *Race – A Study in Modern Superstition,* USA, Harper & Row

Beatty, J (1998) *The World According to Drucker,* New York, The Free Press

Berle, A & Means, G (1933) *The Modern Corporation and Private Property,* New York: The McMillan Company

Berlin, Isaiah (1953) *The Hedgehog and the Fox; An Essay on Tolstoy's View of History,* London, Weidenfeld & Nicholson

Bonaparte A & Flaherty J (1970) *Peter Drucker, Contributions of Business Enterprise,* New York, New York University Press

Brech, E F L (1946) *Management – It's Nature and Significance,* Norwalk Conn. Easton Press (1989)

Brech, E F L (2002) *Vol 1. The Concept and Gestation of Britain's Central Management Institute 1902-1976,* London, Nicholas Brealey (1996)

Brech, E F L et al (1953) *The Principles and Practice of Management,* London, Longmans

Brech, E F L, Thomson A & Watson J F (2010) *Lyndall Urwick Management Pioneer – A Biography,* Bristol, Thoemmes Press (2002)

Burnham, J (1941) *The Managerial Revolution,* Harmondsworth, England, New York: Penguin Books Ltd

Cantillion, Richard (1755) *Essai Sur La Nature du Commerce En Général (The General Nature of Business),* London, Holburn

Carlson, Professor Sune (1951) *Executive Behaviour,* New York, Arno Press

Carnegie, D (1913) *How To Win Friends and Influence People,* Surrey, The Worlds Work

Chandler Jnr, A. D (1962) *Strategy and Structure: Chapters in the History of the American Industrial Enterprise,* Massachusetts, London: The MIT Press

Child, J (1969) *British Management Thought – A Critical Analysis*

Churchill, W.S.C (1939), Times Literary Supplement, London; Times Newspapers

Clark, Wallace (1923) *The Gantt Chart,* New York, The Ronald Press Co., (1922)

Cordiner, Ralph J (1956) *New Frontiers of Professional Management,* New York, McGraw Hill

Davenport, Thomas H & Pruzah, Laurence (2003) *What's the big idea? : creating and capitalizing on the best management thinking,* New York, The Free Press (1999)

Dean, Joel (1951) *Managerial Economics,* American Economic Association

Dostoevsky, F (1880) *The Grand Inquisitor,* New York: A Frederick Ungar Book Continuum

Drucker, P. F (1939). *The End Of Economic Man: A Study of the New Totalitariansim.* London & Toronto: W. Heinemann.

Drucker, P. F. (1942) *The Future Of Industrial Man: A Conservative Approach.* New York: The John Day Company.

Drucker, P.F. (1946). *The Concept Of The Corporation.* New York: The John Day Company Ltd.

Drucker, P.F (1950) *The New Society; The Anatomy of the Industrial Order,* Melbourne, London, Toronto, Willian Heinemann Ltd,

Drucker, P. F. (1954). *The Practice Of Management.* London: Heron Books.

Drucker, P. F. (1959). *Landmarks Of Tomorrow.* New York: Harper Brothers.

Drucker, P. F. (1964). *Managing For Results.* New York: Harper & Row.

Drucker, P. F. (1969). *The Age Of Discontinuity.* New York, Harper & Row.

Drucker, P. F. (1974). *Management: Tasks, Responsibilities, Practices.* London: Heinemann.

Drucker, P. F. (1979) *Adventures Of A Bystander.* New York. London: Harper & Row.

Drucker, P. F. (1985) *Innovation And Entrepreneurship.* London: William Heinemann.

Drucker, P. F. (1986) *The Frontiers Of Management: Where Tomorrow's Decisions Are Being Shaped Today*. London: Heinemann.

Drucker, P. F. (1995). *Managing In A Time Of Great Change*. London: Butterworth – Heinemann.

Drucker, P. F. (2002). *Managing In The Next Society*. Oxford, London & New York: Butterworth – Heinemann.

Elbourne, Edward Tregaskis (1934) *Fundamentals of Industrial Administration – An Introduction to Industrial Organisation Management & Economics*, London, MacDonald & Evans (1934)

Emmett, B & Jeuck, John E (1950) *Catalogues and Counters – A History of Sears Roebuck & Company*, University of Chicago Press

Flaherty, J.E (1999) *Peter Drucker, Shaping the Managerial Mind*, San Francisco: Jossey-Bass

Fayol, Henri (1916) *Administration industrielle et Généralé*, France, Paris: Dunod Editeur
(Translated into English 1949 - *General and Industrial Management*) USA, Eastford CT, Martino Fine Books

Gabor, Andrea (2000) *The Capitalist Philosophers: The Geniuses of Modern Business -- Their Lives, Times, and Ideas*, New York, The Crown Publishing Group

Gantt, Henry L (1919) *Organizing for Work*, New York, Productivity Press

Gilmore, R E(1948) *A Practical Manual of Organization* [s.n.]

Given, W.B (1949) *Bottom-Up Management*, New York: Harper & Brothers

Graham, P (1995) *Mary Parker Follett Prophet of Management*, Boston, Massachusetts: Harvard Business School Press

Greenwood, Ronald G (1981) *Management by Objectives: As developed by Peter Drucker assisted by Harold Smiddy*, New York, Academy of Management

Gulick, Luther , Urwick L F & Graicunas, V A *et al* (1933) *Papers on Scientific Management*, Institute of Public Administration (1937)

Hamel, Gary & Prahalad, C K (1990) *The Core Competence of the Corporation*, University of Illinois

Hamilton, Sir Ian Standish (1921) *The Soul and Body of an Army*, London: E Arnold

Handy, Charles (2002) *The Hungry Spirit; new thinking for a new world*, London, HarperCollins (2000)

Harmondsworth: Penguin Books Ltd (Published by Sage in U.S.).

Hawley, Cameron (1954) *Executive Suite*, New York, Ballantine Books (1952)

Hayek, Friedrich, August von, (1994) *The Road to Serfdom*, UK Routledge Press

Heller, R (2000), *Warren Buffett The Man Who Made Billions With a Unique Investment Strategy*, London, Dorling Kindersley

Heron, Alexander R (1954) *No Sale No Jobs*, USA Harper

Hoopes, James (2003) *FALSE PROPHETS: The Gurus who created modern management and why their ideas are bad for business*, Mass. Cambridge University Press

Juran, Joseph Moses (1951) *Quality Control Handbook*, New York, Tokyo, London: McGraw-Hill

Juran, Joseph Moses *et al* (1962) *Quality Control Handbook, Revised Edition* [s.n.]

Kantrow, A (1980) *Why Read Peter Drucker?* Boston Massachusetts: Harvard Business Review, Harvard Business School

Kaplan, R.S & Norton, D.D (1996) *The Balanced Scorecard*, Boston, Massachusetts: Harvard Business School Press

Katona, George (1951/1975) *Managerial Economics; Its growth and methods of operation*, New York, W W Norton (1948)

Kaufmann, S A (1993) *The Origins of order: Self-organization and selection in evolution*, New York, Oxford; Oxford University Press

Kennedy, Carol (2002) *Guide to the Management Gurus 4th Edition*, Random House Publishing.

Keynes, J.M (1936) *The General Theory of Employment, Interest and Money*, London, McMillan

Kierkegaard, S (1843) *Syrgt og Bievem (Fear and Trembling)*, London: Penguin Books

Knauth, Oswald (1948) *Managerial Enterprise; Its growth and methods of operation*, New York, WW Norton (1948)

Knight, Frank Hyneman (1921) *Risk Uncertainty and Profit,* New York, Cosimo Classics (2000)

Kuznets, Simon (1953) *Economic Change – Selected Essays in Business Cycles, National Income & Economic Growth* [s.n.]

Le Bon, Gustave (1895) *Pyschologie des foules (The Crowd: A study of the popular mind)* [s.n.]

Levi, Anthony (2000) *Cardinal Richelieu: The Making of France,* Robinson

Lewis, Joseph Slater, (1896) *The Commercial Organisation of Fractories*

Leys, W A R (1941) *Ethics and Social Policy,* New York, Prentice-Hall Inc.

McGregor, D (1960) *The Human Side of Enterprise,* New York, Toronto, London: McGraw-Hill

McNair, Malcolm Perrin (1954) *The Case Method at the Harvard Business School,* New York, McGraw Hill

McNair, Malcolm Perrin & Hansen, Harry L (1949) *Reading in Marketing,* New York, McGraw Hill

Maciariello, J.A (2011) *A Year with Peter Drucker: 52 weeks of coaching for leadership effectiveness,* New York: Harper Collins

Maciariello, J.A & Linkletter K.E (2011) *Drucker's Lost Art of Management,* New York: McGraw Hill

Magnetta, Jean & Stone, Nan (2002) *What Management Is... How it works and why it's everyone's business*

Maslow, A (1962) *Eupsychian Management,* Homewood Illinois: Irwin – The Dorsey Press

Mayo, Elton (1933) *The Human Problems of an Industrial Civilization,* New York, Macmillian Company

Mayo, Elton (1949) *The Social Problems of an Industrial Civilization,* Division of Research Graduate School (1945)

Metcalf ,H C et al (1926) *Scientific Foundations of Business Administration,* UK, Norwich, Hive Publishing Company

Metcalf H C and Urwick, L F (1941) *Dynamic Administration – The Collected Papers of Mary Parker Follett,* New York, Harper and Brothers

Micklethwaite, John & Wooldridge, Adrian (1996) *The Witch Doctors; making sense of the management gurus,* New York, Times Books

Mooney James D & Reiley, Alan C (1931) *Onward Industry! The Principles of Organization and their significance to modern industry,* New York, Harper & Brothers

Nadar, Ralph (1965) *Unsafe at any speed,* Berlin, Grossman Publishers

O'Toole, James (1995) *Leading Change – Overcoming the Ideology of Comfort and the Tyranny of Custom,* New Jersey, Hoboken, Wiley

Odiorne, George S (1965) *Management by Objectives – A System of Managerial Leadership,* Texas, Fearon-Pitman Publishers

Odiorne, George S (1978) *MBO – A Backwards Glance,* USA/UK Elsevier Inc

Peters, Tom & Waterman Jr, Robert H (1982) *In Search of Excellence,* Harper Business

Pigors, Paul & Myers, Charles A (1947) *Personnel Administration,* London, McGraw Hill

Plachy, F (1926) *Britain's Economic Plight,* Mass; Boston, Little, Brown, and Company

Polanyi, Karl (1944) *The Great Transformation,* USA: Rinehart & Company Inc

Pugh, Derek S & Hickson, David J (1989) *Writers on Organisation*

Rathenau, Walther (1917) *Von Kommenden Dingen (In Days to Come),* London, MacMillian (1967)

Rathenau, Walther (1919) *Der Neue Staat (The New Society),* London, Oxford University Press (1946)

Rautenstrauch, Walter & Villers, Raymond (1949) *The Economics of Industrial Management,* New York, Funk & Wagnalls (1957)

Richardson Jr, F L W & Walker, Charles R (1948) *Human Relations in an Expanding Company,* New York, Arno Press

Roethlisberger, Fritz Jules & Dickson William, J (1939) *Hawthorne Effect,* Cambridge Mass, Harvard University Press

Saint-Simon, Claude, Henri de Rouvroy, comte de (1952) *Selected Writings 1760-1825* Oxford: Basil Blackwell

Say, Jean Baptiste (1803/1964) *A Treatise on Political Economy or the Production, Distribution and Consumption of Wealth,* New York, Augustus M Kelley Publishers (1964)

Schumpeter, Joseph A (1911) *Theory of Economic Development* , New York, Harcourt Brace & Company, Republished and translated 1968 Mass: Cambridge, Harvard University Press

Schumpeter, Joseph A (1939) *Business Cycles: A Theoretical Historical and Statistical Analysis of the Capitalist Process,* CT, Eastford, Martino Publishing (2014)

Schumpeter, Joseph A (1952) *Ten Great Economists from Marx to Keynes,* London, Weidonfeld & Nicholas publishers

Sheldon, Oliver (1923) *The Philosophy of Management,* Oxford, Routledge

Sloan Jr, Alfred P (1964) *My Years with General Motors,* New York, Doubleday & Company

Smiddy, Harold F &Naum, L (1954) *Evolution of a Science of Management in America 1912-1956* [s.n.]

Spates, Thomas G, (1937) *Industrial Relations Trend* [s.n.]

Spates, Thomas G (1948) *The Scope of Modern Personnel Administration* [s.n.]

Spates, Thomas G (1960) *Human Values Where People Work,* New York, Harper & Brothers

Stewart, Rosemary (1963) *The Reality of Management,* New York, Random House (1999)

Stewart, Rosemary (1967) *Managers and Their Jobs; a study of similarities and differences in the way managers spend their time,* Harmondsworth, Middlesex UK, Penguin Books (1924)

Tarbell, Ida M (1932) *Owen D Young: A New Type of Industrial Leader*

Tarrant, John J (1976) *Drucker: The Man Who Invented the Corporate Society*

Taylor, F W (1911) *The Principles of Scientific Management,* New York, London: Harper Brothers

Tead, Ordway & Metcalf, Henry C (1920/1933) *Personnel Administration – Its Principles and Practices* [s.n.]

Tichy Noel M &Stratford Sherman (1995) *Control Your Destiny or Someone Else Will,* New York, Harper Business

Tocqueville, A de (1835 & 1840) *De La Démocratie en Amérique* (*Democracy in America*), London: Oxford University Press

Trompenaars, Fons (1993) *Riding the Waves of Culture: Understanding Diversity in Global Business,* New York, McGraw Hill Companies Incorporated

Urwick, Lyndall Fowndes (1929) *The Meaning of Rationalisation*, London, James Nisbet & Co

Urwick, Lyndall Fowndes (1933) *Management of Tomorrow,* London, James Nisbet & Co

Urwick, Lyndall Fowndes (1943) *The Element of Administration*, New York, Garland

Urwick, Lyndall Fowndes (1956) *The Golden Book of Management,* London, Routledge (2001)

Urwick, Lyndall Fowndes (1957) *Leadership in the Twentieth Century Thirteen Pioneers,* London, Vintage Classics (2011)

Urwick, Lyndall Fowndes and Brech E F L (1945) *The Making of Scientific Management, the thirteen pioneers*, London, Bloomsbury Publishing

Urwick, Lyndall Fowndes and Brech E F L *Historical Perspectives in Management: A Critical Essay Embodying a Review of The Making of Scientific Management* Bristol, Thoemmes Press

Walker, Charles R and Guest, Robert H (1952) *The Man on the Assembly Line*, Mass. Cambridge, Harvard University Press

Watson Jr, Thomas J (1963) *A Business and Its Beliefs and the Ideas that helped to build IBM*, New York, McGraw Hill Education

Weber, Max (1922) *The Theory of Social and Economic Organization*, USA, University of California Press

Weber, Max (1927) *General Economic History,* New York, Greenbert

Wheen, Francis (1999) *Karl Marx: A Life,* Indianapolis, Liberty Fund (2007)

Wolf, William S & Urwick, Lyndal Fowndes (1984) *The Golden Book of Management – New Expanded Edition in two parts* [s.n.]

Wren, Daniel (1994) *The Evolution of Management Thought,* London, Bloomsbury Publishing Plc (2015)

Wren, Daniel A & Greenwood, Ronald G (1998) *Management Innovators: the people and ideas that have shaped modern business,* Bristol, Thoemmes Continuum (2005)

Xenophon (circa 450 BC) *Cyropaedia* (*Life of Cyrus*), London: The McMillan Company (1914), William Heinemann

Yost, Edna (1949) *Frank and Lillian Gilbreth: A Life,* New York, John Wiley (1994)

Zimet Melvin & Greenwood Ronald G (1979) *The Evolving Science of Management – The Collected Papers of Harold Smiddy and papers by others in his honour,* New York, AMACOM Books

INDEX

Accountants, 66, 83, 118-123, 125-126, 135, 174, 221-223, 240

American Telephone and Telegraph Company (AT&T), 15, 68, 75, 91, 148-149, 151, 239

Automation, 87, 92, 96-97, 109, 111-112, 114, 118, 139, 141,143, 156, 158, 169, 173-174, 202, 206, 219, 248

Balanced Scorecard, 119, 250, 257

Barnard, Chester, 43-45, 53, 56-57, 75, 176, 219, 228, 238, 239

Barzun, Jacques, 21, 33, 41, 182, 231, 253

Beatty, Jack, 44, 181, 225, 253

Bennington College, 19, 22, 24, 236

Berle & Means, 36-37, 39-40, 83, 120, 228, 237, 253

Berlin University, 81

Bonaparte & Flaherty, 180, 198, 200, 208, 217, 229, 253

Bonn University, 234

Brailsford, Henry Noel, 20

Brake Shoe Plant, 162-163

Brech, E F L, 45, 180, 206, 210-213, 218, 220, 224

Brown, Donaldson, 22, 45-46, 50, 89, 99, 102-103, 107, 118, 149, 172, 174, 197, 240

Burnham, James, 34, 37, 56, 58, 237-238, 253

Burt, Cyril, 43, 45, 85

business cycles, 67, 83, 103

Cadillac, 125, 127-128

Cambridge University (Kings College), 235

Cantillon, Richard, 174, 200, 219, 253

Capitalism/Capitalist, 25, 29-32, 34, 39-40, 51, 55, 57-58, 65, 69, 71, 73, 83, 100, 177, 193-194, 230, 236, 243, 245

Carlson, Sune, 90, 163-164, 172, 253

Carnegie, Andrew, 35

Carnegie, Dale, 147, 253

Chandler, Alfred, 76, 104, 250, 253

Chevrolet, 106, 128, 224

Chief Executive Officer (CEO), 15, 22, 98, 106, 123, 137, 149, 155, 163-164, 167, 170, 223, 249

Christian/Christianity, 7, 20, 25, 28-30, 32, 38-39, 42, 55, 58, 79-81, 98, 183, 219, 234, 237, 242

Churchill, Sir Winston, 17, 32, 236, 254

Clark, John Maurice, 45, 73, 92, 124, 214, 215

Communism/Communist

(Russian/anti), 19-20, 25, 27, 33, 57, 73, 115, 143, 245

Cordiner, Ralph Jerron, 45, 75-76, 89, 146, 149, 164, 253

Critical Path Planning Analysis, 124, 213-214

Crown-Zellerbach Corporation, 15, 91, 98, 148, 152, 203

Dean, Joel, 90, 117-118, 120-121, 172, 174, 191, 220, 254

Decentralisation (Federal/Functional), 15, 38, 47-48, 52, 56, 62-63, 96-97, 105-109, 112, 141, 151-152, 156, 164, 166, 173, 185-186, 188, 199, 201, 230, 239, 242, 248

Depression, 38, 50, 54-55, 60-61, 65, 67, 122, 128

Diebold, John, 90, 92, 173, 202

Doering, Otto C, 90, 149, 151,

Dostoevsky, Fydor Mikhailovich, 29, 39, 254

Dreystadt, Nicholas, 125

Drucker, Doris (neé Schmitz) 235

Drucker, Peter Ferdinand, 5, 7, 17-93, 95-177, 179-215, 217-252, 254-255

Econometrics, 121

Economics (business/classical/equilibrium, industrial/micro/socio/totalitarian), 18-19, 23-25, 28-29, 31, 49, 70, 73, 81, 92, 114, 118, 121, 123-125, 146, 183, 185, 211, 224, 234, 238

employment fund, 50, 55, 238

entrepreneur(s/ial/ship/function), 61, 83, 96-97, 99, 126, 174, 194, 200, 202, 205, 207, 219, 224, 228, 240, 243, 249

Fascism/Fascist, 27, 29, 32

Fayol, Jules Henri, 30, 43, 85 45, 90, 111, 162, 176, 197-198, 227, 248, 252, 255

Federalism, 105

Flaherty, John E, 181, 206, 212, 230, 255

Follett, Mary Parker, 43, 57, 73, 85, 92, 138, 176

Ford, Henry, 58, 90, 151, 176

Ford II, Henry, 90, 149-151

Ford Motor Company (The), 15, 31

Fords River Rouge Plant, 56

Fords, 15, 31-32, 34-35, 39, 49, 51, 55, 63-64, 76-77, 81, 84, 91, 98, 110-111, 128, 148-151, 153, 221, 237, 239, 242, 246

Frankfurt University, 234

free market, 40, 55, 68-70, 72, 109, 149

Gantt, Henry Laurence, 43-45, 64, 68, 75, 85, 90, 111, 124, 213-215, 219, 255

General Electric Company (GE)

15, 25, 43, 50, 72, 75-76, 91, 98,
101-102, 123, 129, 135, 145,
146, 151-15, 155, 165, 167, 220,
246

General Motors Corporation
(GM), 15, 22, 25, 37, 42-44, 46-
48, 50-52, 54-56, 71, 74-77, 89,
91, 99, 103, 105-107, 109, 118,
127-128, 139-141, 148-152, 156,
170, 173, 181, 202, 221, 224,
228, 239-240, 246

Gestalt, 18, 77, 114, 124, 207,
233

Gilbreths (Frank & Lillian), 24,
43-45, 84-85, 90, 111, 176, 252

Given, William Barnes, 90, 149,
162-163, 255

Graham, Pauline, 43, 255

Greenwood, Ronald G, 76, 99,
101-103, 172, 181, 227, 255

Guest, Robert H, 90

Hamburg University, 233

Hamel & Prahalad, 150, 250,
255

Hamilton, Sir Standish
Monteith, 43, 45, 76, 85, 153-
154, 256

Harvard Business Review, 15,
242

Hawley, Cameron, 90, 170, 256

Hayek, Friedrich, August18,
100, 187, 193, 196, 230, 233, 256

Heron, Alexander Richard, 90,
133, 172, 180, 256

Hofstede, Geert, 219

Hopf, Harry A, 43-45, 84,
90,103, 111, 146, 176, 197, 205-
207, 220, 238, 252

Hoopes James, 181, 212, 215,
256

Hoshin Kanri, 220

Howe, Qunicy, 21, 41

Human Relations (HR), 136-
138, 145, 221, 223, 240,

Hurni, Melvin L, 92, 104, 173,
202

Innovation, 35, 51, 83, 98, 115,
126, 128-131, 158, 200, 202,
207, 213, 237, 249

International Business Machines
(IBM), 15, 84, 86-87, 91, 114,
135,137, 141-145, 148-149, 152,
156, 165, 169-171, 190-191, 202,
220-221, 241, 246, 250

Japanese art, 195, 229

job security, 117, 134, 172

Juran, Joseph Moses, 90, 111-
112, 118, 124, 128-129, 138,
174, 195-196, 218, 220, 248,
252, 256

Kaizen, 114, 142, 220, 250

Kantrow, Alan M, 74, 181, 194-
195, 229, 252, 256

Kaplan Robert S & Norton
David P, 119, 250, 256

Kauffman, S A, 231, 256

Kennedy, Carol, 151, 256
Keynes, John Maynard, 31, 49, 56, 65, 82, 121, 221-222, 224, 235-236, 243, 256
Kierkegaard, Søren Aabye, 28-30, 39, 80, 234, 236, 256
Knauth, Oswald Whitman, 90, 120-121, 174, 220, 256
Knight, Frank Hyneman 49, 56, 65, 70, 85, 121, 238, 247, 257
Knowledge Society (The), 61, 82, 212, 245
Kuznets, Simon Smith, 90, 110, 117, 120-121, 174, 257

Labour Unions (Unions), 15, 20, 35, 37, 48, 55, 59, 77, 85-86, 91, 116, 134-138, 140, 145, 148, 187-188, 190, 193-194, 224, 243
laissez-faire, 38, 238
leadership, 37, 53, 56, 82, 85, 100, 146-147, 151, 239
Levi, Anthony, 63, 257
Levitt, Theodore, 175, 180, 198, 205
Leys, Wayne Albert Risser, 18, 92, 257

McCormick, Cyrus Hall, 59, 90, 127
McGregor, Douglas, 45, 90, 100, 137, 197-198, 205, 230, 250, 257
McNair, Malcolm Perrin, 79, 90, 110, 121, 124, 129, 174, 257
Management by Exception, 160, 250
Management by Objectives & Self Control (MbO), 15, 84, 86, 90, 95-97, 99-105, 108, 115, 119, 124, 146, 154-155, 159, 172, 174, 182-183, 199, 201, 203,, 220-221, 226-227, 230, 248, 250, 252
marketing,52, 56, 110, 115, 122, 126-129, 131, 133, 145, 156, 158, 174, 180, 204, 207, 249
Marxism/Marxist, 18, 34-35, 37
Marx, Karl Henrich, 27-28, 31, 34-35, 38, 41, 49, 65, 71, 81, 99, 184, 237
Maslow, Abraham, 92, 100, 197, 230, 257
mass production, 40, 48, 51, 53, 57-58, 71, 87, 111-113, 151-152, 174, 187, 237, 241-242
Mayo, Elton, 43, 54, 64-65, 75, 85, 90, 134, 137, 140, 145, 171, 180, 197, 243, 249, 257
Metcalf, Henry Clayton, 45, 72-73, 92, 136, 257
monopolies, 31, 34, 224
Mooney, James D, 40, 44-48,, 53, 56
Mooney & Reiley, 45, 53, 56, 84, 109, 240, 258
motivation, 82, 85, 92, 126, 133, 138-139, 143, 158, 162, 239, 251
Münsterberg, Hugo, 43, 85, 136
Myers, Charles Andrew, 90

new economists, 121, 126, 226
New York University (Graduate Business School), 24, 242
Nordling, Rolf, 45, 90, 164, 172

Owen, Robert, 20, 30, 43, 82, 236

performance, 49, 69, 77, 79, 82-83, 86, 89, 91, 97-98, 100, 105-107, 109, 114-116, 118-120, 123-126, 129, 132-136, 145-147, 159, 161-163, 165, 167-169, 171-172, 175, 182, 185, 210, 222-223, 244, 246, 248, 251
Personnel Administration, 136-138, 141, 166
Personnel Management (PM), 52, 56, 135-136, 139, 141, 143, 145, 152, 159, 167, 180, 230, 241, 244, 251
PERT (Programme Evaluation Results Technique), 124, 213-214
Pigors, Paul J W, 90
Pigors & Myers, 137, 258
Porter, Kendrick, 91-92, 104
privatisation, 27-28, 204, 236
69, 236
Priestley, John Boyton, 17
productivity, 60, 67-68, 81-82, 89, 92, 98, 109-115, 117-118, 132-134, 142, 144, 146, 191, 243-244, 247-248
'profit motive', 49, 65, 115

proletariat, 28, 71
property rights, 36-37, 40
Protestant, 7, 28, 31, 81, 219, 234
Purdue University, 24

Race, Hubert H, 90, 153-154
Rathenau, Walther, 24, 29-31, 34, 36, 39, 43, 53, 56, 59, 81, 85, 88, 159, 189, 197-198, 201-202, 224, 236-237, 240, 252, 258
Rautenstrauch, Walter, 45
Rautenstrauch & Villers, 90, 121, 123, 258
Reiley, Alan C, 40, 75
responsibility, 31, 38-39, 51, 64, 68, 70-72, 76, 83, 85-89, 92, 96-100, 107-109, 117, 123, 129, 132-133, 135, 141, 143, 147-148, 153-154, 156-157, 163, 165, 167-170, 176, 189, 239, 247, 249, 252
Richardson, Frederick L W, 90
Richardson & Walker, 90, 141, 144, 150, 171, 220, 258
Rosenwald, Julius, 90, 149-151

Sarah Lawrence College, 19, 236
Scientific Management, 40, 44-45, 53, 64, 83-85, 110-111, 134, 138-139, 161, 174, 199, 207, 252
Schumpeter, Joseph, 28, 31, 35, 39, 49, 56, 65, 70, 75, 81, 83, 89, 99, 120-121, 131, 174, 184-185, 193, 196-197, 200, 202, 204, 207, 224-225, 227-228, 233-234,

267

237-238, 243, 247, 251, 259

Sears, 75, 91, 128, 136-137, 141, 143, 148-152, 155-156, 159, 223

Sears, Richard Warren, 90, 150

Self-governing plant community (autonomous), 38-40, 54, 56, 59, 60, 64, 82, 190, 199, 202, 237-238, 242, 245

Sloan, Afred P, 22, 45, 47, 55-56, 63, 75, 89, 99, 101-103, 106, 109, 149, 172, 181, 197, 199, 238, 240, 249, 259

Smiddy, Harold Francis, 45, 75-76, 86, 90-91, 101-102, 104-105, 176, 207, 220, 221, 259

Social Organisation, 25, 30, 51, 53, 56, 65, 84, 127, 132, 202, 238, 240

Span of Control, 85, 96, 135, 153-154, 156, 249

Span of Managerial Responsibility, 155-157, 249

Spates, Thomas Gardiner, 90, 136, 145, 259

Taylor, Frederick W, 30-31, 35, 39-40, 43-44, 53, 55, 64, 68, 75, 79, 83-85, 90, 97, 110-111, 122, 139, 142, 144, 160, 174, 176, 197-199, 202, 237-238, 241, 250, 252, 259

Tead, Ordway, 41, 43, 45. 56, 85, 92, 238, 239, 241

Tead & Metcalf, 45, 136, 145, 259

The American Cast Iron Pipe Company, 63, 245

The American Telephone and Telegraph Company (AT&T), 15, 68, 75, 91, 148-149, 151, 239

the Corporation, 22, 37, 40, 44, 47, 52, 55-56, 91, 95, 100, 109, 185-186, 202, 237-239

The Law of Loss Avoidance, 66, 243

Tichy & Sherman, 72, 75-76, 259

Tocqueville, Alexis de, 30-31, 39, 71, 80, 100, 236, 259

top management, 22, 48, 55, 62, 64, 68, 95, 97-98, 100, 107, 141, 149, 156, 163, 167, 172, 182, 239, 244

Totalitarianism, 24, 27, 29-30, 33, 37, 40, 184

Trompenaars, Fons, 219, 259

unemployment, 38, 54-55, 60-61, 67, 117, 186

Urwick, Lyndall Fownes, 39, 43, 45, 75, 85, 92, 153-155, 176-177, 180, 191-192, 197, 205-207, 209-211, 217-220, 241, 260

Vail, Theodore N, 90, 151

Vertical Integration, 63, 151, 249

Walker, Charles Rumford, 90, 141, 145

Walker & Guest, 138-139, 140-142, 144, 169, 171, 206, 260
Ward(s), Mongomery, 127-128
Warwick University, 220
Watson Jr, Thomas 220, 260
Watson Snr, Thomas J, 91, 145, 149-150, 152, 221
Weber, Karl Emil Maximillian (Max), 31, 53, 64, 80, 176, 224, 228, 252, 260
Wolf, William B, 45, 260
Wood, General Robert Elkington, 91, 149-151
World War I, 79, 84, 136-137, 209, 213, 218
World War II, 18-19, 42, 131, 152, 181, 212
Worthy, James Carson 89, 155-156
Wren & Greenwood, 75, 102, 181, 260

Xenophon, 85, 91, 147, 260

Young, Owen D, 36-37, 237, 242

Zimet & Greenwood, 155, 260

**Endorsements of Peter Starbuck's work on
Peter F. Drucker**

Charles Handy CBE

World renowned Management Philosopher

'Peter, you are indefatigable! Drucker should be very grateful.'

December 2018

Philip Kotler

The Father of Marketing

Professor Emeritus of Marketing at the Kellogg School of Management

'Your work on Peter Drucker is monumental and an excellent resource for scholars

and managers.'

June 2019

'Your research and Drucker books will be appreciated around the world.'

January 2021

Dr. Joseph A Maciariello

Joseph Maciariello worked and wrote with Peter Drucker for 26 years.

He is regarded by many as Drucker's successor.

My first exchange with him was in 2010, when of my report, **'A personal**

refection on the Global Drucker Forum, Vienna, November 2009',

he wrote;

'What a wonderful paper- thank you!'

Our exchanges continued until his untimely death in 2020

Prof. Dr. Dr. h.c. mult. Hermann Simon

Founder and Chair Simon Kutcher & Partners

'Your work on Peter Drucker is extremely impressive. You are without doubt the world's leading expert on Peter Drucker.'

June 2021

Dr Richard Straub

Founding President of Drucker Society Europe host of the Global Peter Drucker Forum

'Often Drucker is misquoted; in case of doubt, you might also ask Peter Starbuck – who has the most complete documentation about everything Drucker ever said and wrote.'

July 2018

'It is really important that your outstanding work get wider visibility'

March 2021

Dr Peter de Toma

IBM Business Management Consultant

Of Peter Starbuck; *'the only man I know to whom I can talk comprehensively about Peter F. Drucker. Unfortunately, very rare moments.'*

2008

'Maybe there are not more than 20 Peter F. Drucker true experts with Maciariello, Cohen and you [Starbuck] leading such a group.'

February 2018

Jorge A. Vasconcellos e SA

MBA Drucker School / PhD Columbia University /

Jean Monnet Chair Professor at Swiss Business School / AESE (IESE)

'None is better than Peter Starbuck, with his deep knowledge and care for detail.'

September 2015

Dr Julia Wang

President Peter F. Drucker Academy Hong Kong

'I am very much enjoying your books. It's very impressive and really appreciate your efforts.'

March 2021

Professor Morgan Witzel

Writer, Management Historian, Teacher

Fellow of the Exeter Centre for Leadership at University of Exeter

'What an impressive body of work you have created. This is a real landmark of scholarship.'

July 2021

ALSO BY Dr PETER STARBUCK, ONE OF THE ACKNOLWEDGED AUTHORITIES ON PETER F DRUCKER 'THE FATHER OF MODERN MANAGEMENT'

PETER F. DRUCKER, LANDMARKS OF HIS IDEAS

Highlighting and outlining Drucker's ideas and placing them in a biographical framework, this thoroughly researched, fully referenced and sensibly indexed slim volume represents an excellent starting point for anyone interested in learning about the man and his contribution to the field.

Landmarks was distributed at the 4th Drucker European Conference in Vienna 2012, 'The World Management Forum', to the delegation from countries across the world, one of the recipients was the Nobel Prize winner Israeli Dan Shechtman who requested a signed copy.

DRUCKER'S EUROPEAN INFLUENCES by DR PETER STARBUCK

'Drucker's European Influences' is the first of a trilogy of Peter F. Drucker's research which is being republished with the addition of indexing essential for researchers.

Originally my PhD Thesis entitled: The Formative European Influences That Shaped The Thinking Of Peter F. Drucker And How They Manifest Themselves In His Later Ideas; the only thesis on Drucker in the British Isles deposited at the British Library.

A DRUCKER MISCELLANY

This book includes profiles of 111 influences Drucker considered to refine his ideas together with tributes to his immediate participants, including obituaries in The Guardian of two of them Edward Brech and John Humble and also that of Drucker.

Also explored is how MbO (Management By Objectives) has evolved in the Japanese practice of Hoshin Kanri.

275

REVIEWS OF HIS CONTRIBUTIONS

A collection of reviews stemming from Peter F. Drucker's achievements and contributions towards the nature of modern management as seen across the globe.

DRUCKER'S CAMEOS

A collection of 20 stand aside stories, that connect directly or indirectly to Drucker, including his FBI investigation and the crediting of both to him and a different Peter Drucker.

STARBUCK VIKINGS

From the Viking's first arrival onto America's eastern shores to Cape Cod's whaling industry of the 17th and 18th centuries, and to how the Starbuck name became known as one of the leading coffee brands across the globe, a fascinating book exploring the history behind the Starbuck name.

HOW NATURE MANAGED FIRST

Illustrating the essential role of management by analogy within the natural world Dr Peter Starbuck takes the reader through the vast sweep of history.

From reviewing man's progress from the earliest civilisations through to the Industrial Revolution, Dr Starbuck succinctly explores the development of management theory and its major management gurus.

Examining the Natural World and illustrating how management's key principles can be observed at work in nature, How Nature Managed First brings the two worlds together, with helpful analogies and further questions considered.

An excellent guide to the major works of leading management thinkers and the fascinating parallel behaviours of the animal world.

276

PROFILE - DR PETER STARBUCK

FRICS, FCIOB, FCMI, DBA, Ph.D
Alumni, The Open University
Founding Professor, University Centre Shrewsbury
Visiting Professor, University of Chester as a member of their Business
Research Institute, China Centre

Dr Peter Starbuck was born on 5th February 1936 in Birmingham and grew up in Wolverhampton, in the heart of the industrial West Midlands. He qualified as a construction professional but his career was interrupted by conscription for National Service in the Corps of the Royal Engineers. Following training in England, he was posted to the British Zone in West Germany from 1959 to 1961.

A successful businessman in the construction industry, Peter was an adviser to 10 Downing Street on affordable housing. As a strategic director for the City institutions, he worked with the financial regulator, stockbrokers, merchant banks, investment companies and the financial press.

His entrepreneurial endeavours continue to this day as a contributor to non-profit organisations and prolific writer on management concepts.

In April 2022, Dr Starbuck received an Honorary Degree from the University of Chester, putting him in distinguished company. Previous recipients include HRH Charles III King of England, Baroness Joan Bakewell DBE, raconteur Gyles Brandreth, former poet laureate Sir Andrew Motion and actress Dame Joanna Lumley DBE.

An entrepreneur and logistician, Peter is an acknowledged world expert on Peter F Drucker (1909-2005), the hugely influential Austrian-born management consultant and writer, whose ideas shaped the modern business corporation. Dr Starbuck is an Honorary Member of the Drucker Society – Europe

In the 1970's Peter moved to the Welsh-border town of Oswestry, Shropshire, where he developed his award-winning construction and house-building business.

For years, Peter and his Welsh wife Heather have enjoyed international travel, visiting 179 different countries and territories in all, mainly to explore the natural world. In March and April 2022, the couple embarked on their latest African safari that saw them out in the bush encountering some of the planet's most exciting, dangerous and endangered wildlife.

Printed in Great Britain
by Amazon